Conversations
with
Writers II

Conversations • Volume 3

Conversations
with
Writers II

Stanley Ellin   **Anita Loos**

James T. Farrell   **James A. Michener**

Irvin Faust   **James Purdy**

Barbara Ferry Johnson **Ishmael Reed**

Roger Kahn   **William Styron**

Eudora Welty

A Bruccoli Clark Book

Gale Research Company
Book Tower Detroit, Michigan 48226

Editorial Director: Matthew J. Bruccoli

Managing Editor: C. E. Frazer Clark, Jr.

Project Editor: Richard Layman

Editors
Margaret M. Duggan
Glenda G. Fedricci
Cara L. White

Transcriptions: Rhonda W. Rabon

Interviewers: John Baker, Matthew J. Bruccoli, Jean Todd Freeman, John P. Hayes, Richard Layman, Cameron Northouse.

Library of Congress Cataloging in Publication Data

Main entry under title:

Conversations with writers II.

    (Conversations ; v. 3)
    "A Bruccoli Clark book."
    1. Authors, American--20th century--Interviews.
2. Authorship. I. Ellin, Stanley. II. Baker,
John, 1931-   III. Series: Conversations with ;
v. 3.
PS129.C58   810'.9'005   77-27992
ISBN 0-8103-0945-9

INTRODUCTION

Conversations with Writers II has been planned with three chief goals in mind: first, to provide a forum for leading authors by preserving their comments on their work and careers; second, to provide readers with insights into the profession of authorship in our time; third, to present an accurate image of writers as individuals—to reveal their aspirations, their feelings about writing, and their responses to the world they live in.

The interviewers for this series were selected for their knowledge of the material and for their interviewing experience. They were asked to submit cassette tapes of their interviews along with short biographical sketches of their subjects and short descriptions of the settings of the interviews. The tapes were transcribed at the *CONVERSATIONS* editorial office. Transcriptions were then sent to both interviewers and subjects for approval before final editing.

Recordings of these interviews are being preserved and will become part of a permanent archive of oral history.

CONTENTS

Conversations with Writers II

Stanley Ellin was born in New York City in 1916. He became a full-time writer after being discharged from the Army at the end of World War II, and each of his first seven stories won an award from Ellery Queen's Mystery Magazine. Since that time Ellin has won three Edgars (1954, 1956, and 1958) and Le Grand Prix de Litterature Policiere (1975). His novels include Dreadful Summit *(1948),* The Key to Nicholas Street *(1952),* The Eighth Circle *(1958),* House of Cards *(1967),* The Valentine Estate *(1968),* The Bind *(1970),* Mirror, Mirror on the Wall *(1972),* Stronghold *(1974), and* The Luxembourg Run *(1977). Two volumes of his short stories have appeared:* Mystery Stories *(1956) and* The Blessington Method *(1964).*

Stanley Ellin

Stanley Ellin was interviewed by Matthew J. Bruccoli at the author's Brooklyn apartment on 19 August 1977. The Ellins are among the few white families in a black neighborhood, and Mr. Ellin explained that his choice of residence is a result of his liberal convictions. The interview was conducted in Mr. Ellin's businesslike study, which contrasted with his informal manner.

Conversations: Mr. Ellin, how—or why—did you become a mystery writer rather than a so-called "straight writer"?

Ellin: A very complex story, I suppose. I think that writing is an aptitude of personality, the persona. I guess it is the question of how I became the person I am. As a kid I was an avid reader and developed the idea of becoming a writer very young—dreamed of it; put it aside when I was unable to make any living at it; returned to it at thirty, and discovered that something had happened in between: that what I wanted to write and the way I wanted to write it was now finding the market. I don't exactly know what goes into making you the writer of a particular type of story or style. I think the greatest influence is very likely to be the things you loved to read during your adolescence. I was never an addict of mystery writing in the old-fashioned whodunit sense. I came of the generation that discovered Hammett, who was reaching his peak in 1930, and Graham Greene. Writers like that hit me hard.

I found myself gravitating more or less toward the idea of a crime being the most dramatic thing you could write about. I did not know when I submitted my first book, *Dreadful Summit,* that I was writing in the mystery category which still at that time, 1946, was still largely a whodunit category—whether a hard-boiled or soft-boiled classic or whatever. This was a novel which I thought was simply a story exploring the nature of a crime and the

3

criminal. There was never any secret or mystery about who did it or how it was done; and, as a matter of fact, it rather floored Lee Wright, the editor at Simon & Schuster who accepted it. Well, she felt the emphasis on crime made it a novel in the mystery field; but she felt that the peculiar treatment didn't put it squarely in the field, and, in effect, a new category was created at that time for what she called "suspense specials." But it was intended to be a *novel*—and not a mystery novel. In a sense I was hijacked into the mystery field.

Conversations: Did you feel at that time that you were trying to write a new genre?

Ellin: No, no. I was simply writing the kind of story I would have wanted to read—picking up an event and developing it dramatically. We lived on the West Side of New York then, in the Chelsea section, and there were scenes and events which struck me very deeply. I simply picked one up—an event—and developed it into a story which was the study, I thought, of a character under duress. It's the sharp division in America of the novel called the "straight novel" and the mystery genre—I was balanced between the two. I had intended to write a straight novel. I was balanced between the two and put over into the mystery genre because, as Lee Wright said very bluntly, "You have an assured sale if this comes out under a mystery colophon." That was the Inner Sanctum which she had created for Simon & Schuster.

But if it comes out as a straight novel, it can drop dead and be a most discouraging experience. I needed the money very much at the time; I desperately wanted that first sale, and I settled for the genre. I have all along, by the way, been uneasily balanced between the genre and the straight novel. I only wrote one straight novel as such, and the others were over on the mystery-writing side, or regarded that way. Now I have reached a point in the last few books where they are not put out under a mystery imprint or regarded as mystery books. The feeling was after awhile that I could claim my mystery audience on the basis of my name, and then expand into the realm of a larger audience. It's worked out pretty well that way.

One problem you'll meet in becoming defined as a mystery writer is that it's always hard to break away when you make the effort to write the straight novel. I ran into that with my straight novel. I rather baffled readers at that time who had expected something else. Of course, there are authors who did make the break successfully, notably Marquand, who created Mr. Moto and eventually turned to the straight novel with *The Late George Apley*. On the other hand, Graham Greene, always living uneasily between genres, used to list his crime novels as "entertainments," with the others as "novels." Then I noticed, as the time went on, there was a blurring of the distinction. I don't know whether he liked it or not, but some of the so-called "entertainments" are taking rank as straight novels.

It's a world, I think, in which the effort to sell—to mark a product clearly—creates the situation where you, in a sense, become a writer of a certain type of thing more than you might have been. Now when I sit down to write a novel, I automatically think of the crime, the treatment, as I would if I were a born-and-bred mystery reader and writer, which I am not. I find myself very easy now in that approach to it. I find that I can deal with any subject I choose as long as it's a criminal subject, and that it does me good to subject myself to the discipline of mystery writing. I insist on creating a story for myself with a beginning, a middle, and an end, which is not altogether in fashion on the straight-novel level. Circumstances, I suppose, all around created the writer I am; and then circumstances, economically and in the book trade, create the direction I will take.

Conversations: Do you resent—personally or on behalf of your colleagues—the fact that few mystery novels are given review space? Most mysteries have to make their way by word of mouth.

Ellin: Well, I again fall out of the category because I have been fortunate in one way. My books, by and large, have gotten what might be called more properly standard reviews. That is, I will get a column in the Sunday *Times* Book Review section instead of the paragraph in what Tony Boucher, a marvelous critic, used to call the "ghetto page." So I have that break. I do get the full column or two more often than not, although I can be hammered at greater length that way. But I resent it very much on behalf of those mystery writers who are, without any question, fine novelists. It is a delight to see, for example, a Ross Macdonald get some of the kudos he deserves. I would like to

Stanley Ellin

see John D. MacDonald get that. There are some other writers who deserve it, and the feeling that that distinction must be made, that their books are shoved aside for want of reviewing space is a cruel injustice to them. I don't know if one way or another the reviews—those mystery patchwork reviews—are any real damaging factor in selling a book, because there's a certain amount of reader recruiting as you go along.

If you live long enough as a writer you attain a following and a status and a comfortable existence, so that I don't know for the established writers if the reviewing problem hurts that much. For a young and new writer, I think it's damaging, but I think it's also damaging that many newcomers to the straight novel can't get proper reviewing. In my own case I have a peculiar out. Whereas I might feel resentment at not getting the widest possible press, I have been very fortunate in hitting the British, West German, Italian, French, and Scandinavian markets very often as a novelist—a straight novelist. I get the glory transatlantic in that way, which is a great ego gratification and which helps to—at bad moments—buoy the spirits.

Conversations: Your novels have been praised for their accuracy of setting. Do you write from memory or do you research them?

Ellin: Yes, at great length. I put in months of research to check out every possible piece of information which I may use. I also enjoy, and I think readers enjoy, novels which are set in what to a local person is an exotic place, European cities and so on. I have a close acquaintance with the ones that I write about, street by street. There's a marvelous routine we have where my wife and I take these European trips, settle down in a city and every day simply walk the city, live the city. In the evening while I'm enjoying the local television, whatever language, she has to sit there and make out a daybook, compressing every possible bit of information into clear, lucid form, which she then at home—when we get back to New York—types up.

I have a set of these volumes which are 300-page books in themselves and invaluable. As I get closer to the novel I will have gone over and through the material—all the material—at such length that most of what is useful is solidly imprinted on my mind. I will then take all the notes and put them away before I start the book. I very rarely refer to notes while I'm writing the

6

Stanley Ellin

book. I have a feeling that whatever I don't have imprinted by then is not essential to the book. When you go back to a reference while you're working on a novel—for myself, at least—I find it inhibiting. I find it stalls me, breaks whatever flow there is.

Conversations: The dust jacket of one of your books notes that you literally write one page at a time. Is it true that you can't leave a page until it is in final form?

Ellin: It's unhappily true. There are some writers I know of great distinction who have, in effect, painted themselves into this corner, typed themselves into this corner. It's a compulsion. I suppose the page, being a perfect unit itself, represents the end of something each time you come to the last word on it. I find that when I try to just gallop ahead, I am frozen with the thought that there's something wrong on that preceding page and I will work and rework it at length, until I am as satisfied as I can be with it. This is about as bad a method as you can get for writing. In one way it means terribly tedious amounts of time producing something which really should be dashed off and then gone over as a whole. I have discovered it has one advantage—not one I preach, but one that I accept—and that is: because of this there is a tautness obtained. When I read my own stuff back, I find that each page has a tension in manuscript, and if they all interlock properly they create tension throughout a book.

Conversations: Does this writing method save you from writing complete working drafts that you then have to discard?

Ellin: It does. However, I have, on a couple of books, gone so far off the mark with what I thought was good when I was finished that the whole thing had to be dismembered and done over. But again, from the beginning entirely—patchworking bothered me, so I simply thought it over and went through the same process. If you swerve off the broad pattern that you establish in writing a structured book, it can lead possibly to a very exciting and rewarding aspect of the book, but much more likely it will lead you into a disaster. It will take you away from your story into something else, and you will wind up in a sort of dramatic cul-de-sac. I've done that a couple of times, and in each case I have simply gone right back from the beginning, rediscovered my

Stanley Ellin

original story line, and finished off what amounts to a new draft in its entirety.

Conversations: Are you able to salvage any of the rejected drafts in these cases?

Ellin: No, no. I never try to salvage anything. The thing I've learned is that if you are anchored by any of these bits and pieces in a drawer, they're distractions to what you want to do. Every time you set at the task—the whole task and then each chapter and then each page—every time you yourself, I believe, are going to respond to instant-by-instant development and change. You are making a unity at that time. You are a certain person at that moment writing that thing. That is what makes the novel very much alive. It's what makes an oil painting much more alive than a photograph in a way—that the painter has each instant that he has painted been going through the lightning changes of personality, mood, and so on—development within himself. A painting done by hand reflects that, where a photograph freezes everything at one peak. When I do a chapter or page I am compressing myself into that area totally. If I were then to say that I thought I had in my desk a good scene which might fit in here, I would soon find that the scene is out of my past. It may be yesterday; it may be a month ago; but it's now out of my past. It will not ring true to me at that instant. It becomes, in effect, a purple patch to be inserted; it's all wrong. By the way, all of this—anything I say—it must be made explicit that it is always entirely in terms of myself—not as writing advice or writing guidance. I think my writing method is atrocious. I have found it damaging to productivity. Where I might have done three dozen books in the thirty years I've been writing, I believe my work method may be the element that has restricted me to a dozen.

Conversations: Can we talk about your writing habits? Do you work on a schedule every day?

Ellin: I used to have a capacity for writing ten and twelve hours a day; and then I discovered, as age hit me, that writing actually takes physical stamina, and now I'm only good for about six hours at a stretch. And the six is hard, but I haven't given up on the six. I have a feeling that it's an acknowledgment that I've arrived at really old age when I get down to four.

8

Conversations: Is that six hours of actual writing or does that include fooling-around time?

Ellin: No, that's six hours of writing. Usually I try to make it one unit, and if it's broken I will be back at the work late at night to get in that amount.

Conversations: Seven days a week?

Ellin: Six days a week, allowing a few days here and there.

Conversations: How long, on the average, does it take you to write a novel?

Ellin: It takes me fourteen or sixteen months.

Conversations: How much help do you expect or require from your publisher's editor?

Ellin: Oh, to start with my wife herself was a professional editor. By marrying her, I have now her editorial genius all to myself. As I complete anything, she does the first editing. She goes over the entire thing—story structure, Englishing, and all. She's an old-fashioned girl who demands precision in the use of words and structure and a clean prose and a very, very accurate use of language. So she does a marvelous job on this, and I will then do a typescript from her edited manuscript.

Conversations: Your first draft is a longhand manuscript?

Ellin: No, no, it's always typed. I can't write in longhand. Jeanne, my wife, does a job on my typescript. Then I do the final typescript from that, which goes to the publisher. I have, by the way, been very fortunate in that Bob Loomis is my editor at Random House, and he's a splendid editor. He also will have greater objectivity than both Jeanne and myself, so that he can contribute there, and he has been invaluable.

Conversations: Several of your novels have been made into movies. Have you worked on these screenplays?

Ellin: In three cases I simply sold the rights. In one case I also did the screenplay, that was from the first novel, *Dreadful Summit*, which was made as *The Big Night* with the late John Barrymore,

9

Jr. And recently I sold the book, *The Bind*, and have completed the screenplay on that.

Conversations: Do you find satisfaction in adapting your novels?

Ellin: I enjoy doing a screenplay while I'm doing it. I always have a terrible sense of disaster impending, because there are so many people going to be involved in it—the producer, and his oldest child, and the butcher boy who serves him, and so on. This is a familiar story to anybody who knows the movie business— everybody is involved. It's an enormously insecure bunch of people you're dealing with, and after awhile they're all over you and making you very unhappy because you know you're starting to make concessions in rewriting that you shouldn't make. It is really a money business in that sense. But I love the screenplay writing itself, and I find it comes fairly easily.

Conversations: Have you had a particularly satisfying experience working with any of the movie people?

Ellin: I worked longest on the very first one with Joseph Losey. We never met; we haven't met to this day. I did a draft; he took the draft and redid it. I was in New York, and he was in California. We worked back and forth on this a couple of times, and I had the very, very good information he could supply by way of the revised script. On the first draft of *The Bind* I worked with a director who was temporarily on the job, and again I learned something, and I again found the problem of the multiple image. I had a picture of what I wanted in my mind, but as you go along working with somebody the picture starts taking on different aspects. You slowly lose a grip on your own work. And that I don't like. I do like the solo effort, the solo creation. I'm very much addicted to it—it's hard to break from.

Conversations: One of my favorite movies is Nothing But the Best, *a 1964 English movie made from one of your short stories. How did it happen that an American story became a typically English movie?*

Ellin: Well, it was a very funny thing in its own way—that is, the story was called "The Best of Everything" here. It was an *Ellery Queen* story, and it was simply a story of a young man on the rise. In the story I had certain difficulties, in a way, of projecting the difference between a young man starting pretty crudely and emerging polished. Now this was picked up by English television originally, and it had a success there; and then, very fortunately, it was bought by David Deutsch for Domino Productions in London, and then—doubly good break—he got Frederick Raphael to do the screenplay. Raphael is a superb novelist and a marvelous screenwriter. The advantage he had in this case is that in England it is much easier to define class levels than in America.

What Raphael did was to transmute the image I had into a series of class steps through language and mannerisms. The young man, who was close to blue-collar, moves through lower middle class, middle class, upper middle class, and right into the aristocracy. And in England, because just speech mannerisms will convey each step, in effect all he had to do was stress those speech patterns. Then we were all given the break of having Alan Bates do an absolutely marvelous job in the role itself, and with great support. I was very happy to see that in an old *Saturday Review* an actor I always admired was praised for having given in *Nothing But the Best* one of the great performances in modern film—that was Denholm Elliott as the high-class remittance man who trained the young man on the rise in his proper manners.

I must say that ordinarily and in other pictures, the author who has sold film rights to his novel or story suffers agony when he finally sees the finished product. In this case, however, I was absolutely delighted with this thing. I had the pleasure of meeting Bates and Deutsch and telling them that. I absolutely delight in it, and when it pops up on TV, even though slightly mutilated, I still watch it faithfully. I think it is one of the most delightful pictures made, and I rejoice in the contribution I was able to make to it.

Conversations: Many of your stories were done by the Alfred Hitchcock television series. Did you work with Hitchcock?

Ellin: I've never had a personal contact with Mr. Hitchcock. That was the old half-hour Alfred Hitchcock series, and, as far as I know, Joan Harrison was the one in charge of the complete work. That's Eric Ambler's wife, whom I did have the pleasure of meeting as I've had the pleasure of meeting him—and incidentally, learning from him that he is as much in awe of her editing of his work as I am of Jeanne's. As I gather, Joan Harrison

11

was very much in charge of the whole thing. My stories, breaking with the standard whodunit thing, were exactly what the Hitchcock program wanted at that time.

So quite a few of them were picked up; and Joan always respected the author of the original enormously, and would actually call up to find out if he minded certain changes that might have to be made—an astonishing experience, because ordinarily the author of the original is totally overlooked. I was happy with the arrangement—several of the productions are small classics of TV in their own way. But Hitchcock I never did meet and never had any direct dealings with at all. His role, I dare say, was largely left to Joan Harrison.

Conversations: You've mentioned how you research your books while traveling. Are you consciously seeking material when you travel, or do you relax and osmose? Do you regard it as work or pleasure?

Ellin: I regard it as pleasure. Jeanne and I between us have what you might call a working command of French, Italian—she has some Spanish and can make out in German fairly well. Wherever I go I think one of the great pleasures we have is that we very rarely touch what might be called the high spots. I'm unabashedly a tourist. I dropped the idea long, long ago—which is an idea of youth—that when you go to a place, you must lose yourself in the population. But we're touring among all the parts of town where people live and work—that is, working-class sections, lower-middle-class sections. We head immediately for the nearest variations of what would be the American Woolworth's—the local markets and stores. We get the local paper and we, of course, fix on the local TV.

Recently, I found myself in Brussels one rainy night watching with fascination as they gave basketball scores of a French town league. About sixty teams make up French basketball town leagues. I would never have known this if I weren't watching it. I watched every score faithfully. They were all very low, by the way—good defense, but no big offense. This is the great pleasure, I think, of traveling if you are lucky enough to be able to stay in a place long enough, not to make the routine trips. Of course, to see the museums and visit the places of importance, but then to move into the town itself—become part of the local life—that is a great pleasure. You do meet people that way, and if you are open—and Jeanne is just fantastic at falling into casual conversation with any woman who hovers nearby—if you are open, you find that very quickly you have made acquaintance locally.

Conversations: Do you look for any particular things that may be useful as literary material?

Ellin: I turn Jeanne on, and I turn off. She is the one that must be aware that the zone we are going through is maybe to be used in a story. She must be acutely aware much more than I am of subtleties of language we hear when we pass—an idiom or a sign in a window or a street address or a housefront or anything like that. She does all that. I am very much simply enjoying the experience. It's only when bit by bit as I go along, usually near the end of a trip, that pieces start falling together—that I myself become acutely aware that I now have the makings of my story material. But most of the trip is a working trip for me in only one part of the brain, far away—and she is working with all parts.

There are two fine old sayings: if you want to be a writer, marry an editor; and if you want to learn a subject, write a book about it.

Conversations: You mentioned your European readership. In which country do you have the largest audience?

Ellin: West Germany—I am hot stuff there, much in demand. I think it is because—I've tried to put this together from the reviews that are shipped across to me—I am regarded there as an expressionistic writer in the Germanic mode. Interestingly, I do happen to be a worshiper of German expressionistic painting. Anyhow, my books are regarded in West Germany as samples of expressionistic outlook and writing, and are enormously popular.

Conversations: Do your German editions outsell the American editions?

Ellin: Well, you have the population difference. That is, if you go per capita, yes, definitely, in Germany I outsell the American editions. I have German book clubs, German newspaper and magazine serializations much more than I do in America. In Italy, depending on the book, I have an occasional fine sale and book club. And in England I do well. In France, again, depending on the book—which generally has to be a short one for the French readership—I will hit a French book club. Oh, yes, given a short enough and unusual book—with a book called *Mirror, Mirror on the Wall* the French awarded me the Grand Prix in 1975 for mystery writing, a pleasant compliment.

Conversations: Are you regarded as a literary celebrity in any of these countries?

Ellin: In England and West Germany to some extent.

Conversations: Who is your English publisher?

Ellin: Now Jonathan Cape. But it was a previous publisher, a dear man, who decided that instead of putting . . . . I think he had an appropriation of over £2,000 for advertising, and instead of putting it all into newspaper and magazine advertising, he'd leave it up to me as to whether I would come over there for two weeks—a week before and a week after publication—and commit myself to a heavy-duty BBC and public appearance and interview schedule. He would pay for a deluxe two weeks for Jeanne and me, and see what happened that way.

So Jeanne and I went over and had two wonderful weeks, absolutely deluxe, with the pleasant experience of being given red-carpet treatment by the radio, TV, *London Times*, and so on; and we enjoyed it immensely. Then when the smoke cleared away about a year later, the results came out, and the sale of that book was precisely the sale of the previous book.

Conversations: Which book was that?

Ellin: That book is called *The Valentine Estate*. It had a good healthy sale, but no better than the previous one, no worse. From Jeanne's angle and mine we much approve that form of advertising because, after all, you're living high and enjoying it, and all, as they say in Las Vegas, on "house money."

Conversations: Would you say that you have found your own public: they know who they are and you know who they are?

Ellin: Yes. By now I would say that at the age of sixty, after thirty years in the business, I have found my public, and in the international sense, too. That is, by and large, sales around the foreign countries where I'm published do run very close to each other. They're guaranteed to make the publisher a profit, which makes me happy. And they do, on occasion, rise to very good levels, depending on a certain book hitting a national taste. So that one way or another you do over the years obtain a readership and an economic base, which are very important.

Conversations: Do you agree with the observation that the mystery story —or "thriller," as they call it—is in some ways the last British colony? The English seem to have produced many highly competent thriller writers, whereas in America there are a handful of excellent mystery writers and a lot of hacks. Certainly the good English thriller writer enjoys a greater respect than his American counterpart.

Ellin: Well, I would disagree with one premise at the start: that England has a large number of high-quality thriller writers, and America has a handful, but a large number of hacks. I don't know statistics, but I will say that in England—there are fewer writers by and large, naturally—the proportion probably remains the same, except that in England a hack-writer cannot find a ready market and may give up on his career. Otherwise, considering English rates of pay, he'd starve to death very soon. Bad American writers, hack-writers, turn out stuff which at its worst has a sort of power to it. It grips by raw violence and sexuality. Bad English writers are stupefyingly dull.

You have to do—as I once did in setting out to draft some critical analysis—you have to wade through the works of the lesser English crime writers to discover how tedious they can be, and marvel that anybody could manage to stagger through the first fifty pages of one of those books. As I say, American writing at its worst has a vitality that English writing at its worst doesn't have. But the English rejoice in the idea, which I don't believe is well-founded, that they are the masters of the thriller and—the term "thriller" has such a broad connotation today—that they're masters of the crime novel, and the Americans are second in that. But they concede that the Americans are masters of the short story, and that the British are really lagging behind in that department.

15

Stanley Ellin

I think all these glittering generalities really are, you know, just blather. But one thing England does have, and that is a very tight literary establishment. America is simply too large geographically for it. In England when you get through the front door there in literary terms and start making the rounds, you discover you're meeting the same people: that this man, who admires your thriller in the pages of the *London Times*, is also next week going to do a write-up of some very, very sober and heavy novel that recently came out, and that he himself is a distinguished scholar of this and that. You know Pamela Hansford Johnson, who is a superb novelist herself, is an authority on our Thomas Wolfe and on a couple of other major literary figures, and at the same time is a superb critic of the thriller.

So that there you're meeting people who read in a catholic sense and appreciate in a catholic sense, much more than is done in America. So it's very refreshing to go to England, but I don't know an English writer who doesn't yearn desperately to be picked up by an American publisher, if he wants to make a living. Of course, it is difficult making a living as a writer in England unless you're fantastically successful. Book prices are too low; sales are too limited.

Conversations: Are you willing to comment on some of the mystery writers you read for enjoyment?

Ellin: A pleasure. I am incurably addicted to Dorothy Sayers—at the same time I deplore so much of what I read in her. That famous snob quality of hers. By the way, such splendid British crime writers as Julian Symons and Colin Watson, among others, have done devastating studies of the snob quality in the English thriller, in the English low-down novel. Some of the most astute criticism of Ian Fleming has not been done by Americans. I think the most devastating was done by the Canadian writer, Mordecai Richler. They have a very keen sense of the snob elements in such novels. And so I say I read somebody like Sayers, whom I much enjoy, while at the same time there's a censor working in my mind, troubling me. Crossing the Atlantic, I would say that Dashiell Hammett is the writer who most truly lives up to the high regard he's now held in.

Conversations: Do you rank Hammett as number one?

Ellin: Yes, I would rank Hammett as number one.

Conversations: Why?

Ellin: I suppose because he, bit by bit, worked his way to the point which I admire, which is the most precise use of language in telling a story. For example, in 1930 he wrote *The Maltese Falcon* which is, I suppose, in terms of plot and characterization—just plain vivid characterization—the most memorable of his works. But it's a book with the writing style spoiled for me in a sense by carry-overs of strained writing, carry-overs from the gaudy old pulp days which he had brought along with him into his later novels.

By 1934, four years later, he came out with *The Thin Man*, and in *The Thin Man* he had evidently, over those four years, set himself to write a prose which was so precise, so clean, it was as if it were etched with a sort of steel-edged tool. I have found in my own writing—again, this is very highly personal—I found in my own writing a tendency to overwrite, to let a flood of words carry a scene—it's dangerously easy to fall in love with your own beautiful words—and I strain to achieve what Hammett did in his ultimate style.

Conversations: Do you find Raymond Chandler self-indulgent in this regard?

Ellin: I think Chandler is definitely self-indulgent, although I think that Chandler did as good a job in defining the Southern California middle class and its mores as any writer could have done. I believe that, after you've read the Chandler lower-California texts, you will find no writer can quite compare in creating that ambience, and in defining it. I do find his plotting totally confusing, but, as I understood from some people later on, so did he. But even more than Chandler, Hammett was a writer with a very sharp perception of social conditions and of social crises—both stemming from the boom times of the twenties and carrying into the depression of the thirties. Hammett was a man who really lived in a real world, and had his characters in that sense living in a real world. So that whether

17

high life or low life, there is a sense of validity in the Dashiell Hammett texts for me.

Then there's Graham Greene whom I first met in short stories and then in *Brighton Rock* and later on in, of course, the other so-called "entertainments." Abroad I hit on Nicolas Freeling, a British writer who went Dutch and who, after creating for Holland what Chandler did for Southern California. . . . I had a correspondence with him about this which was fascinating. He killed off his series hero. He had a most profitable series going and one day killed off his hero because, as he said, he couldn't any longer live—when he was growing older—with a man who could not really afford to grow older. I admire his work and get much pleasure from it.

When I think it over, my preferences in crime fiction really seem to be very largely outside of someone like Sayers. I suppose I incline toward writers who will tend to be realistic, tend to probe somewhat into situations rather than simply give you an exciting story—and who will also demonstrate a command of the language.

Conversations: You admire writers who have social concerns. Do you feel that you are making a social or political statement in your own work?

Ellin: I know I'm making one. I'd never try to make one deliberately, because sermonizing is deadly. It's deadly to me when I read it or become aware of it. I imagine it's deadly to any reader. But I know that since I am intensely socially aware, a follower of events and definitely drawn into them, my feelings are part of my stories. I don't hesitate to have characters come out with it. That's a quality, by the way, I admire in John D. MacDonald, in the series he's done with Travis McGee. His hero is definitely a man who reads the newspaper from front to back every day and feels strongly about news events.

Conversations: Is a mystery better if it shows this social concern or social awareness?

Ellin: I think that a book may benefit if the author doesn't hold back. This is not saying that every writer has to have some kind of social outlook; but I think if he has and it's part of him, there's no use in his saying that a story is entirely entertainment and let us avoid anything that might make the reader uncomfortable. For example, there's James McClure who has come out with an engrossing and disturbing series of crime novels set in South Africa, using a white detective and a black assistant. In Scandinavia you hit a number of crime writers who in their novels achieve superb studies of psychic and social conditions in their countries.

So again and again there's this social awareness which you cannot deliberately make a book of, but which, if the writer has simply invested himself entirely in his story, will emerge from it. That's why I say I can read Sayers who was an atrocious snob and yet enjoy the books immensely, at the same time saying to her invisible presence: "You're too smart a girl for that; you shouldn't really, you know, come on with this apple-polishing for the upper crust." But I find the books as entertainment simply delightful. I love the use of the background which, bit by bit, becomes much larger than any plot in the book.

I always have the feeling in all mystery writing that you must have a sound and valid plot, and that is the skeleton. But as you build and as you work, the skeleton should properly and will properly sort of disappear. And in the end, in the far reaches of review, I imagine that most people don't remember what the plots in their favorite mysteries are. I've challenged people on this—avoiding, of course, the Sherlock Holmes fanatics who know every word and every plot by heart. But ordinarily you get people saying that they're enthusiastic about a certain mystery, and when you ask them what the plot was, they find that they can't really remember.

Conversations: It has been said that the lasting appeal of the Holmes stories derives not from the plots, but from their value as social history.

Ellin: Right. It was the creation of his character and ambience that made Sherlock immortal, not the adventures he underwent. If everything moves along, if the characters—particularly the main character—are alive and the ambience is vivid and interesting and entertaining, that is what makes the book. There must be a story to tell, but that story will gradually lose its place as a prime force. I'm always wary—when I'm talking to neophytes

19

Stanley Ellin

in mystery writing, I'm very wary about telling them this simply because they then feel that, well, the plot isn't important. And it is.

Conversations: You regard the mystery novel as a sociological document?

Ellin: Oh, yes, yes, very distinctly, yes. They mark—I hit on this long ago—their times very clearly, as Holmes and his people marked London at that period. You had in the twenties Hammett coming along—the cynical era, because Hammett's books are invested with a powerful cynicism—and Chandler picking that up. You had Mickey Spillane coming along at the McCarthy time, because Spillane's Mike Hammer was the quintessential McCarthy hero: the "I-am-the-judge-jury-and-executioner" thing was implicit in that time. And during the nadir of the Cold War Bond came along, but Bond had to be transformed as social events were transformed. In the latest Bond treatment in the movies, he is now allied with the Russian spy—the two of them—because this is the way the situation has evolved and that's right for the time. So that there is always a picture of the time and place.

I think readers, by the way, like most in mysteries an accurate sense of time and place. And you will get very heated letters if you in any way offend a reader's sense of time or place: this could not have happened, or they would not be wearing this, or this was not the street where such a thing goes on.

Conversations: What quality in your own work do you regard as most important?

Ellin: I suppose character. That is, I know my characters when I start. I know my characters' prehistories and I know what they will be doing after the book is over. That's important to me in planning the book: so that when I start I have a feeling I know the characters; and when I'm successful at it, I'm pleased that the characters do come alive in that sense and will sustain the story.

James T. Farrell was born in 1904 in Chicago. After working at various odd jobs, he first attracted literary attention with Young Lonigan *(1932), the first volume of the Lonigan trilogy, which also included* The Young Manhood of Studs Lonigan *(1934), and* Judgment Day *(1935). Since that time, Farrell has become one of America's most respected and most prolific authors. His canon consists of fifty-two published volumes and a number of unpublished works. Farrell's work spans many genres, including novels, short stories, poems, and literary criticism.*

James T. Farrell

James T. Farrell was interviewed on 23 September 1977 at his eastside Manhattan apartment by Matthew J. Bruccoli. Farrell has recently moved and was still in the process of shelving his library—cartons of books were stacked all over. He made a point of showing the interviewer a file cabinet full of unpublished manuscripts; at the age of 73, he is still writing faster than his work can be published.

Conversations: The English critic, Walter Allen, has said that the twin influences on you are James Joyce and Theodore Dreiser. Would you agree with that?

Farrell: Well, yes. I would say that Joyce was more of an early influence; that Dreiser, as an influence, was more of an inspiration. That is, Dreiser is the kind of a writer who doesn't influence other writers technically.

Conversations: Did Joyce influence you technically?

Farrell: Oh, yes. The first one who noticed that was Ezra Pound. You know, Ezra Pound was one of the first well known literary people to like my work. And when *Young Lonigan* came out he wrote me and said, "You know, of course, that this is influenced by *A Portrait of the Artist as a Young Man.*" In Paris in early 1932 or late '31, I was rereading *Ulysses*, and at the time I was working on *Gas-House McGinty*. I had my first book, *Young Lonigan*, accepted. Originally I'd planned the *Lonigan* as one book, and it grew into three books. To start, I'd planned for it to end with his death in his young manhood. When I reread the Night Town scene I thought to describe his death as—that suggestion, of course, came from the Night Town scene of his dying consciousness—a grand fantasy of the day of judgment. That's how I came to the title, *Judgment Day*. In preparation for that I added a chapter to *Gas-House McGinty*—I believe it's chapter

James T. Farrell

seven—of McGinty's dreams. Finally the Lonigan books grew into three volumes; and I wrote that scene, but it wouldn't fit the book after Studs in *Judgment Day* receives the last sacraments of the church. The scene would have been out of proportion. I never could get it published separately. The publishers were either afraid on the grounds of censorship or else uninterested.

I had a fire in my apartment on East 58th Street late in 1946. That manuscript was almost completely destroyed. I had only one copy. In those days I didn't make carbons—that is, in the early thirties. I rescued about thirty half-pages of it, which were published in a magazine called *Tri-Quarterly* in the sixties, and are going to be published as an epilogue in the new edition of *Studs Lonigan* which Vanguard Press is bringing out. In the case of Joyce there was so much that I recognized, because he had been brought up a Catholic and I had been brought up a Catholic. If ever I felt what Edmund Wilson called "the shock of recognition," I did when I read Joyce—especially *A Portrait of the Artist as a Young Man.* I believe until this day I favor that among Joyce's books.

Conversations: Where and when did you first read Joyce?

Farrell: In 1927 and '28, in New York and in Chicago. I read everything I could read of Joyce's at the time.

Conversations: Did you stumble on him or did somebody point you at him?

Farrell: Oh, no. I had heard about *Ulysses* and about Joyce as early as '26, and had been planning to read him.

Conversations: Let's talk about the Dreiser strain. You've been called "the last American naturalist." Would you accept that label?

Farrell: Well, I don't know what they mean by it.

Conversations: What do you mean by the word "naturalism"?

Farrell: I've given up being concerned with it. I did give a lecture on naturalism which I published in my book, *Reflections at Fifty.* I analyzed the one coherent presentation of any theory about naturalism with which I was familiar—that was Zola's *Le Roman experimental,* which he published in 1880. And, of course, I couldn't agree with that. Scientifically it does not hold today. I mean, Zola based his ideas on the writings of Claude Bernard, a great scientist—particularly on an introduction to the *Medecine experimentale,* which is a great and exciting book to read in itself. My writing is much different from Dreiser's. As a matter of fact, it was more influenced by Hemingway. Hemingway, along with Ring Lardner, gave me the idea of using dialogue and using vernacular, and from that I developed. So I use dialogue in many different ways: I use it to continue a story; I use it to create a sense of atmosphere; to give an added sense of reality; to characterize; to continue the story; and merely, sometimes, for its own sake.

Conversations: Of those two influences—the Lardner influence and the Hemingway influence—the Lardner would have been earlier, because you would have been reading Lardner in the Chicago Tribune *when you were a boy, is that right?*

Farrell: Yes, but it was unconscious. The Hemingway influence came after I had started to write. If you read one of my first short stories, which was written in 1928 called "Mary O'Riley," you will see how different that is from some of the writing I did as much as a year later. It's a story of a woman, a virgin, who dies. It's interesting—I was twenty-four, and it began by stating that one morning Mary O'Riley looked at herself in the mirror and discovered that she was an old woman. She was over fifty. When I looked at it recently, I was amused when I considered that I'm now over seventy. But that story is much different. As a matter of fact, there is nothing in it that predicates Studs Lonigan; there is something in it that presages the O'Neill-O'Flaherty books and the character, the mother Liz O'Neill. When I first began writing I didn't know that I could write dialogue.

Conversations: And reading Hemingway and Lardner broke this block—if that's what it was?

Farrell: Yes. Yes, it was. Hemingway's technical influence in America was very great. I believe that dialogue—that it's largely due to him that there have been changes in the use of dialogue in America.

25

James T. Farrell

Conversations: And your exposure to Hemingway dates from what—1925, In Our Time?

Farrell: '27 I first read him. *Men Without Women* I read in the New York Public Library.

Conversations: But you'd been reading Lardner for a long time before that.

Farrell: Yes, yes. Then, of course, George Ade, too, whom to this day I admire greatly. He's one of our many lost writers—lost in the sense that few members of the younger generation know of his work. His writing, it's almost like he were painting. I mean, it's extremely colorful. There's one phrase of his I always quote. In one of his stories he describes an employer as every Saturday crowding $3 upon the working girl who works in his factory. I was influenced by many books outside of literature, too; I was never solely interested in literature or reading simply literature. When I went to the university I majored in social sciences, not literature, not English. And books like *The Economic Consequences of the Peace*, and the writings of John Dewey, R. H. Tawney, and many others influenced me.

Conversations: In a sense you escaped from the environment that destroyed Studs Lonigan. I take it that your own Chicago background in terms of neighborhood, in terms of locale, in terms of setting, was much like the one described in the Lonigan trilogy.

Farrell: Yes. I would say yes, but I would say this also: whether people escape or don't escape has something to do with themselves and their characters. I've been described as being an environmentalist.

Conversations: Are you?

Farrell: No.

Conversations: You feel, then, that what happened to Studs— Studs' fate—was a result of his character. He was not shaped by the forces of environment.

Farrell: Well, he was shaped by them because he didn't resist them. I conceived the characters of Studs Lonigan and Danny

O'Neill simultaneously, practically. The work I planned to write was the one which became the O'Neill-O'Flaherty series. It grew into four books: *A World I Never Made, No Star Is Lost, Father and Son, My Days of Anger*. Then, ten years later, I wrote a new beginning to it called *The Face of Time*. Now if you examine Studs and Danny O'Neill in those five books, I think you'll see that Studs never makes the right decisions concerning his future estate and his destiny, and Danny does. And furthermore, as I've stated already, I began *Studs Lonigan* with the idea that he was going to die young. Then I asked myself the question: What happened in his life before he died?

Conversations: I once heard a critic say that Studs Lonigan *was an old-fashioned book in that the simple message of it is that the wages of sin is death.*

Farrell: Well, I've always contended that's the Protestant conception; and furthermore, that if you're a religious person and you take on to yourself the power of God and say that the wages of sin is death, you are becoming quite arrogant and presumptuous. Furthermore Studs doesn't do so much sinning.

Conversations: Yet Studs' fate is, as I read the book, the result of all the mistakes he makes. Or, if that's putting it the wrong way, all the right moves he does not make.

Farrell: Yes.

Conversations: Aren't these secular sins?

Farrell: They're not sins in a religious sense. Some of his mistakes do not violate the Ten Commandments or the seven capital sins. But Studs' death is enigmatic—deliberately so. You can not say with definite assurance that Studs died because of the way he lived. It could be that he was born with the defective heart, because other characters drank as much as Studs, and they didn't die.

Conversations: Did your conception of character in your novels written during the thirties result from your Marxist thinking at that time?

Farrell: More from the thinking of Dewey and George Herbert Mead. There was one article of Mead's I read about 1930, "The

James T. Farrell

Genesis of the Self and Social Control," and that book, *Human Nature and Conduct*, which I think is one of Dewey's outstanding books, and parts of William James's *The Principles of Psychology* influenced me very much. It was through the work of the pragmatists that I developed a functional sense of the relationships of character and environment, and environment and character, and the sense of continuity and of process. Also Whitehead's work influenced me, and Eddington. Studs is a reflection of his environment. He carries in himself all the values of his environment or many of the values of his environment. And he affirms some that he doesn't abide by, as everybody does.

But you can also consider it a psychological novel. Much of the world as presented in *Studs Lonigan* is presented through Studs' consciousness—even the streets, the descriptions. He walks along and more or less describes them to himself or notes places or remembers. Now I had a stronger environmental bias then than I do now. But as I wrote the book—you can't take a theory and create a character out of a theory.

Conversations: Which was the point of your 1936 book, A Note on Literary Criticism.

Farrell: Yes. And Studs, of course—see, I didn't have a full conception of Studs when I began to write it. I wrote a story called "**Studs**" that was printed in *This Quarter* in 1929. That story is definitely different from *Studs* in the writing. It's written in the first person and there are a few metaphors. As I worked on *Studs* I decided to write the book using words that he would use or that were in his working vocabulary—that is, that were comprehensible to him. I sort of created a style for *Studs* as I wrote it.

Conversations: A Note on Literary Criticism *created a furor. The* New Masses, *for example, devoted some space to rebuttals of that book. In* A Note on Literary Criticism, *as I understand it, you say that literature cannot be created in accordance with a theory of economics or politics or even of human conduct. Do you see literature as a social instrument?*

Farrell: Yes, but that is not necessarily the aim of the artist. That is true in terms of its effects, its consequences.

Conversations: Would you say, then, that the job of the artist is to create character, and whatever "message" the book has is incidental to the main job of the novelist?

Farrell: Well, I believe the message may be incidental, or the message may be contradictory, or there may not be a message. Joyce had a message in the sense of rejecting Ireland, but that's not so important in his work.

Conversations: You do not, then, hold that literature is valuable—permanently valuable—only in so far as it has social impact, social effect?

Farrell: Well, no, because how are we going to explain many of the books of the past? How can I explain my liking of a writer like Ronald Firbank, or how can I explain my liking of Celine, who is one of the most powerful and greatest writers of this century?

Conversations: Critics have discerned a pattern from a social awareness in your earlier work to a socially uninvolved position as your work developed. Would you agree that in your earlier work you were trying to deliver a message?

Farrell: Well, yes, but the message was more general. It was fundamentally a rebellion at the misery of life. I explained it to myself differently as I learned and observed and changed.

Conversations: Do you still believe in the misery of life? Are you still rebelling?

Farrell: Oh, I've seen it all over. At my age people are dying like flies. I can tell you some terribly sad stories of friends dead and dying. My last book, of course, *The Dunne Family* is a terribly sad book.

Conversations: Before the point of death, do you see life as being unfair, accidental, random—or do you feel that people get what they deserve?

Farrell: By the time I began writing I felt that there was no retribution. I had the feeling that the artist, at least, gives the illusion of retribution.

Conversations: But isn't character fate?

James T. Farrell

Farrell: Yes, but, again, some of the things that strike men, some of the mistakes we make, some of the most incidental mistakes have the greatest of consequences. It's too big a question. I could say that everybody gets what they deserve. Very early in my career I made the distinction that there are two tragedies of men: the social and the biological.

Conversations: Would you elaborate, please?

Farrell: The social tragedy is when man pays the consequences for the actions of himself or of others. The biological tragedy is based upon the frail mortality of man, and that can be postponed but it cannot be averted.

Conversations: But looking at the social tragedy, would you say that in your experience there are certain characters, in fiction as well as in life, who seem to be masters of their fate—who seem to dominate life?

Farrell: Yes. Well, that was always my ambition—that was the idea behind the creation of Danny O'Neill. I changed his name to Eddie **Ryan** in my current series on which I'm working.

Conversations: Do you think the writer is a life-dominator or, at least, tries to be a life-dominator?

Farrell: He has to be or he's out of luck. Some writers do not. For instance, writers like Kafka and Strindberg you couldn't describe in that way. You could Ibsen. The writer whom you could say was determined to dominate life more than any other I can think of—the two writers were Tolstoy and Balzac. You know, Balzac had this bare room in which he wrote. Almost bare—he had a statue of Napoleon, and he scrawled on a sheet of paper under it: "What he has not conquered by the sword I shall with the pen." And whenever his energies flagged, he would look at that statue. And, of course, Napoleon was one of my first heroes, and I've been interested in Napoleon and reading about him, and I've written about him all my life.

Conversations: Let's go back to your boyhood. I take it you were not exposed to books—

Farrell: Oh, yes. There were books around. My uncle was a traveling salesman. He was a very successful one—as a matter of fact, in 1913 he made as much or more money then Ty Cobb. Ty Cobb's salary was $9,000 a year, and his was at least $10,000. See, I lived with my uncle who was a prosperous, successful salesman. My father was a poor man, a teamster, and then a scripper at the express company. But I lived with my grandmother. They were much more prosperous. I was never in want or anything like that, but I saw two environments—a more prosperous one and a working-class one.

Conversations: Your grandparents' home was filled with books or, at least, books were available?

Farrell: He used to read books and leave them around, and many of the first books I read were books he left around. I realize he left them around hoping I would read them: *The Way of All Flesh, Lord Jim, Smoke* by Turgenev, *Babbitt*, one of the books by the de Goncourts—I think it's *Renee Mauperin*, and a number of other books. Well, in my boyhood I read sports books. I read *The Saturday Evening Post*. There were always things around the house to read. I read some of O. Henry and Kipling and Shakespeare. But I wasn't really a reader; I was more interested in sports. I think I read more than other boys. I read *Penrod, Penrod and Sam, The Adventures of Tom Sawyer, The Adventures of Huckleberry Finn.*

Conversations: At that time Chicago was going through its so-called literary renaissance.

Farrell: Well, I knew nothing of that.

Conversations: That didn't touch you?

Farrell: No. I learned about that after I went to college.

Conversations: Ben Hecht, Sherwood Anderson—

Farrell: That was after I was twenty. Ben Hecht was the first.

Conversations: When did you first know that you were going to be a writer?

Farrell: Even in high school I wanted to write, and people tell me they always knew I would be a writer, but maybe they're imagining. But by the time I was out of high school that ambition

James T. Farrell

was there. I was working in the express company, and every word that I didn't know I'd write down. I'd come home every night, and I'd look them up and write sentences of five words, and I'd even keep copies of my letters. When I decided definitively was on March 17, 1927.

Conversations: What happened that day?

Farrell: Well, I took a course in advanced composition from James Weber Linn.

Conversations: You were twenty-three years old at the time.

Farrell: I didn't start to college until I was twenty-one.

Conversations: This was where?

Farrell: At the University of Chicago. And I became so interested in writing that I neglected my other courses. Now I was on my way to having a phenomenal university record. I worked forty-eight to fifty-four hours a week, six to seven days; did more work in all of my classes; and in my first thirteen courses I got ten A's and three B's. I won a freshman honor scholarship as one of the twenty highest freshmen. But I became so interested in writing, and he published one of my compositions on a B & G Sandwich Shop in his column. It was printed on that day—that was the day interim between the winter and spring quarters.

Conversations: He had a newspaper column?

Farrell: Yes. And he printed this composition of mine.

Conversations: What paper was it?

Farrell: *Chicago Herald-Examiner,* for which I later worked. And I decided I'd be a writer; I quit school.

Conversations: The first time you saw your work in print.

Farrell: Yes.

Conversations: The first time you saw that by-line.

Farrell: Yes.

Conversations: You knew you were a writer.

Farrell: Yes.

Conversations: In a sense you're the last of your breed, having outlived most of your contemporaries. Looking back from your vantage point, who were the greatest talents that you knew personally, that you were associated with as a writer? Who are the ones you most envied, most admired, most respected?

Farrell: Mencken, Dewey, Trotsky, Dreiser, Anderson, Fred Lewis, Ernest Hemingway—although I gradually reduced my appreciation of Hemingway. Marya Zaturenska, the wife of Horace Gregory, whom I believe is a genius and a great poet— terribly neglected—Horace Gregory.

Conversations: You knew all of these people more or less well?

Farrell: Yes.

Conversations: Is there any one of them—

Farrell: Well, the most inspiring figure was Dreiser because I read. . . . I was working for R. R. Donnelly selling advertising in what's now called the yellow pages but was then called the *Red Book* out in Queens. This was in 1927. I was on my way to winning a prize, but I became so interested in Dreiser that I worked it out so I could go out on my territory four to six hours a week and sell enough to keep my job. I spent the rest of my time reading Dreiser, and I read one book after another. I read about eight books of his in succession.

Conversations: When did you first meet Dreiser?

Farrell: In 1936.

Conversations: How and where?

Farrell: At the Democratic National Convention in Philadelphia. I saw Mencken on the street and he told me, "Dreiser is in town. Why don't you go up and see him?" I went up to see him, and when I left he forgot who I was.

Conversations: Did you see him again?

Farrell: Once, but I had a correspondence with him, and I read his last two novels for him and wrote him very long, detailed letters on them—about twenty-five typewritten pages.

James T. Farrell

Conversations: Looking around today, who are the ones who matter in your judgment?

Farrell: Solzhenitsyn, Brian Moore. I don't know who else.

Conversations: Neither one of them is an American. Are there any Americans?

Farrell: There are some Americans whose work I like, but, you know, it's not of that stature. I like some of the writing of Kurt Vonnegut. I don't read too many contemporary novels. I don't have time. I'm trying to think—there's a writer who wrote a book of short stories that I like very much: Richard Yates, *Eleven Kinds of Loneliness.*

Conversations: You have been a lifelong baseball buff. You were living in Chicago and about sixteen years old at the time of the Black Sox scandal. I have read the statement that the Black Sox disclosure shook American confidence; that the belief in the essential innocence of American life was damaged by the revelation that the players conspired to tamper with the national game. Is that an exaggeration?

Farrell: I think it's an exaggeration; I really think it's an exaggeration. My feeling was: I was kind of hurt and I wished that they could have been given a second chance.

Conversations: It wasn't a personal trauma for you, though.

Farrell: No.

Conversations: Were you a White Sox fan?

Farrell: Oh, yes. I used to go to the ball games and pray that they would win. I later met a few of the players on that team: Buck Weaver, Ray Schalk, Red Faber. You know, I wrote a book on baseball. I called it *My Baseball Diary.* I have two drafts of a novel on that scandal—good first drafts.

Conversations: Are you going to publish it?

Farrell: I hope so, but then I have so many first drafts.

Conversations: When I walked in today you showed me your file cabinets, and you said that these were the drawers filled with finished but unpublished works.

Farrell: Finished or almost.

Conversations: How many? What's the total in there?

Farrell: Well, let's see. There's one called "When Time Was Cliche"; two volumes called "The Call of Time," almost finished.

Conversations: This is all fiction?

Farrell: Yeah. There are two volumes of one called "Equal to the Centuries"; there are over 800 pages of one called "When Time Was Running Red"; there are two drafts of a baseball novel; there's a novelette called "Anita Nelson"; there's a novelette on a trade union conflict; there are about 400 or 500 pages of a book called "Paris in the Spring of 1949"; and there are over 400 pages of a book really untitled, it's set in the sixties, called "Hotel Sequence"—that's a designation; there are several hundred pages of one called "A Trip to Hollywood"; there are more.

Conversations: The obvious question is how did you accumulate this backlog? Are you writing faster than the publishers can publish them?

Farrell: Yes. In 1941 when *Ellen Rogers* was published, I was in California, and my wife at that time was Hortense Alden, the actress. She was very disturbed by the critical licking I was taking for that book, and I wrote back. I said, "Don't worry; I'll write books faster than those sons of bitches can condemn them." At that time I had seen a lot of the actress, Alla Nazimova, who admired my work. She had noted the reviews, and she liked *Ellen Rogers*. She said, "Jim, you have one alternative. You must win by weight, like Zola." I have a great admiration for Zola, but I never read Zola until about '36 or '37.

Conversations: Obviously one of the ways you've accumulated this backlog is by spending a lot of time at your desk.

Farrell: Yes.

Conversations: I take it you write seven days a week.

Farrell: Yes.

Conversations: How many hours a day?

35

James T. Farrell

Farrell: I used to write sometimes as many as twelve. I still write two, three, four, five, six, eight, nine, ten, and crowd in what reading I can.

Conversations: You're still on occasion putting in ten-hour days?

Farrell: Oh, yes. When I travel I don't allow my traveling to interfere with my work; I continue to work while I travel and lecture.

Conversations: You write in hotel rooms; you write on trains; you write on planes?

Farrell: Yes.

Conversations: As long as you're awake you write.

Farrell: Yes.

Conversations: How much sleep do you get?

Farrell: Well, now I get about eight or nine. I used to get four.

Conversations: When were you in Europe?

Farrell: I was in Europe in 1931 to '32.

Conversations: How did you get over there?

Farrell: I had a chance to go, and I was in a lot of trouble so I went.

Conversations: I won't ask about the trouble. When you say you had a chance to go, did you get a grant?

Farrell: No, a ticket. We went with $80 or $100. We had a baby there, who died after five days. Lived there a year. I got an advance on Young Lonigan and an advance on Gas-House McGinty. I came back with the help of Travelers Aid.

Conversations: Was this period spent entirely in Paris or did you travel?

Farrell: No, in Paris.

Conversations: You were there in '31-'32, so you arrived after the golden period was over.

Farrell: Yes, the exodus was on.

36

Conversations: At the time when most of the Americans were fleeing Paris, you came for the first time.

Farrell: Yes.

Conversations: Who was still around?

Farrell: Well, I met Pound. He lived in Rapallo. I met him once. Sam Putnam, Peter Neagoe, the people at *Transition*, but I didn't meet them.

Conversations: Now you were published in This Quarter.

Farrell: Yes.

Conversations: Was Walsh still alive?

Farrell: No. Titus—and Sam Putnam was working on it. Titus didn't like the story, and Sam Putnam slipped it in. Some months later I sent a manuscript to *The New Republic* and received a reply from Slater Brown, asking if I was the same James Farrell who wrote a story called "Studs" in *This Quarter*. I learned it was published, and I wrote Titus a letter and asked him to pay me. He wrote me back an indignant letter, and the next day he wrote me a second letter. He discovered that it was in *This Quarter*, and he sent me a twenty-five-dollar check.

Conversations: Was "Studs" your first fiction publication?

Farrell: No, it was a story called "Slob" printed in *Blues*, edited by Charles Henri Ford and Parker Tyler from Columbus, Mississippi, in June 1927. It also wasn't the first story I wrote that was since published. In 1928 I wrote three stories. One is called "Mary O'Riley"; one is called "Calico Shoes"; and one is called "The Open Road." The first two were published in my first book of stories, *Calico Shoes*. "The Open Road" was published in my second book, *Guillotine Party*. I call attention to them because the three of them are different, and they don't predicate *Studs Lonigan*. Curiously enough, "Calico Shoes," my first story, is really an ethnic story; people read those stories today and like them.

Conversations: You wrote Young Lonigan, *or what became* Young Lonigan, *in Paris?*

37

Farrell: No, I finished it. It was written and turned down by five publishers. I left it with a friend of mine, Walt Carmen, who was managing editor of *The New Masses*. He took it to Henley, and Henley accepted it for Vanguard Press.

Conversations: Then you revised that draft in Paris.

Farrell: Yeah, I put back a section or two, and Henley made a very good suggestion about a new beginning. I wrote a new first chapter. It began with the graduation scene. Also I took out a scene—gang shag scene. Well, I had that directly described and Henley said that there wasn't any chance at all of getting it by the censorship. So I took it out. I later published it in my book, *A Dangerous Woman and Other Stories*, under the title of "Boys and Girls."

Conversations: What else did you write in Paris during that period?

Farrell: I wrote, actually, two novels and a novelette.

Conversations: All published?

Farrell: No, the novel was *Gas-House McGinty*. I revised it back here. I was going to make that a trilogy, and I had a connecting section which I published as a story called "Omar James." Then I had another volume about a character, Willie Collins. There are some Willie Collins stories which were salvaged out of that work, but in my fire in 1946 that and three other books were burned.

Conversations: You made no attempt to rewrite them?

Farrell: No.

Conversations: You mentioned the critics and said that you were going to beat the sons of bitches by weight: You'll overwhelm them. It is an unhappy fact that the critics have not been kind to you for the last decade or so. Do you feel that this is because your work is now unfashionable, and, if so, what makes a writer's work unfashionable?

Farrell: You know, there's a market for novelty and there's this trendiness and there's Eastern snobbery. Every Mid-Western writer who has come here, or almost every one, has run this gamut of snobbery. When *Young Lonigan* came out they decided I was a natural and an ignoramus; and they hold to that position, more or less. Now it's just become a cliche not to like my work. It doesn't really bother me. I recall when *Young Lonigan* came out I read a couple of reviews and learned of all the things I was doing that I didn't understand, and I decided: Well, if I pay attention to this stuff, I'll go nuts.

Conversations: Do you read the critics now?

Farrell: I start reading a review and the minute I see that the reviewer is faking or lying, I put it in the carton and send it to my archives. Maybe some candidate for a doctorate will take the trouble to finish it. You know, the last communication I received from Edmund Wilson was a postcard: "Dear Jim, The only thing we can do is outlive the sons of bitches. Edmund."

Conversations: And you're doing that.

Farrell: Well, I hope to. You see, we talked about my early work, but I'm interested in my current work. I'm always interested in the books I'm writing or going to write—not the ones I've written. I don't like to read my own work.

Conversations: Do you feel the Studs Lonigan books may have warped or distorted the understanding of your career in that people feel if they read the Studs Lonigan trilogy, they've read Farrell?

Farrell: Yeah, that's a fact. Of course, to a considerable degree it was deliberate and intended and calculated, because many people who didn't like *Studs*, liked it to criticize my other books. See, *Studs* to me is no longer a major work of mine. *Studs* was finished—when it was finished there were no problems. It didn't lead to anything further. The O'Neill series was meant to lead to something further. After I had begun writing I decided that my works would be one collective life-work and nobody would accept that. Or almost no one.

Conversations: One of the charges that hostile critics bring against your work is that it hasn't shown any development; that you keep writing the same novel over and over again with different names.

James T. Farrell

Farrell: That's because they don't read it.

Conversations: What is the principle of growth and development and evolution in your works?

Farrell: Well, all I can say is to keep learning and saying and thinking.

Conversations: Mr. Farrell, looking beyond your shoulder, I see three autographed baseballs. Who signed them?

Farrell: This is signed by four umpires—Tata, Bill Williams, Andy Olsen, and Ed Sudol. I walked in to see the umpires with Jerry Holzman, a Chicago sports writer, at Wrigley Field and they gave me this. This one is signed by Joe DiMaggio, Monte Irvin—a number of players in the old-timers game at Shea Stadium a couple of years ago. It was signed for a friend of mine, Ron Taylor, who was a pitcher for a number of years. He was a relief pitcher with the Mets, among others, and he's now a doctor in Toronto. He drove me home, and he wanted to give me a present. So he gave this to me. This was gotten for my seventieth birthday, signed by Walt Alston, whom I also knew because I took a trip with the Dodgers in 1955.

Conversations: Do you still get to games?

Farrell: Oh, yes, I go at least once a week. I always sit in the press box, and I sometimes go out on the field. I talk with Red Smith and all the writers and a number of friends—Gabe Paul is a friend of mine. I like Billy Martin very much. I like Yogi Berra. I've met quite a few ball players. I've written some stories about ball players. Some of them were published in a book—two books were in paperback only.

Conversations: There's a cliche that says there is no great American baseball novel. Would you agree?

Farrell: Well, there are two very good ones, at least—*You Know Me Al* and *The Southpaw* by Mark Harris; then another one, *Bang the Drum Slowly*, is sort of a novelette. They're all good works. Mark Harris has written very well about baseball. There's a good biography of Babe Ruth, but that's not a novel. But there's not much good writing about sports. I've tried to take in a number of sports: I have one story about a tennis player; I have two prizefight stories; I have some high school basketball and football stories; I have stories with a baseball atmosphere; and I have this unpublished novel about baseball. I have a few other stories on baseball unpublished. And I may write more yet.

Thomas Wolfe had touches about baseball that were good. Thomas Wolfe, at first I didn't care for him, and I feel it was a great mistake. Thomas Wolfe was a real combination of genius and adolescence. There was kind of an overwhelming genius about him, and he should be more remembered.

Conversations: I can't leave that list you recited of the great figures you'd known, which included Hemingway, Mencken, Dreiser, Sinclair Lewis, Sherwood Anderson. Are there any golden memories that you especially recall—time spent with any of these people?

Farrell: Not golden moments. I used to enjoy Mencken more than most of them.

Conversations: Was he the one you saw the most often?

Farrell: Yes, I corresponded with him for years. See, Mencken read a lot. He was interested in ideas; he was more receptive; he was more interesting to talk to. Socially speaking, he had a more interesting personality.

Conversations: Would you see him in Baltimore or New York?

Farrell: I'd run into him at political conventions, and I'd see him in Baltimore. I'd run into him in New York. I would see him several times after his illness. His parting words always were: "Tell my friends I'm a hell of a mess." Well, the Gregorys I've had very many fine times with—they're both fine poets. Dos Passos used to come to see me, and I always enjoyed and liked Dos—a very decent man and a good writer. Incidentally, in my new book of stories I have tried something—I've got two stories about Southerners.

Conversations: Is this a departure for you? Are these the first Southerners to appear?

Farrell: Yeah, except incidentally. I never knew Frances Newman, but I admire her work. I took the idea of her life, then I imagined a writer.

Conversations: This was the Georgia writer.

Farrell: Yeah. The story has nothing to do with Frances Newman, but she gave me the idea of this cogitative woman—who dies young—who is a gifted, cultivated, Southern woman. And in the other I imagined a Southern boyhood of Maxwell Bodenheim. He came from Mississippi, I believe.

Conversations: Did you know Bodenheim?

Farrell: Yes. He was a pathetic person, and he wasn't a good writer.

Conversations: Ever?

Farrell: No, I agree with Marya Zaturenska: he didn't know the English language. He was an incurable alcoholic. Ben Hecht's best book is about Bodenheim, *Count Bruga*. It's a very funny book.

Conversations: You knew Hecht in Chicago?

Farrell: No, I never met Hecht.

Conversations: Did you have a Hollywood period? Did you ever go out to Hollywood and write for them?

Farrell: Two weeks and I came home.

Conversations: You left.

Farrell: I wrote a story on that called "$1,000 a Week." I wrote two other Hollywood stories. One is "To Whom It May Concern"—it was put in the form of a diary of a Hollywood writer. And one called "Patsy Gilbride"; it was based upon a very successful figure of the silent days. The story I never published was based on Alla Nazimova, called "Two Ibsen Girls from Yalta."

Conversations: When you went out to Hollywood for this two-week stint, what were you brought out to do and who brought you out?

Farrell: My agent was determined to sell me. He brought me out, and they paid the expenses, and he didn't do anything. Finally I was leaving, and he made a deal for the day I was supposed to leave. It was all idiotic.

Conversations: You left anyhow.

Farrell: Yeah.

Conversations: So you never put in a day on the payroll?

Farrell: Two weeks. He made a deal for a two-week contract with an extension.

Conversations: Which studio was this?

Farrell: Twentieth Century-Fox.

Conversations: They brought you out there; they gave you $1000 a week for two weeks; and gave you nothing to do?

Farrell: Yeah, they gave me some old source to do a script on, and I wrote a couple of drafts of it.

Conversations: At the end of two weeks you said the hell with it.

Farrell: Yeah, I came home.

Conversations: My recollection is that the only one of your books Hollywood has done is Studs. *Have they bought other properties?*

Farrell: No. I've never seen it, but I understand it's coming out on television.

Conversations: In an eight-part series, I believe.

Farrell: That's what I was told, but I don't—

Conversations: On ETV.

Farrell: Yes.

Conversations: Will you have any part of that?

Farrell: I have nothing to do with it. I may get something out of it. I don't know how much.

James T. Farrell

Conversations: You won't write the script or have any role in the making of the series?

Farrell: No, and I wouldn't want to. I wouldn't want to work on *Studs Lonigan.*

Conversations: You've been there already, is that it?

Farrell: Yes, that's a long time ago. I finished it February 1, 1935, and I was thirty years old.

Conversations: I noticed twice during our conversation that you've mentioned specific dates: the date of your first appearance in print, the day you finished the Lonigan trilogy. Does it just happen that you remember these dates?

Farrell: I remember a lot of dates. I sailed for Paris on April 16, 1931. I believe I came back on April 15, 1932.

Conversations: Is this just accidental or do you make some attempt to record dates?

Farrell: I don't make an attempt, but I do have a good memory.

Conversations: Mr. Farrell, looking back over a writing career that is now more than forty years duration and what—forty-odd books—

Farrell: Fifty-two to come out, and I don't know how many in my archives and in process.

Conversations: If you were planning your career or replanning your career would you have played it more cautiously, or would you have done it just the way you've done it?

Farrell: No, I've done a lot of incautious things, but I imagine that I would have made other mistakes.

Conversations: Different mistakes?

Farrell: Yes. It doesn't do much good to regret the past. If you've acted badly, you just do the best you can about it and forget it.

Conversations: Most writers have a pet project that didn't work out. Some book they weren't able to write or weren't able to finish that they regret in the small hours of the night. Do you have one of these projects?

Farrell: Well, I have all kinds that I could never get to. I wanted to write a book called "An Amateur Looks at Philosophy." I wanted to write plays.

Conversations: You've never written a play?

Farrell: Yes, I wrote a one-act play. It's never been produced, but it was read at Kent State University. And I wrote a three-act play with my former wife, Hortense Alden, which was published but never produced, called *The Mowbray Family.*

Conversations: If you were writing your New York Times *obit what would you say about yourself?*

Farrell: I don't know. I wrote a book of bad poems—or I don't think they're very good anyway—and I wrote my obituary. I'll read it:

One James (T. for Thomas) Farrell
Who might have been this,
And who might have been that,
But who might have been
Neither this nor that,
And who wrote too much,
And who fought too much,
And who kissed too much,
For all of his friends,
(He needed no enemies)—
That man, J.T.F.
Died last night
Of a deprivation of time.
He willed his dust
To the public domain.

Irvin Faust was educated at City College of New York and Columbia University. He holds a doctorate in education and is a full-time guidance counselor at a New York high school. Since 1964 he has published six volumes of fiction: Roar Lion Roar, The Steagle, The File on Stanley Patton Buchta, Willy Remembers, Foreign Devils, *and* A Star in the Family.

Irvin Faust

Irvin Faust was interviewed by Matthew J. Bruccoli in May 1977 at the Fausts' apartment on Riverside Drive near Columbia University. Trim and energetic, Faust speaks forcefully, tempering his strong convictions with humor.

Conversations: You mentioned a few minutes ago that you're working on something that's exciting to you.

Faust: It's a novel that takes place primarily in the thirties, but moves back into the twenties. I haven't talked very much about it before, but I think I've reached the point where I'm able to talk about it now. I guess I'm about three-fifths of the way through, and it's the first thing that I've attempted in which a black man is the central character—the hero or the villain, as will be determined. It ranges from the South to Harlem to Africa and, perhaps, back to Harlem. And, as I say, I'm about three-fifths of the way through. When I say a black hero, I guess back in the thirties we would have called him a "colored" hero. But I'm excited to the point that I'm driven to the typewriter every night. When I do that, I know something's happening.

Conversations: Is that unusual for you—to feel driven to the typewriter every night?

Faust: When I stop being driven, as has happened even after 500 or 600 pages, I know that's the end of it.

Conversations: You're not a compulsive writer normally?

Faust: No, but I'm compulsive in the sense that when lightning strikes, I go. But I don't set myself a quota or say I have to sit down every night. In fact, I've gone six months or a year without a word on paper.

Irvin Faust

Conversations: Can you endure these vacations? You don't suffer like hell?

Faust: Not at all. No. As a matter of fact, in the end I find that things have happened down in the well. Then something may click like the Memorial Day parade down Riverside Drive, which turned on *Willy Remembers* after about a year or two of nothing happening externally. The Nixon trip to China suddenly resonated with a failed short story I had written five or six years before, which clicked into place as the novel within the novel in *Foreign Devils*—the foreign correspondent bit. And, as you may know, I have a compartmentalized existence: during the day I'm very busy as a guidance counselor in a public high school. I find counseling very therapeutic for me as a writer, and I find the writing very therapeutic for me as a counselor. They complement each other beautifully. And since I came to writing rather late in life, my other career had been established.

Conversations: How old were you when you had your first professional appearance?

Faust: My first story, "Into the Green Night," was published in the *Carleton Miscellany*, the Carleton College magazine, when I was about thirty-seven. So that's sixteen years ago. But actually, the first time I broke into print was in 1956. A case study I wrote as a class project, "Angel and the New Teach," was published by Teachers College in a book of case studies—which was a great surprise to me because I didn't know I was a writer. Then I decided to do a group of case studies for my doctoral thesis—which later was published by Teachers College, in 1963, as *Entering Angel's World*.

Conversations: Before that there were no high school publications?

Faust: I was on the sports staff of my high school newspaper, *The Newtown X-Ray*—Newtown being a high school in Elmhurst Queens—very often called "Newton," to our consternation. I wrote sports for *The Newtown X-Ray* for about a year or so. My great thrill then was getting a by-line. But other than that not much—a few piddling things like an essay contest for *Scholastic Magazine*. I can remember writing an essay called "The

Ramifications of the Sino-Japanese War" for which I got an honorable mention pin from *Scholastic Magazine*. I hadn't thought too much about writing except that the sports editor of the high school newspaper said to me, "You know, Faust, I think maybe you should be a journalist someday." And that was kind of interesting for me to consider, not at all knowing what I wanted to do. And so I sat down at that point and wrote a sports story about an Italian runner named Luigi Beccali, who was the 1500-meter champion at the 1932 Olympic games. Never again won a race as far as I know. Beccali would come to New York City every winter. I was an indoor track nut—still am—and I'd go to the Garden and sit up in the balcony in seventh heaven. I'd watch these mile runs with people like Glenn Cunningham and Gene Venzke. And Beccali used to be invited over every winter to run, but the poor guy could never win a race, and here he had won the Olympics in '32. I found this very sad, so I sat down and I wrote a—I guess a sports essay about this fact. Because my high school editor said I might have a future as a journalist, I sent the piece to Dan Parker, who was the sports editor of *The Daily Mirror* at the time, telling him that somebody told me maybe I should be a journalist. I said: "I know something about sports. Does this piece have any merit? Do you think I should do anything after this?" And Dan Parker, who must have been a lovely gentleman, wrote me back a long letter saying it was an interesting piece and never to become discouraged, and that if this was what I wanted to do, I should go on and do it—all the right things to say to a kid. It was probably a terrible piece; to this day my wife and I collapse over the final sentence, which went something like this: "And as you watch poor Beccali plod around the Garden track in last place, you sit back and wonder: 'Whatever happened to the amazing speed that once infected his legs in 1932?' "

And that's about it. I went to Queens College for a year and a half, then enlisted in the Army—World War II. I was in Europe and the Philippines and then Japan for the Occupation. I came back, and like a lot of guys during that period was so confused and mixed-up that I didn't think about going back to college. I knocked around for a year and finally decided to go back, but I just didn't want to do anything academic, although I had been a very good student in high school. Because I was a good ball player, I decided to major in physical education at City College, of all places, which is kind of a contradiction in terms. One does not major in physical ed. at C.C.N.Y. One majors in engineering or takes English Lit. and becomes Bernie Malamud. But I took physical ed. with a minor in biology, and got my teaching degree. Then I went to work in Harlem for four years. Much of what I experienced in Harlem later appeared in *Roar Lion Roar*—the street sense, the jargon and so on, the Puerto Rican thing.

I learned that although I enjoyed working with the kids as a teacher, it wasn't enough for me. There had to be another way of working and reaching kids, I thought. And at that time the guidance counseling movement was getting off the ground, particularly at Teachers College, Columbia. So I took a leave of absence and went back and got a master's and then decided to go for a doctorate in the field. It was at that point when I became a graduate student that I had a lucky break: an advisor who understood and encouraged me—Dr. Raymond Patoullet (who's now teaching at the University of South Florida in Tampa). He helped convince the department that my case studies were material for a doctoral thesis. We worked together and—as Dan Parker used to say—"putting one little word after the other," the thesis emerged and was called "As They See It: A Series of Subjective Case Studies." T. C. decided to publish it under the title of *Entering Angel's World*—An-hel's World.

I guess then I got the idea that I might be able to write. I took a course in short story writing with Martha Foley. Halfway through the course, she became ill and was replaced by R. V. Cassill. I wrote a story about a kid who lives his life in the movies and is turned on by numbers, dates, which become very crucial to his life. This story turned out to be "Into the Green Night," which Cassill liked very much, announcing to the class: "This story is ready for publication." "What do I do with it?" I said. I had no idea, but I showed it to Jean, who's an excellent critic, and she said, "This is good." If she and Cassill said it was good, I thought maybe it was good. I went to the Martha Foley anthology—in the back they have the list of magazines and addresses—and I started sending it around. I'd get nice comments, but "it-does-not-meet-our-editorial-needs" kind of thing. Finally, I sent it to the *Carleton Miscellany* where Reed Whittemore was editor at the time. He liked it and printed it. That got the pump started. Whittemore took a couple of more stories. Then came "Roar Lion Roar." I've always been a Columbia football nut, which is an exercise in masochism, if there ever was one. This goes back to those Sid Luckman days. Oddly enough, no New York magazine wanted to touch it. I finally sent it out to the *San Francisco Review Annual*, which was published by New Directions, and they loved it and printed it. I can still remember getting a phone call one Sunday morning from Plimpton, the editor of *Paris Review*, who in the meantime had accepted "Philco Baby," the story of the kid with the transistor radio that is physically a part of him. He said, "Have you seen today's *Herald Tribune?*" I said, "No, we haven't seen it yet." He said, "Well, in *Book Week*"—or *Book World*, whatever the thing was called at that time, on the page where they review four or five novels— "there's a review of 'Roar Lion Roar'." I said, "You mean they've reviewed a story in the same way as a novel?" He said, "Yeah." So we rushed out on the way to a Japanese flick. I remember it was called *High and Low*, with Mifune. We got a copy of the *Tribune*, and sure enough, there was a review of "Roar Lion Roar" in the section devoted to four or five novels discussed by R. V. Cassill, and the title of the RLR part was "Pure Gold." We walked around on cloud nine that day.

Conversations: Your first book after your thesis was the short story collection, Roar Lion Roar, *and good as the stories are, it's a great break when a collection of short stories by an unknown writer, or at least a writer who has not a novel behind him to back it up, gets published. How did that come about? Did one of the editors spot and approach you?*

Faust: Yes, in a way. I began to publish stories in places like *Carleton, San Francisco, Transatlantic,* and I would keep getting letters from editors who would say, "I've seen such and such a story; am very impressed with it; do you happen to have a novel?" Or another letter—"Vance Bourjaily out in Iowa has told us about your work in the short story. Do you happen to have a novel?" I guess the breakthrough came when Plimpton published "Philco Baby" in *Paris Review*. This guy was great to me. He mentioned me to an editor at Random House named Robert Loomis, and Loomis said to me, "I've heard about your stories from Plimpton and Rose Styron, Bill's wife, and I understand at this point you don't have a novel, but do you have a number of stories to make a collection? If so, would you send them to me?" I had about ten stories at that time, seven of which had been published. I sent them to Loomis and got a quick reply, saying, "I love them. They really talk to me, but as you know, it's very difficult to make any money from a story collection"— something to that effect. "And much as we'd like to do them, it just does not seem right for your first book, your first fiction. When the novel comes along, by all means see me." And so I thought that was that, but later I heard from him again: "I can't forget *Roar Lion Roar and Other Stories*. And my wife, Gloria, keeps saying: 'Don't let this one get away.' I've talked to Mr. Cerf, and he says if I want to, do it." They did it, and the rest, as they say, is at least personal history.

Conversations: May one ask why you left Random House?

Faust: That's a good question. They did *Roar Lion Roar*. It was reasonably successful—certainly in the literary sense—and I don't think they lost any money on it. During the period of gestation, between the time I handed in the manuscript and when it was finally published, I did begin work on my first novel, *The Steagle*. The missile crisis in 1962 spoke to me in a stimulating way, and so I began writing. And naturally they published that. It was pretty well received, I thought. Next I wrote a novel about a New York City cop—I guess one of the earlier cop novels—kind of a triple agent in the old Russian sense, the nineteenth-century triple agent, on whom everything acts rather than his acting on anything—until the very end, of course, to his dismay. I guess I was expecting rather big things in a variety of ways, which didn't quite happen for one reason or another, and it's hard to know why. Could be the title; I guess it was the world's worst title.

Conversations: The File on Stanley Patton Buchta.

Faust: *The File on Stanley Patton Buchta*, right. I'll never have a title like that again—or that long or unpronounceable. By that time, Random House had moved from that beautiful landmark building on Madison Avenue over to a fancy corporate structure on Third Avenue. I began to get itchy. I thought perhaps I wasn't as appreciated as I could be, which, perhaps, was partly true and partly the eternal author's quest for Maxwell Perkins somewhere out there—who probably never really exists. At that point I had begun work on *Willy Remembers* and was very excited about it. When I finished it, my agent and I decided that perhaps Random wasn't the place for it. "Let's try a small house," she said, which turned out to be Arbor House. That's it. I guess I'm still looking for Maxwell Perkins.

Conversations: One of the marked characteristics of your work is the accuracy of it. The details are right: the names, the places, the dates, the song titles; everything is right. Does that just come out of your computer bank, or do you have to do a lot of research with old newspapers, old magazines?

Faust: It comes mainly out of the computer bank. I seem to have that kind of mind. My wife will do a double take when I come up with something ancient, and then wonder why I can't remember what happened to something I laid down five minutes before. I guess all husbands have gone through that routine. But yeah, it comes out of the computer bank mainly—on occasion just to make sure the computer bank hasn't failed me, I will check it out. I can remember discussing with Loomis an actress in *Rashomon*, my insisting that it was Machiko Kyo, and his thinking it was somebody else. I was willing to go to the mat on that one, and I turned out to be correct. I usually do turn out to be correct; but on occasion I will check the fact or the date. I'm not infallible. But mainly, it does come out of this well of New Yorkiana that's been simmering and cooking, lo these many years.

Conversations: I believe that this fund of information and a respect for detail differentiates your generation, my generation, from the young people today. Would you say that is an accurate comment?

Faust: Very accurate, very accurate. I just spoke about that recently with a couple of colleagues of my generation. As you know, I work in a public high school. . . .

Conversations: Where?

Faust: Garden City, out in Long Island. I deal with kids constantly, and one of the things I notice is there doesn't seem to be that continuity, that personal historic past. It's almost as if they were born yesterday. To me, there's a great sadness in this. Their life has missed so much richness.

Conversations: You blame it on the telly?

Faust: To a large extent I blame it on the telly, yeah. And in some ways, I blame it on my generation that came out of World War II and was determined to give a better life to our children, and in so doing have showered so many material things on them. . . the telly, the cars, the trips to Europe if you pass your geometry Regents; you name it. But the kids haven't had a chance to introspect and find out who they are, where they are. And there seems to be some kind of yearning toward this, at least in the kids that I deal with, but they're very confused. So yes, I blame the telly, and I blame my generation—both parents and educators. Of course, I'm talking about the middle-class kid with whom I deal.

Conversations: Would you also say that in addition to the showering of material gifts, benefactions, there is an absence of intimate contact with the parents? I spent big hunks of my life listening to my parents talk. As you say, the young people of today were born yesterday with no past at all.

Faust: Exactly. I had the same experience in a Brooklyn-Queens Jewish household. They may not have spoken to me as much about these things, but I got an awful lot through osmosis and a tremendous amount from my father whose heroes were men like Cardozo and Sol Bloom and Emanuel Celler. And Liebowitz, the retired judge who was a big criminal lawyer; Max Steuer— people like that. And this osmosed into me, much of it. But I just don't see that kind of thing with kids. I suppose one of the things that the kids are missing in some peculiar way is the sense of being an outsider becoming American—which I as a Jewish kid at that point was really trying to do. Not that I knew I was trying to do it, but that was what it was all about.

Conversations: Your parents were immigrants?

Faust: My father was; my mother wasn't. And my mother's background is very interesting because her mother was from Germany, but her father was born here and was an amazing character about whom I should do a novel someday. In fact, he appears, or some material about him appears, in my last book, about the comic, *A Star in the Family,* where Goldwine goes to live with his eighty-year-old grandmother and she tells him about her husband. Well, the husband is actually my grandfather, who fought in the American-Indian wars against the Apaches—against Geronimo, of all people—under General Crook. I remember his telling me how Crook was deprived of all the credit for capturing Geronimo, and how Nelson Miles came in and took all the glory. I guess till his dying day that was a tremendous injustice. That scene does appear in *A Star in the Family.* I think some people at Doubleday probably would have liked to cut it because it didn't add much to the story, but I wanted it in there because of my grandfather. One of these days I'm going to write to the War Department and get his military records and see what else I can do about him. When he came back from the war he was about twenty-one. He married my grandmother; they went on a honeymoon all over the country by rail, winding up in California. My grandmother, who was a very young immigrant, about seventeen at the time, insisted that a girlfriend go along on the honeymoon. So they traveled all over America with this girlfriend. When he came back he got a job at Louis Tiffany, and became a very expert craftsman in mosaics and worked there for fifty years, settled down, became a marvelous family man after being one of these crazy wild kids— probably the only Jewish soldier who fought Geronimo. As I grew older, I began more and more to appreciate him.

Conversations: Do you regard your work, in addition to the fictional aims, as an effort at social history? Do you feel that you are getting it down?

Irvin Faust

Faust: I find I'm in touch with my talent most tellingly when I write out of a realistic base. Some of my good friends, for example, said re: *The Steagle*: "Why did you use the missile crisis? Why don't you just talk about a crisis in general?" Universality, I suppose. I resisted that. I said, "It's important for me that Heshie's liberation must spring from the missile crisis which involved Kennedy"—who was a very important figure in my social and personal history. "My President," as Goldwine refers to him in the book on the comic. And yes, I feel that I am attempting to say these things, especially in *A Star in the Family*, and this is something few critics picked up—maybe it's my fault. The great watershed for this era of American history, I believe, was November 22, 1963. I think our whole consciousness and subconsciousness were altered by that day. And of course, the comic begins to disintegrate from then on. He picks up a little; then when R. F. K. gets killed he goes down completely. I think J. F. K.'s murder was the beginning of the breakup of the American Empire; things like that are said in the book.

Conversations: Do you see other writers trying to fulfill the same rationale of getting down the history of their times in fictional form? Or using it as a basis to make the fiction better, more convincing, stronger?

Faust: I saw a lot of this, I think, in the earlier work of Bellow and to a lesser extent Malamud. I saw some of it in Roth's *Goodbye, Columbus*, which I loved. I didn't care all that much for the title story, but I liked the other stories very much. And I'd like to see him return to stories one of these days. I guess I can't say that I know too many other people that I admire for that reason. I admire other people, but for different reasons.

Conversations: What do you think of the now classic social-fiction writers—O'Hara, Marquand? Do you recognize that in their work they were shooting at the same things that you are shooting at? Or do you feel that's a different tradition entirely?

Faust: I feel it's a different tradition simply because I feel both of these people are rooted very deeply in the American realistic tradition—the William Dean Howells school. They themselves are very—were very—comfortable as indigenous Americans. I see myself starting from that base, but then taking off with a great deal of fantasy involved within the realistic base—some of which works better than other portions of my work. I thought it worked probably the very best in *Foreign Devils*—the combination of the fantastic, the aspiring, the yearning, the Jew turning into the American, and the realistic base. In retrospect that probably was the most successful blending of those elements for me.

Conversations: Do you think of yourself as a Jewish-American writer?

Faust: No, I really don't, but I'm very aware of that base. I suppose it's a little bit like being a character actor—Robert Redford is always Robert Redford, but Alec Guinness is many things and yet he is still always Alec Guinness, basically. Naturally he must imprint himself upon his roles. So I have this Jewish-American base, but I don't think of myself in that sense as I think perhaps people refer to Malamud or Bellow, whose heroes are almost consistently Jews. One of my most successful books, at least in a commercial sense, was *Willy*. He's fairly anti-Semitic—anti-everything in many ways. And yet in the end, I think he emerges rather sympathetically. Buchta: I suppose his heritage is middle-European, but certainly not Jewish. Some of my stories don't deal with it, and, of course, my latest book will not deal with it at all—except tangentially. So no, I don't see myself as a stereotype Jewish-American writer, and yet I suppose that out of that wellspring much has developed. One of my most painful stories was a story about an anti-Semitic Jew in *Roar Lion Roar*—"Jake Bluffstein and Adolf Hitler"—a very painful story to write and to publish, for which I received some criticism from Jewish sources. I felt that it was important to talk about self-hatred. I think it's important to bring it out in the open, even to the extent that it becomes a psychosis, which it did in Jake's case. The funny thing is that right after that story came out and there was this criticism and my own feelings of pain, a member of the Ku Klux Klan killed himself when it was found out that he was brought up as an Orthodox Jew, bar mitzvahed and everything else. When he was exposed as being Jewish he couldn't handle it and killed himself. I said to myself: "My God, you know, life *does* imitate art after all."

Irvin Faust

Conversations: Do you have any comment to make on what could be called the Jewishization of American literature, at least in the last fifteen years or so, when most of the top writers are Jews and drawing on Jewish materials? Read the roll call of the most prominent, most influential, most successful, best, living American writers and you've got Faust, Markfield, Heller, Bellow, Malamud, Mailer, Roth. Any ideas about how this came about?

Faust: I subscribe to the Edmund Wilson theory of the wound and the bow. I think some of the greatest psychic wounds in American groups were felt by Jews prior to World War II, in particular as we saw what was happening in Germany. Our parents saw this, and their parents were involved as my grandparents were over there. I'm sure they were killed; we never found out—that's my father's parents. The World War II experience was critical for Jews: we could get out and fight this devil. I guess it's a cliche by now to say that was the last good war. No war is good, but in a personal sense I subscribed to that concept—which is one reason I enlisted, I suppose. Earlier, in 1942, I was inspired to work on a farm in the Volunteer Land Corps run by Dorothy Thompson, an experience which emerged as a story—"Miss Dorothy Thompson's American Eaglet." There was this three-day convention in Burlington. I can remember Thompson getting up and talking to us and seeing Sinclair Lewis kind of wandering around. To me, at that time, Sinclair Lewis didn't mean much, except that he had written *Arrowsmith*, which I was required to read in high school. So this farm project was part of the pre-World War reaching. Then came the war itself; and after that the experience of trying to find a place in America—I was hurting badly—as I think all Jews were. That well of experience, of reaching out, of yearning, of wanting to be an American in the way that we had perceived it—which of course, was incorrect. But we perceived it in movies; we perceived it in the novels of Ralph Henry Barbour and the Frank Merriwell stories and the Boy Scouts, which I joined—which was not at all like the *Boy Scout Handbook*, you know. All these elements produced the drive to write. Somehow it was part of getting to be American—though in that struggle Jews aren't the only ones who hurt.

Conversations: But they write best about their hurt?

Faust: Well, yeah, but Southern writers have been doing something there. There are women like O'Connor, who had a number of psychic hurts—Southern, Catholic, female, ill all her life—she turned it all into art. Maybe she didn't write so personally about her hurt, but I think out of it came much of what she did. That's about the best that I can do with the question. But I've taken off from that starting point. I've become tremendously interested in history, as you've probably inferred from reading *Willy* and *Foreign Devils*. And I've become tremendously interested in the overlay and the juxtaposition of history and what's happening today and the bouncing back and forth of themes. So I have begun to move out from the sense of personal hurt, but I guess it still exists.

Conversations: Do you have in your own head a career plan, a game plan for Faust's career? Do you have a body of work you would like to accomplish? Or do you take it one book at a time?

Faust: I pretty much take it one book at a time, except that I would like to see it all as a type of socio-realistic-fantastic journey from the thirties through the seventies and whatever years I am granted. And also to continue to live and work in my job.

Conversations: You lead a double life as a guidance counselor and as a writer. Do you ever feel that one interferes with the other—not conflicts, but interferes?

Faust: On the contrary, I find that they enrich each other and that if anything I've become more productive by doing both. I think I've done a book about every two or three years. I'm sure that wouldn't have happened if I didn't have the other life. And as I've begun to do this over the years, I'm feeling more and more that I'm part of the European tradition, the Chekhovian tradition of the man who is a dedicated doctor and also writes. Malraux involved with government and so on.

Conversations: Or English civil servants.

Faust: Yes, exactly. I think American writers have missed something by not doing that. It happened to me almost casually and accidentally. I don't claim any credit for consciously choosing this way of working, because I had this other career before I became a fiction writer. I have to be involved in a real way with the world, and when a kid says to me: "What have you done for me lately?" he couldn't care less about the fact that I've written a couple of books—some of which he knows about and some of which he doesn't.

Conversations: In purely practical terms, your job structures your day so that you don't sit around either waiting for something to write about or feeling guilty because you're not writing. Your day is laid out for you—at least five days a week.

Faust: Right, and when I am compelled to write, as I am now, the pressure of my life—the external pressure of the job and the internal pressure of the fiction—makes me much more productive. It drives me to that typewriter at night, weekends, holidays, what have you.

Conversations: When you're having a streak—when you feel that this stuff is coming out right. . . .

Faust: Good word, "streak."

Conversations: Do you resent the fact that you have to go to work the next day, when you would rather stay home and write?

Faust: No, because working sweeps out the cobwebs and clears the deck each day to get ready for that next evening.

Conversations: And you're not tired when you hit the typewriter at night?

Faust: I'm revived. I'm a bit of a physical exercise nut. I come home; I do a little yoga; when I can I jog or ride a bike; and then I'm ready to roll. I have an understanding wife, and I guess that's one of the things you need in this game. And when she sees me possessed she backs off and does other things.

Conversations: You hit the typewriter about eight o'clock at night?

Faust: A little earlier, maybe about 7:30, and go through till about 9:30 or ten, weekends, and so on. But I find that when I am not busy with this other kind of life, I'm not terribly productive.

I've never taken a sabbatical—a leave of absence. I've been urged to write for TV, for Hollywood—my own stuff and other things—and I've always said: "What for?" I happen to love working with kids, and I suppose someday I'll be doing stories and novels about my work in suburbia. You know, I lead a different life by day: What happens in Garden City is completely different from the reality of Morningside Heights, very clearly. I'm a wrong-way commuter—I commute from the city out to there.

Conversations: Why do you commute? Why don't you live in Garden City and walk to work?

Faust: I'm strictly a city boy—that I couldn't do.

Conversations: You don't begrudge the two hours a day in the subway?

Faust: Well, I did that for many years and then I finally got a car, because it was just too tough. No, because I find the ride relaxing. And the work is therapeutic for me.

It works both ways. Being a writer, I think, makes me a better counselor. Once in awhile the English teachers ask me to come in and talk to the kids; and the kids see me in a different dimension, which is important, I think. They see me as somebody other than the guy who gets them into college.

Conversations: Is that your primary job?

Faust: College guidance is a big item out there, yeah. That's a big one. At least that's the way my efforts are perceived by the community and the Board of Education. If I don't produce, they're very unhappy. I see it a little differently in that the college thing pays off in the natural course of events.

Conversations: You don't teach any classes at all, then?

Faust: No, except when I go in and lecture.

Conversations: You're a full-time guidance advisor?

Faust: Right, I'm the chairman of the department. So I run the department and I also counsel a certain number of kids. I love working with kids. I dearly love it, and I find that over the years

Irvin Faust

my work in schools has paid off as a fiction writer. I talked about my four years in Harlem which materialized into some of my best stories, and authentic ones, too.

Conversations: Do you find yourself consciously looking for material in your work?

Faust: No, no. I wait for that moment. My best moments are the things that hit me—the Memorial Day parade and the two remaining survivors of the Spanish-American War. The Red China thing. The reinvasion of China by Nixon, putting me back in touch with the Boxer Rebellion, which was the first invasion by America. A moment that strikes me going up on the subway to Baker Field: seeing across the aisle the little Puerto Rican kid who may or may not be going up to the game, then the click of "Roar Lion Roar." I can remember once the final sentence of a story hitting me and the problem then being to develop this story, to materialize it into the final sentence.

Conversations: Which story was that?

Faust: This is an uncollected story that appeared in the *Paris Review* called "Operation Buena Vista." It's about a little colored boy—"colored," you can see my background—a little black boy whose father has worked and scrimped and saved to get them out of Harlem. So they finally get an apartment on 95th Street, which looks over to New Jersey. To the kid *that's* America out there—that's the *mainland*. He lives on an island and that's the mainland; that's where America is. That's where he wants to be. That's where he wants to go. The father thinks he is nuts. The boy becomes the pen pal of a little boy in Minnesota named Lance Olson. You know, a good Scandinavian kid. They become pen pals. Lance invites him to spend the summer out in Minnesota.

Then one day he gets a letter from Lance saying all the plans have been cancelled—an obviously phony excuse. The father says, "You see, he found out who you were and he didn't want you over." Of course, the father wrote this kid out there a letter explaining the situation. Be that as it may, the final line of the story which I had originally envisioned was "And he was hung up between Duluth and 95th Street." Because the end of the story

62

occurs when the kid runs away from home, gets to the middle of the George Washington Bridge and becomes terribly frightened when he looks down at the water, clutches the rail, and the bridge swings in his mind, and he's hung up between Duluth, Minnesota, and 95th Street. The challenge was to write the story to lead up to this point. That's the kind of thing that hits me, but I don't look for it.

Conversations: Your most recent novel, A Star in the Family, *did not get much of a reception from the reviewers. In some ways the book was overlooked, and in other ways the reviewers didn't really seem to know what to make of it. Do you feel that the novel got a raw deal or a fast shuffle?*

Faust: Yes, I do, and in many ways it has a star-crossed history, which seemed to carry right through to publication. After I turned in the book, I can remember my agent saying, "Gee, you know, Markfield is also working on a novel about a comic." But when she read it, she said, "No problem, because Markfield's comic is completely different from yours. His is much more Lenny Bruce and yours is not." I said, "Right, he is not." And that was the key ever since. In my mind, Doubleday handled it as a Lenny Bruce comic. The Lenny Bruce thing—the play, the movie, his struggle and what it meant—hit really big at that time. I think that the reviewers immediately dismissed it as a Lenny book— both without reading it and even those who did read it. I think a number of them didn't read it simply because they said, "Oh Christ, here's another thing about Lenny." Those who did read it fell into the same misperception. A few didn't: Lingeman at the daily *Times* picked it up for what it was. The title of his review was "The Comedian as Hero," which was kind of a sardonic comment on what I was saying. But very clearly my man was not Lenny; in fact, I am one of the few people I suppose in New York City who don't particularly admire Lenny Bruce as a comedian. My comic was the all-American straight Jewish-American kid who stood for all the old-fashioned virtues and was the stand-up comic who is perhaps best represented by people like Jerry Lester—if you remember him—Morey Amsterdam, a little of Berle perhaps, but not at all the so-called modern comic. And, of course, what I was trying to do was to show the rise and fall of this nation over the last forty years, using as a vehicle the most vulnerable kind of person in our society—somebody whose business it is to try and stand up and make people laugh. In my judgment, after 1963 there wasn't a hell of a lot to laugh about in America. I'm not so sure there is yet. Now maybe I wasn't terribly successful. I happen to think that I was reasonably successful, but it was misinterpreted because of the Lenny phenomenon. The guy in the Sunday *Times*, for example, just misread it completely.

Conversations: In other words, they were sure it was the roman a clef?

Faust: Yes, yes. And with that mind-set it wasn't the book they wanted to have written. I wrote *another* book. I sent an open letter to reviewers about this—Doubleday, to their credit, did the mailing—and I was able to convince some of them to take another look at it. But it had this history from the very beginning. In fact, I even got racked up on the title. The original title was "The Great Goldwine," the hero being Bart Goldwine. The manuscript had been turned in and edited, and my editor at Doubleday, Betty Prashker—very perceptive woman—who happens to be a vice-president of the company—was not terribly taken with the title nor were the sales people at Doubleday. She said, "Would you consider another title?" I said, "As a matter of fact, I'm not that crazy about it myself. I *would* consider another title." And I came up with *A Star in the Family*, which we all liked. But by that time, Doubleday had gone into production and their lists and their advance things had come out with the title of *The Great Goldwine*. And it even got confused that way in the bookstores. I can remember going into a bookstore on vacation and asking for *A Star in the Family*. "We don't have it." I said, "Could you check the Doubleday list?" She said, "I don't even have it on the list." I said, "Wait a minute. Will you check to see if you've got *The Great Goldwine*." She looked at it—and sure enough, there was *The Great Goldwine* by Faust. I said, "Oh, my God. They couldn't even get *that* straight." So I fired off this hot letter to Betty and told her how disturbed I was.

She said, "Well, you know, in a large company, these things do happen, but I can understand your being upset"—and so on. I'm hopeful that in a few years somebody might go back and read it and see it for what it is: this straight Brooklyn kid who can stand up and make people laugh, and also do great impersonations, which is what his life turns into at the end. And, of course, the high point of his life is the impersonation of J. F. K.—and the identification. When J. F. K. dies, *he* does in many ways. And I hope maybe that will be read for what it is, at some time or other. But I did want to get that off my chest and get it on the record finally.

Conversations: This leads me to a question about the function and the power of book reviewers. Since books are not sold by advertising—the advertising budget even for a great best seller is tiny compared to the budget for deodorants and toothpaste— the form of book promotion is the review. And the reviewers seem to have an almost make-or-break power over the reception of the book. Would you agree that that is true, and furthermore, do you think that most reviewers know what they are doing?

Faust: I agree in large part, although over the years I've been treated pretty well. As for the make-or-break power, it certainly happened in my career. Books that were received with a lot of hoopla like *Willy* and *Roar Lion Roar* did quite well commercially. The others that were a little more puzzling—like *Foreign Devils* and *The Steagle*—were respectfully received, but with a little bewilderment, and so did not do as well commercially. I just described the disaster of *A Star in the Family*. *Buchta* was also not received, in my opinion, properly. So yes, they can do this. I'm not looking for the great blockbuster or commercial success, although I guess I have my share of ego, and maybe even more than my share. All I want is for the book to get a square shake out there with people that I want to talk to, and that's what I'm asking for.

Conversations: But the people you want to talk to, you reach through the reviewers.

Faust: Yes. Which brings me to the second part of your statement, and that is in my judgment many reviewers do not know what they are doing, chiefly because there seems to be no specific background required for reviewers today.

Irvin Faust

Conversations: Are you referring to the hinterlands reviewers as well as the New York reviewers?

Faust: Only partly; I think New York reviewers are just as guilty of this as anybody else—maybe even more so.

Conversations: Are they guilty of something else, which is ax-grinding, back-scratching, helping their friends, punishing their enemies?

Faust: Absolutely, absolutely; the ins, the outs, this school, that school—no question about it. In many ways, some of the best and most perceptive reviews I've gotten have been outside of New York, even though in many ways I'm a New York writer and one would think I wouldn't talk to people out there. I can remember a story that *The Saturday Evening Post* was going to print before it folded—"The Madras Rumble," which appears in *Roar Lion Roar*. They told me, "Oh, listen, that housewife in Ohio is not going to understand this. She'll like the Indian boy, but let's get rid of the narrator." Well, hell, at least half of the story, if not more, is concerned with the narrator and his interaction with the Indian boy—the narrator being the social worker. And I said, "No, I can't see it that way." They said, "Now, listen, this is not the *Paris Review*. We're not giving you fifty bucks here. You're getting $1500 and you're going to be read by 2,000,000 people out there, and not by 200 people in the literary world. So we know what we're talking about. In essence, we've got this clout." Well, I'm not claiming I'm the bravest guy in the world, but I was able to eat pretty well. I said, "Fine. Send me the story back, please." So then they said, "Okay. We'll do it your way." And after it was published I got letters from little old ladies, and it *talked* to them. And I've been getting that kind of reception with most of my books all throughout what you called "the hinterlands." My big beef has very often been with the New York reviewers. The man in the Sunday *Times* who missed *A Star in the Family* . . . the reviewers in the daily *Times*: Lehmann-Haupt is one; Fremont-Smith is the other—were rather nice, but they missed both *Foreign Devils* and *The Steagle*, in my judgment. Probably the most effective review, the best reading I got, was R. V. Cassill in the Sunday *Times* doing *Willy Remembers*. He asked for all my other books. He reread them.

He did a critique on Faust from *Roar Lion Roar* up through all the other books to *Willy*. I thought that was a hell of a thing to do. Cassill happens to be a professor of literature. He *knows* literature. He's got some background. Stanley Kauffmann in *The New Republic* doing *Roar Lion Roar* brought some background to the analysis of those stories. But, you know, so many other reviewers are "ax-grinders," you said, or are one-shot novelists or two-shot novelists who are sent the book and told to review it.

Conversations: And if it's really good react with envy.

Faust: Not so much envy, perhaps, as laziness. An inability to dig into the thing I'm doing, which I think is very different.

Conversations: But how else do you get to your audience, to your public, to your readership—however you think of them? How do you get books to readers if not through reviews?

Faust: It's a good question, and I'll be darned if I know the answer to it.

Conversations: Advertising won't work. The book clubs do it, of course, but the book clubs have a selection a month.

Faust: Yeah, I was lucky enough to hit it with *Willy*. The Book-of-the-Month Club gave it an alternate selection. Well, sometimes you can break into show biz. They made a movie out of *The Steagle*, which was probably the most unsuccessful movie of all time, mainly because it was butchered by Joe Levine, who had the right of final cut.

Conversations: What happened to the movie version of Willy *that was announced?*

Faust: Paul Sylbert, who had done *The Steagle*—and it was a pretty good movie in its original print which I saw—was expecting to make enough money to do *Willy*. But because it was butchered by Levine and it flopped commercially, he couldn't get the money together. "Roar Lion Roar" has been optioned a dozen times both for TV and for films. One of the big stumbling blocks, oddly enough, has always been Columbia University. They don't seem to want to let us use the name or the facilities, and it can't be done any other way. It can't be done at the

University of Chicago or Stanford or anywhere else. It's got to be Columbia, Baker Field, and this whole Morningside area which is my turf and Ishmael's turf.

How do you get it out there? You've got to hope for people, I suppose, to come across books by Faust and writers like me who are not going to turn out *The Godfather* or *Jaws*. And just not worry about it too much, and not get overly concerned—except the one time when I got damn angry with *A Star in the Family*. I really went out there swinging and talking to reviewers. And I felt a little better about that. I felt that I was striking back a little. I got a couple of letters from authors: "Hey, this is great. I read your interview in the *Book-of-the-Month Club News* and you were really steaming mad, and that's just the way I've been feeling, too." But, you know, that's bucking the organization. It's terribly difficult. So I don't know—outside of people who have the background and have the outlets—I don't know what the answer is. Certainly the commercial world of publishing doesn't do it. I guess when I first started I was naive enough to think: "You produce the art, and the rest takes care of itself." It's not quite that simple. But I've stopped worrying about it. You just can't get hung up on that.

Conversations: How have you done in paperback?

Faust: Well, everything has come out in paperback and done reasonably well. *Foreign Devils* is moving in paperback. I'm rather surprised to hear that. I guess it's up to about 20,000 copies now. That's not sensational, but it hasn't been out that long, and it's being done by Popular which is not one of the big paperback houses, although they do some nice things. *Roar Lion Roar* has come out in a couple of editions. So they move. Again they're not blockbusters, but they move a little bit. The life of the book has had some extension.

Conversations: Maybe this is the way you find your readers finally. Somebody in the bus station or the airport picks up the book on impulse for a buck and a quarter.

Faust: Could be.

Conversations: Whereas for $8.95 or $10 you don't get impulse buying.

Faust: Could be, could be. I've also found that, of all places, France seems to dig me pretty well. *Roar Lion Roar* and *The Steagle* came out in France by Gallimard. *The Steagle* got some marvelous reviews, absolutely marvelous. Andre Simon, the translator, sent me a lot of them. I·think they really understood what I was trying to do with that book. The interesting thing about *The Steagle* is that we had to translate it from Faust into English into French. Jean did a lot of work on that, and her correspondence to Simon is almost the basis of another book.

Conversations: Did they call it The Steagle?

Faust: *L'Aciagle*—which, I guess, is some kind of slang pronunciation of *The Steagle*. I was terribly pleased to see that there was a sensibility there that appreciated mine. But I just don't worry about commercial matters anymore unless I feel I've suffered a tremendous injustice as with *A Star in the Family*. I was angry with Doubleday because they promoted it as a Lenny book; I can remember hearing, "Let's try and time it with the release of the movie." I said, "But it has nothing to do with Lenny." But that was *their* end, that was *business*. Very frustrating.

Conversations: "We know how to sell books."

Faust: Yeah, yeah. "Don't meddle—don't get into this." Later on I said something like, "If you know how to sell books, how can you screw up the title on the lists?" "Oh well, once those things go into production it's too late to catch it"—something to that effect. So I now know that when you're caught up in a system and an organization, most of your problems are concerned with the *organization*. When I counsel kids in school, my function is to try to help those kids cope with this organization—I'm the ombudsman to enable them to find strategies to turn their powerlessness into some kind of power with which to cope with the organization. That's a large part of my work, and I see the same thing in the world of literature. It's not literature—it is from *my* standpoint—but to them I guess it's a "property," to use that old show biz word that they kept throwing at me. I'd get these calls at midnight when I first got into writing. I'd get a call from Hollywood on some of the stories and on *The Steagle*. A lot of people were interested in doing *The Steagle*. I would get up at midnight and they'd tell me, "I think maybe Jason might be interested in it, or Paul might be interested in it." Jesus, here I am this Brooklyn kid, you know, grew up in the movies, hearing maybe Robards would do it or Newman. Then I found out it was completely phony. They believed it; they were terribly sincere about it; but they're sincere phonies. And it all would come to nothing. That's why I was so amazed when finally Sylbert did buy it and did do it. He said, "I'd like you to read my screenplay and see what you think of it." Which I thought was very nice of him. It was a good screenplay. It caught the book quite well. As I said, the first print did, too. In fact, Sylbert wrote a book—you might be interested in getting this somewhere. I guess it's a collector's item by now. He wrote a book about making *The Steagle*— originally called "The Voyage of the Steagle"—but the title at publication was *Final Cut*. He names names and he goes right out on the line. I'm sure it was a tremendous exercise in catharsis for the guy, because it was all so traumatic for him. I got a hell of a kick out of reading it. And that tells you what happens to. . . .

Conversations: A property.

Faust: A property—which is what I kept hearing from Hollywood. "You've got a great property here." So you get detached from it in a way and, of course, my work, my daily life at school erases that kind of thing from my mind. It's so useful in doing that, because, you know, you can go nuts if you start to worry about these things.

Conversations: You're not even faintly tempted to go out and work on one of your screenplays?

Faust: I haven't been. I suppose someday it could happen—or the stage. I've been asked quite often to try and do something in drama or TV because they're always hooked on my dialogue. The ear thing always comes up when they talk about my work—you know, Faust's ear.

Conversations: "You've got a great ear."

Faust: Yeah, that's right.

Conversations: That's all it takes—an ear.

Faust: Right. You've got that, so how about a play or how about a TV series? I've never been that interested. I've resisted up to now. I might do a play someday. I am fascinated with dialogue—could happen. But I don't want to get into the Hollywood rat race. It has no fascination for me. I know there is a repulsive fascination for a lot of writers who go out there—sort of being part of it and above it. But I've never been drawn to that. I like the daily thing of being involved with the lives of real people. I spent an hour with a kid yesterday who's flunking his senior math course cold. Cold. And yet is accepted into an engineering program at a fancy college. Now how the hell are we going to reconcile what's happening to him in his major area, once he gets up to college? And why is he doing this? Because he can handle the thing with one hand tied behind his back. He's a brilliant kid in every way. We talked about his possibly being an English major. He said, "Gee, talking about books, I think, is all bullshit." He said, "I apologize to you, Dr. Faust." Incidentally, I'm known as "Dr. Faust" on the job. That was a very traumatic decision to make, knowing that for the rest of my life I'd be known as Dr. Faust. I finally went through with it, though. He said, "I'm sorry. I know you write books, Dr. Faust, but I just think that all the talking about it that the teachers do"—which I guess is some reflection on what happens in secondary school English classes—"is so much bullshit." He said, "So that's why I thought I'd get into engineering where at least there's a problem, and at the end of it you can solve it." I said, "But you're flunking your math course cold, and no matter how much we've talked about it you can't get your ass in gear to do it." He said, "That's right." I said, "So what's going to happen your first year in engineering in college?" He said, "Gee, that's right, I may flunk out." So yes, this is real. What are we going to do about this kid? How do we work with the parents, who are marvelous, caring people? How do they fit in here? Is he sending them a message? Why? Then you fan out; what about all the messages good, conforming, middle-class kids send us? How do they send them? Do we receive? What and how do we respond?

This is the kind of thing I do—much of this—from eight to four, and I love it, tough as it is and even though I can't always put the pieces together. But working with these problems, with kids, getting somewhere, catches me up completely. Whether or not Doubleday has promoted my book successfully, at those moments, is just not terribly important.

At night then, when I can concentrate on the writing, all that matters is my fictive world.

Though Barbara Ferry Johnson is a native of Grosse Pointe, Michigan, her career has been linked to the South. She received the first master of arts degree given by Clemson University; is currently an associate professor of English at Columbia College in Columbia, South Carolina; and her latest novel is Delta Blood, a Southern romance. Mrs. Johnson's first novel, Lionors, published by Avon in 1975, was a success, and Delta Blood, published in spring 1977, is a best seller. Mrs. Johnson recently signed a three-book contract with Avon.

Barbara Ferry Johnson

When Matthew J. Bruccoli interviewed·Barbara Ferry Johnson in July 1977, her latest novel, Delta Blood, *had sold over 700,000 copies after only four months in print. The interview was conducted at Mrs. Johnson's house in Columbia, South Carolina, during a break from her work on a third novel. Though she looked forward to seeing 1,000,000 copies of* Delta Blood *in print, Mrs. Johnson was not content to enjoy that novel's success and was anxious to get back to her writing at the conclusion of the interview.*

Conversations: Mrs. Johnson, how does it feel to see your book on the best-seller list?

Johnson: It feels wonderful. What else can anybody say? It feels great. The first time was exciting; the second time that it was there, unbelievable; it's on for the sixth week now.

Conversations: Where are you this week?

Johnson: It's now number nine on *The New York Times.*

Conversations: The book we're talking about, of course, is Delta Blood. *Do you feel that it was a mistake to publish directly in paperback?*

Johnson: No, not at all. My first novel, *Lionors,* was published by Avon in paperback. People ask me all the time, "Are you disappointed?" I say, "Absolutely not." You get such a tremendous distribution with paperback. It's over 700,000 copies. They're getting ready to go into another printing.

Conversations: And the movies and television are still to be heard from.

Johnson: Wouldn't it be nice?

Barbara Ferry Johnson

Conversations: Have you had nibbles?

Johnson: No, I haven't had any nibbles yet.

Conversations: Well, let's back up. You burst into print, at least in book form, with Lionors, which was 1975. That was the first book you had published. Was it the first book you wrote?

Johnson: No—the first real novel I wrote, yes, yes. I had played around with some mystery stories and some short stories, but this was the first one I had really worked hard at, and the first one that when I finished it, I felt it was right. I felt good about it.

Conversations: How long was that one in the works?

Johnson: Well, over a period of time because I started it, put it aside, went back to it, and finally said, "Look, you're either going to finish it and do something with it or you're going to throw it away."

Conversations: Did you submit it blind to Avon or did an agent handle it for you?

Johnson: I had no agent. I submitted a letter first. Actually, I submitted a query letter to several publishers—saying this was the book, would they be interested in reading the manuscript? Avon happened to be the first one to answer and say yes, they would like to read it.

Conversations: Who was the editor?

Johnson: The editor is Bob Wyatt.

Conversations: And he's also your editor for Delta Blood?

Johnson: Right.

Conversations: He's the one who spotted you? You didn't send the manuscript. He expressed interest on the basis of a letter?

Johnson: Right. To be perfectly honest, I had done what had been suggested. I had sent outlines and a chapter to one or two other publishers, and they had returned them. By this time I was running out of money to pay the price of return postage. So I thought I would try this route instead, and it just happened to be successful. I, in one brief paragraph, said what the novel was about: "Would you be interested in reading it? If so, I'll send the entire manuscript." And that was the result.

Conversations: Lionors *was an Arthurian romance;* Delta Blood *was a complete change of pace—it's a Southern historical novel. Did you say to yourself, "For my second novel, I'm going to write something completely different," or had you been intending all along to write something like* Delta Blood?

Johnson: Well, once *Lionors* was published I guess the bug bit me, and I started on a second novel, which there is no point going into—let's just say the plot was very weak. I realized during the second draft that nothing was going to come of it and actually Bob Wyatt said to me, "What I really want—would like to see—is a second novel with a strong female heroine." Here again, there was the interest in the strong female character. So I went back to the second novel. I looked at it and in it in one very brief episode was Leah in New Orleans, and I said to myself, "Ah-ha! She would make a heroine for a novel." So actually she was plucked from one that I tossed aside.

Conversations: How far had you gotten on this novel before you killed it?

Johnson: Well, I actually finished a rough draft of it. In fact, I had sent the rough draft to Bob Wyatt, and he pointed out a number of weaknesses. The minute I saw them I realized that I was trying for something that just wasn't going to work. The plot was very loose. That's when he said something about, "See if you can think in terms of a strong heroine." That was when I looked at this one character, Leah, and said she definitely could be the heroine of her own novel.

Conversations: I'm interested in your editor's remark that he wanted a novel with a strong female character, which would seem to support the contention that the fiction market is a woman's market, and that most very successful novels are aimed at a female reading public. Would you agree with that?

Johnson: Yes, I agree. I think from my own experience, from talking to people, and also from talking now with bookstore owners, close to 90%—particularly of paperback books—are

Barbara Ferry Johnson

women buyers. People say, "Well, are you publishing for money?" And I say, "Yes. I'm writing to make money at it." I want to write a good book, but I think I'd be lying if I said I didn't want to sell. I think for that reason I'm aiming toward women readers, very definitely.

Conversations: As you write, are you conscious of the fact that you are tailoring your work for this specific audience, this readership of women?

Johnson: I don't know that I'm conscious of it once I have a story outline—that is, while I'm doing the writing I am not. I think I try to choose a subject that I think will appeal to women readers; but *Lionors* very definitely, I think, had a limited appeal—the Arthurian legend. *Delta Blood* seems to have a much wider appeal; I think more men are reading it. So that while I'm writing I'm not consciously saying, "Well, this line will appeal to a woman"; but I think I'm just aware of the fact that I know more women are going to buy the books than men buy them—this type of book, a romantic novel.

Conversations: You waited a long time for your success.

Johnson: Yes.

Conversations: Were you writing all the while?

Johnson: I was writing off and on all the while. I've always wanted to be a writer. My first major was in journalism. I tried my hand at writing all the time. I might be working on a short story, working on a mystery; but I was also bringing up three children and either teaching or going to school, and it really wasn't until the children left home that I finally had the time. I suppose you could say, "Well, if you really wanted to do it, you would have found the time." But everything kind of came together—the time was right, the subject matter was right, and it just all came together.

Conversations: In addition to your writing, you have a full-time job at Columbia College in the English department.

Johnson: I did. I'm now teaching part-time.

Conversations: Lionors *and* Delta Blood *were both written while you were holding down a faculty position.*

Johnson: Right.

Conversations: The obvious question is: How did you fit in your writing—before class, after class, during class?

Johnson: Well, before class, after class. I do a great deal of creating, if you will, in my mind before I put it down on paper, so I might be working over a paragraph or a sentence while I was driving to college. Then I'd get there always, say, half an hour before class started, and so if something would come to me I would jot it down before I'd go to class. Mainly, however, if I taught in the afternoon I probably had the mornings free, so I would write in the morning or the other way around. With college teaching your hours are scattered. Then I would come home in the afternoon. I might do some writing while I put supper on. I just simply found the time. By this time I knew that if I wanted to do it, I had to find the time, and I just took advantage of every bit of time I had.

Conversations: You can break your concentration? You can do half an hour here and an hour there?

Johnson: I can, yes. I don't like it, because sometimes I'd be terribly frustrated. I'd work up till just the second when I knew I had to leave in order to get to school on time, and I might be right in the middle of a paragraph, but I did it. Now I'll have more time, and I don't know if that's going to be an advantage or a disadvantage, but I'll manage to do it.

Conversations: Do you feel that you have any rationale as a writer, or are you simply trying to give your readers a good read?

Johnson: I've always been one who liked a good story. One of the writers I admire tremendously is Somerset Maugham. He was a good storyteller. I'm very much interested in character. I want to develop my characters, certainly. I hope I create well-rounded characters, but I think there's nothing better than a good story. I suppose if anybody asked me, I'd say, "I'm not a philosopher. I don't have something inside of me that has to

79

come out, but I would like to think that I can write or that I can tell a good story."

Conversations: You have no message.

Johnson: No, I have no message. No, I'm not frustrated. I have no message. In fact, my husband used to tell me, "Honey, I don't think you're ever going to be a good writer because good writers have to be unhappy or miserable or have something they need to get out." I don't feel that way at all. I'd like to be thought of as a storyteller.

Conversations: It's no great secret that the audience you write for is frequently disparaged. For example, I don't suppose that your books have been very widely reviewed. Paperbacks which tell a good story, which are aimed at people who want to read for pleasure, make it on their own through word of mouth. They do not receive the kind of publicity that hardbound "serious" books get. Does this bother you?

Johnson: Well, as far as the reviews, in a way, yes. *Lionors* was beautifully reviewed by the *Washington Post*. I was very much excited and thrilled that the *Washington Post*, in fact, gave a whole page to *Lionors* plus another one. *The Atlanta Journal* has reviewed *Lionors*. There are some reviews, but to get to the publicity part of it—this is one reason that I am pleased that I am published by Avon. They spend thousands and thousands of dollars on publicity—the publicity is absolutely tremendous. I might not get the serious reviews that you're talking about, but the publicity and the advertising that they do is absolutely fantastic. Not only that, but they spend a fortune on the covers, and, of course, the covers are the best ads for paperback books. So I think you're right about the reviews, but a tremendous amount of publicity comes from Avon—advertising and publicity.

Conversations: You're going to be stuffed and put into a museum. You're the first author I've ever spoken to who has expressed satisfaction with the publisher's publicity effort.

Johnson: I really can't say too much. The publicity is absolutely tremendous.

Conversations: Space advertising?

Johnson: Space advertising, television advertising, radio advertising. This last time they had radio, television, and newspaper advertising in twelve of the largest markets in the United States. They send out posters. They send out news releases.

Conversations: Have they put you on the road? Have you done personal appearances?

Johnson: Washington. I went up to Washington, D. C., to speak at the Washingtonian Book Festival two weeks ago.

Conversations: Did you like it?

Johnson: Yes, very much. That was the first I had done of that.

Conversations: You're willing to do more?

Johnson: Some more, yes. I've done a lot of autographing sessions within the state; but Washington is the first one outside the state, and it was very enjoyable. In fact, they are very frank to say, they'll tell you that in many ways paperback books now have more money to spend on advertising and publicity than the hardbacks do. And then, as I said, they'll spend a tremendous amount of money on the covers, because the cover is what sells. It is the best ad in the world—that and word of mouth.

Conversations: What was the size of the first printing of Delta Blood?

Johnson: The first printing was 565,000.

Conversations: Obviously somebody at Avon felt that this was a winner.

Johnson: Right.

Conversations: Who made that decision?

Johnson: I don't know. I expect editors have a great deal to do with it. Then there were some prereleases—well, I don't know if you would call it a review or not—but there was a prerelease judgment, let's say, by *Publishers Weekly*. *Publishers Weekly*, even before it came out, said it was going to be a winner, and put it in the winners' column. *Bestsellers* magazine did the same thing—said it was one of the winners that was coming up; it was one to look for. So that helps as far as the bookstores putting in the orders are concerned. Of course, those two magazines go to bookstores. Word of mouth—women talk. When women have found a book that they like, they tell everybody. I was in the beauty parlor today getting my hair done. I didn't let them know who I was—two women were talking about *Delta Blood*. It was all I could do to keep from telling them, "Hey, look, here I am, see!"

Conversations: That's fun, isn't it?

Johnson: It really is. The other day I was getting a check approved in a store, and the woman looked up and said, "Oh, I thoroughly enjoyed your book." I said, "How did you know?" She said, "I recognized you." But word of mouth with paperbacks among women—very, very important.

Conversations: How soon did you and Avon know that Delta Blood *was going to be a hit?*

Johnson: Golly, that's hard to say, because it went on the stands the end of March, and by the first week in April they were going into the second, third, and then the fourth printings. So from orders coming in we knew fairly soon.

Conversations: What printing are you up to now?

Johnson: Sixth. And the last I heard they were getting ready for the seventh.

Conversations: And you're over 700,000 copies?

Johnson: Right.

Conversations: So you can look forward to having 1,000,000 copies of your book out?

Johnson: I was up in New York about two weeks ago, and I jokingly said, "Hey, why don't you just go right ahead now and make it up to 1,000,000?" He said, "Well, we don't move that fast, but it will get there." Summer is coming, and summer is a big reading time.

Conversations: Your book is what used to be called a "hammock book."

Johnson: Right, right, a hammock or on the beach. You walk along the beach and you see women under the umbrellas reading paperbacks.

Conversations: What am I keeping you from doing? Are you writing another novel right now?

Johnson: I'm working on the next one. I was sitting in there looking out the window, watching for you. Yes, I have just signed a contract with Avon for three more novels. One of which I am doing the final draft—well, I might say the final rough draft right now. Then I will be starting on the sequel to *Delta Blood*, which I had not planned to do, really. I thought *Delta Blood* was going to end with the last page. But the word has come that they would like a sequel, so I'm going to be working on a sequel. Then I have a third, which is a Revolutionary War novel located in Charleston. So that will be coming up—I'll start on that in about a year and a half.

Conversations: Are you willing to talk about the one that's almost finished? Is it another change of pace?

Johnson: It's quite another change of pace. This takes us to the tenth-century Vikings. It's a Viking adventure-romance.

Conversations: You've done King Arthur. You've done the antebellum South. Now you're back into tenth-century Vikings. Obviously all of these books depend on the convincingness of the background. How much research do you have to do?

Johnson: A great deal, a great deal. I enjoy doing the research. This I love. I could almost spend most of the time just doing the research. I thoroughly enjoy researching it. The Viking one— incidentally, we joined a history book club. My husband is a historian—a great lover of history. We joined a history book club, and in trying to choose which books, I said, "Oh, look, there's a book on the Vikings. Let's order that. I've always been fascinated by it." So when the book came and I began reading it and really learning about what Viking life was like—which came as quite a revelation to me—I said, "Ah, this would make a tremendous historical romance because of the excitement and the way they live." So then I began working out a plot in my mind, and then began doing a tremendous amount of research because they had a lot of communication and trade with Constantinople and the Byzantine Empire, and all this just opened a whole. . . . Interestingly enough, when you do research, you also come on things that will make marvelous bits and pieces in the novel. So the research itself often leads to part of the plot and brings in characters that you might not have thought about to begin with. I start with sort of a rough outline and then let the research, very often, help me fill in. I do try to be accurate. In fact, with *Delta Blood* I had several people read the manuscript for the New Orleans part, for the voodoo part, for the trial—the adjutant general trial—so that I knew when that manuscript went off there was not a historical error in it. This, to me, was very important.

Conversations: Does plotting come easily to you?

Johnson: I usually start with a very rough outline. I usually know the end. Let me put it this way: I know what I'm heading toward. I will have maybe four, five, six major crises, if you will, or situations to put in some sort of a normal order. Then I find that while I'm writing, while I'm working it out, something will just naturally lead to something else that I wouldn't have thought of originally. You know, this situation—oh, well, naturally, now she'll go in this direction.

Conversations: Can we do a case history with Delta Blood? *When did you get the idea for the novel? When did you get the key plot idea? You said you think of the ending first. How did you get the ending? And then could you describe the steps by which you fleshed out the plot or the story line?*

Johnson: Oh, dear—let's see. I knew what I wanted the ending to be, and that there had to be a triangle in there. I knew there had to be—all right, this is a young woman, an octoroon, whose whole desire is to go north. She's stopped by becoming a mistress. She is stopped by the war. Then after all that was past, I felt she had to meet somebody, meet a man who would take her north. So I had to bring the man into it, the man from the north who would take her north. I guess I just began to try to think,

"Well, why would he be down here after the war?" At the same time he had to be a sympathetic character. That is, he couldn't have been one of those who had remained in a position of power in New Orleans during the war, because those people were very much hated by her. They were tyrants. So he had to be a sympathetic character. I had to find someone who came south after the war who, in some way, was a sympathetic character, who would aid her in some way. He is the lawyer who aids her in the murder trial that she's involved in, so that there is a rapport between them, before there is any notion of love between them. It's almost like a woman with her doctor sort of thing. She is so involved with him when he is trying to defend her in this murder trial, and it is a rapport that no other situation would create. And so then the rapport leads to a more emotional attachment there at the end. Of course, the situation of the war itself is almost an outline for a plot, if you will. I think the same thing was true with the Arthurian legend with *Lionors*. I had the legend, so what I had to do was just simply fit the incidents with *Lionors* in with the outline of the legend.

Conversations: Do you construct a careful outline or a blueprint?

Johnson: Yes.

Conversations: And you follow it as you work?

Johnson: I'll make a rough outline and follow it to a great extent. Doesn't mean I may not change my mind, but I start with an outline. To me this is important. Now I know many people can just start and write. I can't. I may even start listing chapters: Chapter one, this will happen; chapter two, this will happen. I may end up combining chapters. I may end up knocking them out, as I did actually with *Delta Blood*. I threw out the first eight chapters of *Delta Blood*. I started first when she was a little girl, and then I thought, no, let's start in a moment of crisis. Now some of the things that were in those first eight chapters I revealed in flashback or in thought, but the chapters themselves were thrown out because I realized I was wrong. I needed to start in a moment of crisis instead. But I'll start with an outline.

Barbara Ferry Johnson

Conversations: Do you feel that you are a self-made writer in that you developed your technique by yourself, or did you learn some lessons in writing courses?

Johnson: Well, the writing courses were so long ago, when I was in college, that I think probably it would be better to say self-made, in the sense that I do a great deal of reading. A writer that I admire tremendously is Daphne du Maurier. I've read probably almost everything she's ever written. I don't mean I copy Daphne du Maurier—I don't mean that at all. I would never attempt to imitate somebody else's style. But I think, at the same time, I can hope to accomplish the same thing she has accomplished in her writing. Elizabeth Goudge, another English writer, is also one that I admire tremendously. Her writings have a sort of quiet.... Well, mine have gone beyond that now. I think *Lionors* was perhaps closer to that sort of quiet, nonviolent kind of writing. But, yes, I guess you might say self-taught or self-achieved, finally. I think that probably all those years I was trying to write short stories—I guess I was teaching myself.

Conversations: Did you sell anything during all those years?

Johnson: No.

Conversations: Lionors was your first appearance in print, as well as your first novel?

Johnson: Right. As far as fiction was concerned. I did some non-fiction many, many years ago; but as far as fiction was concerned, yes. I think I was going through a very long training period, if you will. That's why when *Lionors* came out I felt good about it. I knew I had finally achieved something.

Conversations: Is there something else you want to say about Delta Blood?

Johnson: Oh, yes. One thing, I think, that disturbed me were the reviews. The reviews have all been very complimentary. I've been very pleased with them except for one thing, and that is the comparison to *Gone With the Wind*. I don't know whether it's because it's a Civil War novel, or whether it's because it has a main female character, or whether it's because the picture of the man on the cover happens to look a great deal like Rhett Butler.

But I don't see it as anything like *Gone With the Wind*. I don't say it upsets me too much, but I just hate to see any Southern Civil War novel immediately compared to *Gone With the Wind*, because *Gone With the Wind* is almost sui generis. It's by itself. There will never be another *Gone With the Wind*. My heroine is nothing like Scarlett, unless you think of two strong women— that's the only thing I can think of. So that just bothered me a little bit—this automatic comparison of a Southern Civil War novel to *Gone With the Wind*. I think they just ought to get on another tack.

Conversations: I gather that a writer writing paperback romances for an audience of people who want to read and not make literary evaluations enjoys a rather special relationship with her readers.

Johnson: The one thing that really, really surprised me—I was completely unprepared for getting fan mail—fan mail from all over the country. People who either were already familiar with the Arthurian legend—this was with the first book, *Lionors*—and so were delighted to see another novel about it, or people who were not familiar with it, and said that this was an introduction to it and they were going to continue reading about it and what could I suggest. You know, what other books could I suggest about the Arthurian legend. They're very intimate, very personal letters. One of them touched me more than any of the others. In *Lionors* she loses three people that she loved within a very short space of time. So I had two paragraphs in there talking about her reaction to death—what death meant to her and what it took away from her—and the fact that quite literally she felt hollow inside because, by losing the people who had known her as a child, the child inside her was gone—this sort of thing. I got a letter from a woman in New Jersey who said that her mother had died. She had picked up the book to read on the train as she was going back and forth between New Jersey and New York preparing for the funeral. And that those two paragraphs were the only thing that carried her through the sorrow of losing her mother, and would I give her permission to have them copied and framed and put on the wall? Well, now what could be more moving or more meaningful than to think that you have helped somebody with two paragraphs in a book that you have written?

Barbara Ferry Johnson

Conversations: I take it you answer every one of these letters.

Johnson: Oh, I answer every letter that comes. I answer them by hand, incidentally. I do all of my first writing by hand. I don't do my first draft on a typewriter. I find it's easier to write by hand, and so the same thing is true with letters. Almost always I answer letters by hand. So I'll sit right down as soon as a letter has come, or just as soon as I can I'll answer letters that come because it is a very personal, very intimate. . . . Very often they'll say, "Dear Barbara." They seem to feel very close to an author of a book that they have enjoyed.

Conversations: Are we talking about hundreds of letters?

Johnson: No, no, we're not talking about hundreds of letters. We're talking about as many as forty or fifty with the first book. Now so far, it's been fewer. I guess I've gotten probably fifteen letters on *Delta Blood*. Most of them are complimentary. One or two of them have been a little bit disturbed, primarily at the ending of the book. I have written back trying to explain what my intent was with the ending of the book. Then as a result of many of these letters and on the advice of the editor—and by the way, I do have an agent now—and on the advice of the agent, I have begun to work on a sequel to it.

Conversations: In some ways your career reads like a bad novel.

Johnson: Let's make it a good novel, please, not a bad one.

Conversations: Your career has been a wish fulfillment.

Johnson: Very definitely.

Conversations: All over America, there are thousands of people who always wanted to be writers, and—particularly in the case of women—domestic responsibilities and one thing or another have prevented them from getting to it. You made the dream come true. Were you just lucky, or do you feel that you had a special streak of determination that carried you through?

Johnson: Well, partly the streak of determination. Partly luck, I suppose, but partly a streak of determination. I was determined with the first one that I was going to do something with it. I thought it was good. I felt good about it, and I was quite determined. In fact, I had finished reading a novel at Christmas time, and I said to myself, "By George, if she can do it, so can I."

Conversations: Would you like to name it?

Johnson: I had finished Mary Stewart's *The Crystal Cave* and *The Hollow Hills,* and of course those are Arthurian books. You see, I had already written several chapters, and that was when I said: "If she can do it, so can I." So I crawled under the bed and I went in dresser drawers, and I pulled out all the chapters that I had worked on over the past years. Between the end of December and the first of March I wrote half that book. You asked me how long did it take: I actually wrote over half the book in about three months—less than that, maybe two months. That's when I sat down and really determined. . . . Writing is hard work, and you'd never deny that. The act of writing is hard work. It takes a lot out of you, and I think you have to have the determination, and I think you have to have a tremendous amount of self-discipline. You ask what hours do I write: You take every free moment you've got to write, if you want to really get some place. You really can't put it off and say you'll do it tomorrow. You have to do it today. You have to take advantage of every opportunity. I think self-discipline is very, very important for a writer. I think writing something every day—all those years when nothing was happening to me, I was still writing whenever I had the chance.

Reading—I think you have to read everything you can get your hands on. I think you need the self-discipline of being a self-critic. I think you have to be able to criticize your own work. I may write a rough draft. Then I go back over it and usually I cross out. I'm apt to be very, very wordy. I'm apt to put in a half a dozen adjectives when really there shouldn't even be an adjective there at all. So I have to be very critical of my own work. Then I'll type up a rough draft, go over it again—add, subtract, whatever. I even type my own final draft. I've had people say, "Well, by this time couldn't you afford a secretary?" No, I have to type the final draft myself because I'm still editing. I'm still changing. I'm still hoping to strengthen weak sentences. So I would say the important things are certainly self-discipline and a critical approach to your own writing, and doing some writing every single day if you possibly can—even if it's just a page or

89

two. I was sitting under the hair dryer today. Half a dozen sentences came to my mind. I had a sheet of paper with me. I've learned never to go anyplace without a pad of paper, because you never know when something is going to come. I'll turn on the light at two o'clock in the morning and write down something that comes to me. I guess it's a matter of just zeroing in on what you really want to do.

Conversations: And cutting other things out of your life.

Johnson: Yes, I think you have to set your priorities. Obviously I have a home; I have a family. Sometimes other priorities get in the way. I may not want to get up and cook supper, but I feel that I have to. But on the other hand, the other night I had been working all day very hard on this rough draft, and my husband wanted to go to the store. He said, "Honey, come on with me. You need to take a break." All right, it requires somebody else, often, to force me to take a break. Or he'll say, "Come on out and help me tie up the tomatoes." Well, I may writhe inside and say, "Leave me at my typewriter," but I know perfectly well he's right. I need to take that break. So that, as I said, sometimes something outside has to force me. This is one reason why I am going to keep on doing part-time teaching. My agent advised me to, among other things. He said, "You need something to force you out of the house from time to time. I know you well enough that if you didn't have something where you had to get out of the house, you'd stay right in there and write the whole time. That's not good." He said, "You need to get out. You need the stimulation of working with young people still." I guess that when I get my teeth into something I don't like to let go. I need somebody else to pull me away from it.

Conversations: Does teaching help your writing?

Johnson: Yes, yes, I think so. I think it's the stimulation of being with other people and working with students.

Conversations: You teach literature?

Johnson: I teach literature. I teach some creative writing, and I teach some journalism.

Conversations: As you are teaching in the classroom, do you find yourself saying things that are applicable to your own work?

Johnson: Only in the sense that I'm apt to give the same sort of advice. When I teach creative writing, of course, those are the things that I tell them. Be sure to write every day. Be sure to do some reading. Be sure to listen. Use all your senses. Listen. Look. Touch. Be aware of everything that is going on around you. That, I suppose, more than anything else in the writing courses. As far as literature is concerned, I'm not really sure, unless I am perhaps more acutely aware now of style and more acutely aware of how a writer has achieved a certain characterization. Yes, I guess I would bring that out in class more. Let them know more about characterization, more about plot, why this story or novel or whatever is so great—because of the marvelous blending of these things without your being aware of them being blended—this kind of thing.

Conversations: How much outside criticism do you look for? Are there people you trust as readers who preview your work for you?

Johnson: My husband for one. In the first place he is a historian, so that helps; and secondly, he is very critical. If I am writing something, for instance, that a man would say, he'll immediately spot it if that's not the way a man would talk. He'll say, "No. No man would say that." He helps me with dialogue or with description, even. He'll say, "Look, you left something out here that is needed." He's my greatest fan, but he is also my greatest critic. Also the agent that I have now is not only a very good agent, but he also was a teacher at Yale. He taught creative writing at Yale. His name is Al Zuckerman. He's in New York, and he also wrote for some of the soap operas. So I feel I am very fortunate because he looked over the rough draft of this novel that I'm doing now. In fact, I was up in New York going over it with him—over several chapters—and he can spot the weak places. This is very helpful. So between the two of them I feel that I do have some very positive criticism.

Conversations: How much editing does your editor at Avon do?

Barbara Ferry Johnson

Johnson: Very little, very little. Usually they bring in a free-lance manuscript editor. The only problem there was with *Delta Blood*: they sent me some pages—one or two pages—they wanted a couple of things changed on, but I immediately spotted some errors. Unfortunately, they chose a person that knew nothing about New Orleans and who knew nothing about the South. He was constantly changing sentences and making them wrong. For instance, I had just two or three phrases in the sort of New Orleans French patois—spoken by the blacks, actually, in the voodoo ceremony—and he wanted to change it to Parisian French. Well, I got on the telephone at that point to Bob, and I said, "Bob, you've got to send me the whole manuscript. I have got to go over everything he has changed, because he is changing things and making mistakes in there." There was one place where I said something about "she thought she heard something," and he changed it to "she heard something." I said, "She couldn't possibly have heard it where she's standing." So from now on, a manuscript editor can tighten. Nobody writes every sentence perfectly, and so he can tighten and, maybe transpose a sentence, this kind of thing. But now I know the danger of one making mistakes or leaving out things. He left out some paragraphs that, to me, were absolutely vital to the meaning of the story, so I put down that these had to remain as they were in the original.

Conversations: Unless you had gotten on the phone this book might have gone to the printer without your having a chance to check on the changes? Don't you see proofs on a paperback?

Johnson: Well, I would have seen galley proofs, as they did come to me later. I made absolutely certain I went through those galley proofs with a manuscript, my own manuscript, page-by-page—line-by-line—to make sure everything was the way it ought to have been. But, you see, I wouldn't have caught it until the galley proof. So from now on I will always insist that I get to see the manuscript after the manuscript editor has been over it, and before it goes to the printer. As I said, there weren't many, but the ones that were made were very serious errors. For instance, I'd described one voodoo charm in there. He knocked the whole paragraph out, and it happened to be a charm that I thought was extremely important to describe. I thought it was interesting. People are interested in how a voodoo charm is made. I didn't want it knocked out. I don't know what his rationale was for taking it out, but I said, "Put it back." And one thing about Bob Wyatt, the editor, he agreed with me. He said, "Everything you want in there will be left in there." He said, "You're the author. You have the final say."

Conversations: When I leave after the interview is over, you're going to get right back to work?

Johnson: Oh, yes, yes. The typewriter is sitting right in there and the pot of coffee is on the stove, so I'll get right back to work.

Roger Kahn was born in Brooklyn on 31 October 1927. His apprenticeship as a writer began in 1947 when, after three years at Columbia University, he took a job as copyboy for the New York Herald Tribune. He made staff in 1950 as sports reporter covering the Brooklyn Dodgers, an assignment that later formed the basis of Kahn's number one best seller, The Boys of Summer. *When he left the Tribune in 1954, Kahn began writing first for magazines and later his own books. He has won the E. P. Dutton Award for the best magazine sports article three times: in 1960, in 1969, and 1970. His books include* The Passionate People *(1968),* The Battle for Morningside Heights *(1970),* A Season in the Sun *(1977). He is currently working on a novel.*

Roger Kahn

Roger Kahn was interviewed on 18 July 1977 by Richard Layman at the author's apartment in Manhattan. Kahn had just completed a four-week tour to promote his new book, A Season in the Sun, and he planned to relax that evening at the All-Star Baseball Game. If Kahn had wearied of interviews, he graciously concealed the fact and thoughtfully discussed his career and his profession.

Conversations: In "Ring," F. Scott Fitzgerald's eulogy of Ring Lardner, he said that Lardner didn't reach his potential as a writer because he had spent his formative years among a bunch of men playing a boy's game, and that as a result his writing world was only as big as Frank Chance's baseball diamond. Do you feel that your career has been inhibited by the fact that your first writing job was covering sports?

Kahn: First helped, then later inhibited. As a sportswriter at the *Herald Tribune*, I had more opportunity to write than if I had been on the city side, covering fires or Mayor Impellitteri—the essentially routine and rather dull beat that a general assignment reporter has at the beginning. Going quickly into an arena where I had Jackie Robinson, Peewee Reese, and Duke Snider to write about, plus the frame of baseball being integrated, and the particular outsized personality of this team, that was a help.

Conversations: You mean, you had good material?

Kahn: I had good material with which to work, and I found markets beyond the newspaper fairly quickly. There were great numbers of magazines looking for people who could write a sports article spelled and punctuated correctly. Selling sports articles came more easily than if I had been a generalist at that point and simply said: "I want to write something about the condition of state legislatures in the United States." The first major magazine story that I did sell was a collaboration with Duke Snider about the sorrows of being a major league baseball player—that it wasn't all fun.

Conversations: Does that magazine article form the basis of a chapter in The Boys of Summer?

Kahn: I refer to it. It was in *Collier's*. That sold easily, and then a fellow named Ed Fitzgerald—Edward Fitzgerald, who now runs The Book-of-the-Month Club—had *Sport* magazine and he gave me regular assignments. So beyond the newspaper, I wrote 10,000-word articles many months. Sports gave me tremendous writing practice. I would write and write and write, and things got published. Whatever writing I had done in programs at school was nowhere near as effective in my development as professional writing. So sports made for a positive beginning.

The other side is that now I'm forever being asked to write something in sports, and, even more than that, to write something in baseball. Of course, the economic forces work to make me do this baseball piece, do that baseball piece, even when I'm tired of doing any baseball piece. So eventually, being regarded as a baseball specialist has tended to impede me.

Conversations: You worked under a superb sports editor, Stanley Woodward. What did he do for your writing?

Kahn: He did a lot with his book called *Sports Page*. He set a climate. His staff was literate. That was probably the best newspaper sports staff ever—that's a limited immortality like being the best three-man rowing crew ever. I went over three years of *Herald Tribunes* for *The Boys of Summer*; there was a lot of good stuff, and a bit of dreadful stuff. There is a tendency to romanticize the *Herald Tribune*. Milton and Homer did not work there. But the *Trib* did present me with people who were good writers—excellent *newspaper* writers, and damned proud to be good. In that company, you didn't refer to second base as "the keystone hassock"; third base wasn't "the hot corner."

Conversations: That was one of Woodward's innovations, wasn't it, to take the slang out of baseball writing?

Kahn: He called that particular kind of slang "the unholy jargon," which is that tendency to call things by names other than their own. Many other sports editors stressed knowledge of the game; at the *Trib*, sports knowledge was assumed. The stress was on good informed writing. And, more than that, literacy. If you had really never read, let's say, *Paradise Lost*, you'd be embarrassed, in that company, to admit it; and you might go home and secretly start to read Milton, as people did—Dickens, Hardy. The backdrop of Stanley Woodward's sports page was a good, strong sense of English literature.

Conversations: How much help in your individual writing did you actually get from Woodward? When you turned in a story, what did he do with it? Did he actually see it, in most cases?

Kahn: By the time I actually got on staff, he was gone. We didn't encounter each other again until later, when he'd used me as a stringer to cover notes and color on a fight between Johansson and Patterson in Miami Beach. I was a little put-off by Jewish vacationers in Miami Beach applauding Max Schmeling, so I wrote in my notes—this was 1960—that I'd agreed to do for $10—

Conversations: Ten dollars?

Kahn: I was going to be in Florida, anyway, so Woodward said, "Ten dollars"; and I said, "Three days' expenses in Miami"; and he said, "All right." So I did the notes on this fight and seeing Schmeling, who had been a paratrooper, I wrote a line that said, "Schmeling, of course, was never a Nazi. As I get the picture, there were never more than six or seven Nazis in Germany, but they worked very hard." Then I thought of the kind of censorship that magazines were imposing, and I thought, "My God, if they see it, they'll kill it." So instead of using the Nazi item as a lead note, I put it way down in the story. I got a letter from Woodward with a check for $50: "I liked your story so much that I decided to give you five times the agreed-upon price, and it would have been more if your expense bite hadn't been so high." With that was an invitation to have a drink.

I was pretty cheerful about the way the notes had turned out. But Woodward's opening remark was: "Why the hell did you bury your lead note?" And I said, "I thought if you saw it, you would kill it." He said, "You're a stupid son of a bitch"; and he turned his back on me and wouldn't talk for twenty minutes. That snapped me away from accepting the kind of expedient writing that was imposed on me by *Newsweek*, that was imposed on me by the old, slick *Saturday Evening Post*. The kind of writing which says, "Let's not offend anybody"—general, American, bland, super-slick writing. Ever since that incident, I've resisted angrily anybody's worrying whether I am offending an advertiser, a Nazi, whatever.

Conversations: One of the marks of your journalism is your political and social awareness; for example, your coverage of the Dodgers. Is the sports page a proper place for politics and sociology?

Kahn: Not to excess. During the time of what Rickey called the noble experiment, baseball was an arena of social change, with Robinson, and later Roberto Clemente. Sports writers all should properly cover social issues—Clemente's saying, "The Latin ball player is no hotdog." Jimmy Cannon used to say it's the toy department.

Conversations: The sports page?

Kahn: The sports page. But then if you read Cannon's writing, it had nothing to do with what he said. Cannon wrote about Miltonic battles. Cannon said, "I write in the toy department"; then he went ahead and wrote about the injustice of a fighter dying, Joe Louis's campaign, Jackie Robinson's loneliness.

I get concerned when I see a sports page which starts ignoring final scores. I looked through the *Los Angeles Times* recently, and it seemed so much into issues that the coverage was buried. Ideally it's a mix. You have to report the news. The reader wants to know how the White Sox did against Kansas City. And you have to put that in. But, at the same time, you can work in why Frank Robinson was fired over in Cleveland—how much that had to do with his being black, and how much it had to do with his inability to make the ball club a winner.

Conversations: Sounds like what you're really saying is that you should cover sports with both eyes open.

Kahn: Yes. Cover issues with both eyes open, but don't forget that the reader wants to know who won the pennant.

Conversations: There's a popular stereotype of the man who reads the sports page, and throws everything else away; he probably doesn't even read the sports page, only the scores. This brings up the question of who you wrote for: How did you envision your audience as a newspaper reporter?

Kahn: Somebody from the *Journal-American*, Mike Gavin, said that the only people who read the *Herald Tribune* were Wall Street brokers and secretaries who wanted to get ahead in Wall Street companies. I didn't have a market research image of the reader. I wrote for a reader who was pretty much like myself: who had read a book, who enjoyed sports, and that was about it. The *Daily News* was a paper. . . . When I was a kid, we were not to have the *Daily News* in the house. The *Daily News* was the paper that wrote about Errol Flynn's seductions.

To crystallize: *The Times* was very stodgy; *The Times* had that standard lead: "The Dodgers drew first blood yesterday and then had it spilled all over them as the Cardinals scored six runs in the fourth inning, overtaking—" you know, awful. One day when Sal Maglie threw at Furillo, there was a confrontation on the mound, an Italian "High Noon" at Ebbets Field. That was my story. *The Times* used "High Noon" as a note. There was a pretty good gap between the strident and vulgar *Daily News* and the stodgy, dull *New York Times*. It was a gap that I was able to fill.

Conversations: Was there some design on your part, then, to write for the Herald Tribune *in the first place? Or was it your father's plan? You describe in* The Boys of Summer *how he got that job for you.*

Kahn: He knew the city editor and got me a job. If he had known somebody at *The Times*, I might have ended up there, which would have been horrendous the way *The Times* was then. After awhile, I had choices—after a year or two at the *Tribune* I was offered a job with the Associated Press, and there was some talk of a job in Minneapolis. I wanted to stay at the *Tribune*. I can remember the first baseball game I covered, which was a college game. I wrote what the score was and how the runs were scored.

99

Roger Kahn

Then Bob Cooke, who had been a baseball writer, and a good one, said, "But that's not the way to write baseball." And then I said, "How do you write baseball?" He said, "Write lines like 'Barney pitched as though the plate were high and outside'" —a line about Rex Barney that he had written. That may not sound like good instructions but he was saying write a light line. I looked up past baseball writing—Ring Lardner, Damon Runyon. You could find the old stories; you could find Heywood Broun's baseball writing where the game becomes a frame within which he wrote an essay. So I sort of put all of that together very quickly.

Conversations: Traditionally, the sports page seems to be a breeding ground for good writers, unlike other sections of the paper.

Kahn: Some sports sections were just awful. *The Daily Mirror* was terrible. In *The Daily Mirror*, a fellow would write: "Normalcy returned to Ebbets Field yesterday. . . ." As a fellow on *The Journal* once told me—I was in some conversation about music—that he knew who "Brahm" was, making Brahms singular. There were batches of writers not only with limited education, but with little reading experience, who wrote jargon and that's all. So you would go from place to place. If you had one baseball writer in a town who was really good, that would be a lot. I can't give you comparative figures on how the business pages were, how the political pages were, but I wasn't awed by the general quality of newspaper writing. Some people were good—there weren't many.

Conversations: Why did you become a writer? Why not something else?

Kahn: Oh, that's what I always wanted to do.

Conversations: Your father was an editor, right?

Kahn: He was an editor; my mother was an English teacher. There's a copy of *Huckleberry Finn* over there which was a second or third grade writing prize. It's pretty much as I set it down in *The Boys of Summer* about this boy who dreamed of playing ball, which is a common dream through generations of unwashed urchins in Brooklyn. But from the time I was really able to form any sort of a sensible thought, beginning with Keats, I thought that would be a fine thing to do. When a dream like that begins, you don't say, "Well, how am I going to make a living at it?" You don't have to get very practical.

I was thirteen or fourteen, and fascinated by Keats's poem on death, "When I Have Fears that I May Cease to Be"—I liked that very much, and that was what I wanted to do. I then decided that I would become a poet like Keats. Writing came reasonably easily; it was an area of early success. I liked it. I could write without great drops of blood. So that was what I was going to be, and all the rest from that point on was how to do it; how to become a writer.

Conversations: Judging from your writing, poetry was a major influence.

Kahn: Poetry was an influence, yes.

Conversations: Poetry as opposed to fiction—the novel or short story.

Kahn: I enjoy poetry best of all forms of writing. And right through the time I was covering the Dodgers I was applying myself and learning. When I went to NYU the poetry teaching was wretched. There was no awareness up there that anybody had written poetry after Swinburne. People like Eliot, and Thomas, and Cummings, and Wallace Stevens were outside of the curriculum. I took a course in '52 with a minor poet, who was a very good teacher, and through him was able to approach sprung rhythm and other forms, and also to determine that I really was not a good poet myself.

Conversations: So you tried to write, but not for publication?

Kahn: If any of it had been acceptable, I would have been pleased. As it is, I craftily used two poems in one of my books which I put in the hands of one of the characters. The closest I came to a poetic triumph came when the editor at William Morrow said, "Don't we need a permission to use that poem?" And I said, "Oh, no, I wrote that myself."

Conversations: Have you then resigned yourself to being an appreciator of poetry, rather than a poet?

Roger Kahn

Kahn: Very much. Last night I was sitting and looking at parts of *The Golden Treasury*. That very, very fine sort of lute-song effect, that extreme delicacy, I can't do. Later, as I was learning that some of Dylan Thomas's poetry was 103rd draft, I thought, "Well, of course he was an alcoholic. He did himself in." There was a poem by Frost—a sonnet—the octave was written fifty years earlier than the last six lines. I've never had that kind of discipline.

Conversations: How about fiction?

Kahn: That's what I'm in the middle of now. My next two books will be fiction.

Conversations: Is it something that you want to talk about, or would you rather not?

Kahn: One has a theme of a father and a son and two women, and that's about as far as I'd better go. I've finished 386 pages. I'm down to rewriting now.

Conversations: This is your first novel, right?

Kahn: It will be, right.

Conversations: Any short stories previous to this?

Kahn: Something in *Cosmopolitan*, which makes me think it couldn't have been very good, but it sold. Then a few, one or two, unpublished things. I sold the first short story I ever wrote.

Conversations: When was that?

Kahn: '54. Then I wrote another one; it was better, and it didn't sell. And that was that. I don't remember whether I was discouraged or whether it was the constant pressure from the market: do a nonfiction piece; do a profile; do the black in conflict. Editors were always coming at me to write nonfiction pieces. There isn't any great body of unpublished work, nor did I ever accumulate a great body of unpublished work. I wrote and I published.

Conversations: Some of those essays are superb. I particularly like the one on Jascha Heifetz in How the Weather Was.

Kahn: I liked doing that; I liked doing the essay. There was a very happy climate for my essays in the sixties and right into the very early seventies, until the old magazines, which I complained earlier about, got into trouble. The trouble had little to do with what they published; it had to do with economics. The magazines were set up so that readers paid a low price, and the balance was made up by advertising.

With the entry of television and the boom in television, the advertising budget went there. No longer were these big magazines able to get the advertising they once had. They were locked into selling five, six, or seven million copies a week for 11¢ a copy. So they then wanted to do something to rebuild advertising. How are we going to get attention? This led to a reexamination of the material they had been publishing. Well, that was marvelous because what they had been publishing was, generally, terrible. Look back at the old *Saturday Evening Post*; this stuff was Clarence Budington Kelland.

The articles were both right-wing and not very good. *Life* had its general view. *Life*'s idea of very good profiles or portraits—you look back and see that they're just not exciting. So suddenly these magazines asked, "Well, what are we going to do?" "Well, we're going to get into the twentieth century." And what happened unawares—nobody really being aware of it— was that the junk, that Clarence Budington Kelland sort of junk, became television's domain. It is today. The old pulp garbage is on every night from eight o'clock until eleven o'clock. ABC is first because it's worst.

The magazines, then, had a whole new area. I remember when *The Saturday Evening Post* decided that it wanted to do grown-up stuff. I was asked if I would update and modernize their sports section. I worked at that for a while, and then I had enough of that. Then, would I go to Harlem? I had never been to Harlem, except on the way to the Polo Grounds. There was a full series of things that I could do: look at Harlem; travel with Goldwater; look at *The New York Times*—how it worked and how it did its job; look at New York through the garbage strikes in a story called "The Politics of Garbage." I would mix in some sports: a piece on Durocher, a piece on Frank Ryan, the Ph.D. quarterback. That was a very exciting time.

Roger Kahn

That the *Post* went out of business had nothing to do with its editorial content, but simply with the advertising forces. Then *Life* found itself in trouble, and *Life* said, "Well, I guess we'd better change the sort of articles we've been doing." Now I was able to get financing for the Heifetz piece from *Life*. They ran about a third of it.

Conversations: The entire essay appears in How the Weather Was?

Kahn: Right. And then that led to the artist resisting the demands of his art, which was the piece on Claudio Arrau. But *Life* fell victim to the same economic forces that wiped out the *Post*; *Look* died. Suddenly they were all gone. There are now no truly general magazines in the United States. If I wanted to do an essay like the Heifetz essay at this point, it would be very difficult. Where would I be capitalized?

Conversations: Do you want to at this point?

Kahn: No. For this period I have the novel that I'm working on, and then there's another novel after that, and then there's a nonfiction book. So my view of the short pieces for this period is that I'll do them when I have time, in and around books. A book seems to take me fairly long—it can take me two years, maybe three.

Conversations: How does one move from making a good living as a magazine writer to the big money in books, best-selling books in particular?

Kahn: The big money is in a best-selling book. I don't think that it's possible, or sensible, to project as you write that a book will be a best seller.

Conversations: But, your books have been, to this point, collections of your magazine pieces that are augmented and revised, haven't they?

Kahn: Not really. The first book was *The Passionate People*, and that was a book. *The Saturday Evening Post* at the outset said that they would take a 20,000-word excerpt. That was delightful. They would finance part of the research. I've never done well with foundations and getting grants. Here, in addition to the advance from William Morrow, I had a guarantee from *The Saturday Evening Post*. I had more time to research. That was followed by *The Battle for Morningside Heights*, which was a book; I don't remember it ever appearing in any magazine.

Conversations: A part of it appears in How the Weather Was.

Kahn: A slightly revised version. *The Boys of Summer* was a book written under a contract between Harper & Row and myself. When the book was finished, it was sent around. *Esquire* then rejected it. Harold Hayes, the editor at *Esquire*, said it would not excerpt. I thought that was nonsense; the very structure made it excerpt easily. It turned out that Hayes didn't want to spend money. He wanted *The Boys of Summer* cheap. But first, he simply rejected it. Andre LaGuerre, the editor of *Sports Illustrated*, never made a serious bid. *Sport* magazine made a generous offer—*Sport* took four different parts. Then *Esquire* came to me and said, "We want the section on the *Herald Tribune*." Suddenly, now that *Esquire* did not have to pay big freight, *The Boys of Summer* became a book which Harold Hayes *could* excerpt. I indulged myself in telling them, "If it didn't excerpt a month ago when I was starving, how come it excerpts now? Go to hell."—which led to Harold Hayes discontinuing my column at *Esquire*. Writers don't like rejections; editors seem to like them less.

Then *How the Weather Was* is a collection of various writings, parts of which had appeared in magazines, some in books. I just revised, edited, and expanded them. The idea of *A Season in the Sun* was pretty much impossible. Somebody in *Playboy*—I don't know who—but a pleasant enough review said it was absurd to do one magazine piece on baseball in America. I always get into trouble with things ending in America. *The Passionate People* was the Jew in America; I got myself accused of being anti-Semitic through that book. *The Battle for Morningside Heights* was the student uprising in America; I got an audit from Nixon's income tax people as a result of that. Now, baseball in America. I'm resolved: For the rest of my life I'm not going to write anything ending in America—money in America, politics in America.

Roger Kahn

Conversations: I wonder if you and Roger Angell have an agreement to publish books about baseball in the same year?

Kahn: No. It's really quite annoying, although it seems to annoy him most. I make a living by writing books and by *selling* books, too. I pay Columbia tuition. I have my indulgences, such as a Mercedes. It's incredible and delightful to me that I've gotten those things through writing. When another book comes along and cuts directly into my sale, which I believe Angell's has, this summer, I am troubled. With *The Boys of Summer*, the idea of comparing *The Boys of Summer*, a book, to a collection of old *New Yorker* pieces was something I regarded with genteel, not to say gentile, disdain.

Conversations: How did the contract for The Passionate People *come about? How did you first become a book writer?*

Kahn: That began with Harlem. To backtrack a little, I had done the Harlem story, which I called "White Man Walk Easy." I worked out a technique quite opposite to, say, Barzini's *The Italians*. Instead of doing broad, sweeping strokes, I did specific individuals. I would say that from these individuals, I wanted the reader to generalize. The Harlem piece stands up reasonably well for periodical journalism fifteen years later.

Following that I heard, "What do you want to do next?" I then wanted to further the same technique. I was working toward my kind of odyssey book: *The Boys of Summer* and *A Season in the Sun*. I had felt an intense alienation in Harlem. I was the only white for blocks. Next, I wanted to experience what it was to be a Jew in Germany. I put my Germany idea in Harlem terms. I'd begun by going from one Harlem bar to another. Now, I said, "I'll go drink beer along the Rhine. And I'll say 'Ich bin ein Jude. Want to fight?' "

The best editor I knew was Otto Friedrich, formerly the managing editor of *The Saturday Evening Post*. We discussed Germany first in terms of a long magazine piece, but I knew then that if this began as a magazine piece, I'd have to finish it as a book. When the Harlem article came out, somebody from Knopf called me and said, "Would you do Harlem as a book?" But I was pretty much written out on Harlem. I had written it once. The idea of starting all over again and writing 80,000 words, probably not as well. . . . I never did that book for Knopf. Friedrich urged me to look at Jews here. A book on the impact of Hitler on *American* Jews. All right. *The Passionate People* had been born. A number of publishers expressed interest—that's a euphemism for money in advance. William Morrow made the best offer. So from the beginning that was a book. Contracts were drawn, and I set out for the Jewish community of Rochester, New York.

Conversations: So there were no agents knocking on doors with your manuscript under their arms; it was editors knocking on your door?

Kahn: Yes. I remember this now, as you bring it up—we went to three or four houses, and there were varying degrees of interest, ranging from no to yes with numbers. And Morrow made the best offer. The agent went from place to place to place; I went to, maybe, two places with him. But I didn't do the book on speculation.

Conversations: How closely do you work with editors?

Kahn: Wherever I can now, I get a clause in the contract that they can't change anything. I had that at *Esquire*, and when I did short essays for *Time*, nothing could be changed without mutual consent. By and large, editors can't write as well as writers. That's why they're editors. I work against them rather than with them in magazines. They might say the same. I don't like to have my stuff ground up. If you look at the *Digest*, if you look at *The New Yorker*, somebody is *editing*—maybe even rewriting—those magazines. I'm never able to read *The New Yorker* on a week-to-week basis. I can only read it once every four weeks, because some enormous figure, or maybe it's a machine, is making everybody sound the same. That doesn't work for me, so I am always putting up barriers and contracts to prevent that from happening.

Conversations: How about discussing ideas in advance?

Kahn: It would depend on whether I'm writing for magazines or books. I like to have a sounding board. Say the editor was Don Erickson, when he was running *Esquire*: "Well, let's think three columns ahead." And "Do you have any ideas?" So we met for lunch three or four times a year. With *Time* I tried to let them know what I'd be doing; find out from them what they were doing. We would talk, and then, "Would I do so and so? Would I do a certain idea?" The answer would be yes or no. If they had a good idea, sure, I'd be delighted to do it; if I thought it was a bad idea, I'd not do it.

I'll give you an example: One of their ideas was something about the Super Bowl, because "We have a Super Bowl cover." I thought I'd try to do the athlete as an actor, the athlete as entertainer. The Super Bowl is an entertainment package with ratings, very much the way any other television is. So I did something, then, on athletes and actors—fairly successful but not a very profound point, perhaps. Then they were doing something on black athletes. Because of my own history in that, I would not get involved in what people I didn't know were going to say about the black athlete. I didn't want to be identified with whatever positions *Time* might take about black athletes. I said no.

Conversations: So you're making a distinction there between being a reporter and being an essayist.

Kahn: Yeah. I have the right in the arrangement with *Time* to say, "Well, you go say what you want. I'm not comfortable in your format writing about blacks. I don't know how my work is going to look, bouncing off what you say, and so I think I'll pass." Books are another story, and book editors exercise a control in that they have purse strings.

Conversations: Better editors?

Kahn: Better editors in a large sense: in a sense of ideas, in a sense of respecting the freedom of the writer and not imposing their ideas on the writer—even in letting the writer make an ass of himself. The sentence editing is, of course, quite different, but I think book editors tend to respect the writer's privilege of controlling his own work. Again, this is very complicated; it's complicated for me now. To give you an example: in *How the Weather Was*, there was another section in my scheme. The surviving sections are sports, deaths of friends, artists, and police. I was going to do politics, and I had essays on Goldwater, Eugene

McCarthy, and "The Politics of Garbage." The editor said he didn't think he wanted all that, because politics dates.

I went along with that, in error. I think Goldwater remains an interesting character; I think that the curious career of Eugene McCarthy is interesting; and I think the politics of garbage in New York City, if it was accurate seven years ago, is only more accurate today. But I acceded to the editor. I won a lot of other points; and I give to get. With the construction of A Season in the Sun, the book editor shot ideas at me, and I'd bounce ideas back at him. "Do Bob Gibson." There was no reason to do Bob Gibson; the angry black had been covered by Vic Power in Puerto Rico, and the docile black was covered by Artie Wilson in Portland, Oregon. We kicked around a number of other components. Finally Harper said, "We would like a book of about 50,000 words, and no more." They then determined what the length was going to be.

Conversations: Why did they limit the size of your book? It's a relatively small book.

Kahn: It is short.

Conversations: So they could price it the way they wanted?

Kahn: I guess.

Conversations: So economics enter in yet again.

Kahn: Unfortunately. Publishers hold the money bags. Then there's a whole economic area beneath the surface: books that are offered that you don't do because they're unacceptable, but for which you are offered a good deal of money. Something I find difficult now is the idea of mass-market paperbacks. I have a friend who runs a paperback house. He'll come up with, "Why don't you look into this; why don't you look into that; there will be riches beyond any telling of them." Usually the ideas are awful.

Conversations: Wasn't there a mass-market paperback deal on The Boys of Summer?

Kahn: There was, but it's very unusual. Sport books are not, I am told, very good mass-market sellers. Nobody gets laid in *The*

109

Boys of Summer and nobody gets murdered, and so I lose the sex and violence audience. I guess it did fairly well. It was a number one best seller, so it would have to do fairly well, just because they could put "Number One" on the jacket.

The good book editor is more involved in your career and is less involved with book-to-book economics. The novel on the father and son and two women is something that I was encouraged by Buzz Wyeth at Harper to go ahead and do. Don't think that you find creative editing now in magazines. I can look ahead; I want to do three more books right now. I don't need editors to give me ideas. I'm three ahead of myself. I need publishing houses to give me financing for the books.

Conversations: And distribution?

Kahn: Distribution, advertising. Then, as I proceed, I need dialogue. After all, a writer goes and sits in a room and an editor who will audit his ideas.... *The Boys of Summer* was originally an idea to get into a car and visit a team from Mother Time: out of that team we would find, as King Lear did, that it's harder to be old than to be young. The autobiographical aspects grew out of dialogue with Buzz Wyeth of Harper & Row. But editors who come and say, "Well, do a book about the manipulations on Wall Street for big money." That's of no value to me; I'm not interested in that; I don't think I'd write it particularly well. I want an editor I can talk to and get a response from; and I want somebody who is honest, practical, and direct, and who understands the line between writing and editing, between prose and commercial tripe.

If *A Season in the Sun* sells 35,000 books—which would disappoint Harper & Row, and disappoint me—I need someone to say, "Go on to the next book"—someone who won't get terribly hung-up about it only making x dollars and, therefore, we have to go and look for an immediate blockbuster.

Conversations: Many authors complain that publishers don't support a book enough after it is published, with advertising and promotion. You have just gone through an opposite ordeal: you've been four weeks on the road promoting A Season in the Sun. *And how many interviews in the past four weeks?*

Kahn: The same set answers. Once in awhile you get a good one—interviewer—but there are always too many each day. I'll go back to *The Passionate People*. I think that was a pretty good effort. I would do it a little differently now. Morrow was chipping away, and they bought a nice ad, and then I got a perfectly awful notice in *The Times* by somebody who would have liked to have written the book himself, but was too busy. He talked about the kind of book that he would have written. It was a standard sour review—a freshman trying to impress seniors at Yale. But Morrow bailed out. When *The Passionate People* got a bad review in the Sunday *Times*, they pulled printing number four off the presses.

Conversations: Morrow quit supporting the book?

Kahn: They quit. Then the next book, the Columbia book—

Conversations: The Battle for Morningside Heights.

Kahn: Here, Eugene McCarthy said, "The most important book written on the issue of student unrest." Now, out came two instant books: one of which was put together by students at Columbia, and another one which was put together by Archibald Cox's investigatory committee. Archibald Cox was working for the trustees of Columbia. Curiously, his report on the Columbia riot did not focus on the faults of the trustees of Columbia University. Well, these two things came out at once. They were superficial, safe, quickie books. First of all, Christopher Lehmann-Haupt said that now everything there was to be said about Columbia University had been said. It was a politic, convenient thing for Lehmann-Haupt to say: a trustee of Columbia is Punch Sulzberger, the publisher of *The Times*. But at that point, Larry Hughes, the president of Morrow, said, "Let's think of the next book." Only three-quarters of my Columbia book was finished. *The Battle for Morningside Heights* was not an instant book. I was looking for certain things that hatched slowly. Well, of course, Morrow would publish the book, because they were contracted to publish the book, but Larry Hughes said, "It doesn't matter how good a book is; it has to be first."

I finished *The Battle for Morningside Heights*. Generally reviews were excellent. I think Morrow bought one small ad in the religious book section of the Sunday *Times;* they had given up. Morrow did not promote either one of those books very well. When *The Passionate People* came under fire, I would have liked them to have promoted it as a controversial book. Some people said it was anti-Semitic because I had the nerve to depict a Jewish stripteaser. These critics knew no Jewish girl ever takes off her clothes. I said Jews were defined by Auschwitz; Jews were defined by Hitler. Jewish leaders didn't like that; they liked the idea that Jews were defined by Abraham and Moses. I said that the relevant definition of Jews is the definition of the Nuremberg Laws—laws that led to the murder of six million.

You can argue with that if you want. Morrow really didn't want the cut and thrust of debate. They hoped, I think, that they had a Stephen Birmingham kind of book on Jews—"Our Crowd Today." But I was saying it is an embattled thing to be a Jew. I was disappointed in Morrow's promotion. About that time they found another writer named Jacqueline Susann and began to promote her books, and she began to promote her books, and I don't feel that Morrow has been hurt by my departure.

Conversations: What about A Season in the Sun? *You have been promoting the book, but, on the other hand, you've spent a month away from your writing. Is it an intrusion on your profession to have to do this?*

Kahn: It is. It is really. I think it's cheaper to use an author's body than to mount a very complicated advertising campaign. First, how good is one as a performer? You're performing for a month—

Conversations: Is your ability to perform evaluated by the publisher?

Kahn: If you have a speech impediment they won't send you out.

Conversations: Do they look for "star" quality?

Kahn: They make an effort to figure out how well you can talk. But, of course, that leads to the preposterous business of the writer who is an excellent performer, but who's a terrible writer, selling a lot of books. But one reason for this is the death of all the newspapers. A very few newspapers have a critical impact far beyond what they should have. When *The Times* was against the *Herald Tribune*, that was a reasonable setup; there were checks and balances. Now there isn't that and, of course, that's going on nationally. So if a paper decides to pan a book or it decides to ignore a book, then the decision of that paper may govern a whole town. What, then, can a publisher do?

Conversations: Also, in TV and radio interviews you don't get book reviews; instead you get exposure. Is that true?

Kahn: There are a few shows where you get real dialogue. Studs Terkel has a good show. Then in very surprising pockets you find reasonable discussion, but mostly I find on the shows: "Would you tell the story about. . . . How did you happen to write this book? What is the state of baseball in America?" That kind of thing. You tell a little bit about the book, then you pitch. I'd like to see publishers pay authors for their pitching time. I'd like Harper to send me $1000 a week for the time that I'm on the road. That would be my idea of an ideal republic.

Conversations: They pay only expenses?

Kahn: Only expenses. One writing society is debating whether an author should pay his own promotional expenses for a tour like this. This is a society of authors and journalists! Members in that debate should be gagged and shot—gagged and/or shot. The way publishers generally are set up, there is a promotion department separate from the editorial function. The people in promotion do a memo saying, "We were able to get Roger Kahn on six shows in Dallas and three in Fort Worth, five in Houston"—and they've done their job very well. Does my pitching sell books in Texas? Well, a promotion department is not directly tied in with the sales department.

And, what about the book you're working on when you interrupt it to go and talk about last year's ball game, last year's book? What is the psychological effect when you suddenly come off the cameras and come away from the microphones to go and sit in a room and begin to type again? I've got a splendid editor in Buzz Wyeth—with whom I've discussed this frankly— "How much time could I give the Harper & Row promotion people?" At one point, when I was having debates about

113

delivery times, they were really pressing me and I said, "Well, then I can't go out and promote *A Season in the Sun*." An executive at Harper & Row said, "It's your book." And I said, "It's your advance." There was a heavy silence, after which we worked out everything. I'm not wild about author tours; I do them more easily now than with *The Passionate People*.

You've got certain set acts ready. You're not offended when somebody hasn't read your book. The interviewers are performers, but so are you.

Conversations: How many of the interviewers had read your book in the past four weeks?

Kahn: Most of them had read some sections. How many read it fully? You can't tell, because in a six-minute television spot there's not time to ask about the whole book. I did Carson for *The Boys of Summer*. I know that a preinterviewer read that book—you go through a one-hour preinterview. Cavett seemed to have read the book, although he may have just read certain sections. But I get annoyed at writers coming back from these tours and saying: "It was horrible. I got a 103° fever in Minneapolis. I found nobody really cares about writing in America." Television interviewers aren't everybody.

If you go out with books under your arm, you're Willie Loman. They're your merchandise; you're out pitching your merchandise. If you agree to do it, then understand for that period in your life—for four weeks—you're a salesman; make the most effective sales pitch possible. You're not a missionary on behalf of American writing. You do that in other climates. Here you're out trying to sell. You get a series of broad, not very incisive questions, and you try to cajole the viewer or the listener into being sufficiently interested in your answers to plunk down nine bucks to buy the book.

Conversations: Does a writer have any responsibility to his readers to make himself visible? I'm thinking of the Robert Frost essay, in How the Weather Was, *which begins with your joy at being able simply to meet him and talk seriously with him.*

Kahn: No, I really don't think a writer has that obligation. I think a writer can be T. S. Eliot, who was very, very difficult to approach; a writer can be a Salinger, who's impossible to approach. I don't think that the writer has any obligation whatsoever to be a performer, any obligation to give audiences. . . . The writer puts his work forth. And, indeed, most of the people we read, we never can meet. They're dead.

The writer has no obligation to write to a mass audience. You write to a very limited number of people—very few Americans read books. Wild best sellers like *The Boys of Summer* sold what, 100,000 in bookstores? I don't remember exactly, but not many more than that. Then some sold through The Book-of-the-Month Club. But the number of people who went to a bookstore to buy it was a fractional percentage of Americans. In practically any other industry it would be an insignificant number. So we're dealing with a very, very small percentage of Americans, maybe 3%. It's a very important 3%: those are the dreamers and the people with ideas—the shapers of the present and the leaders of the future. A writer relates to this very, very minimal fraction.

Then there's a multiplier effect from them that goes on to others. You know, if everybody who read *The Boys of Summer*—I use that because I know it—talked about it to other people. . . . When Gil Hodges died there was a headline in the paper saying, "It's winter for the boys of summer." And then the newspapers would say, or people would say, "You've added a phrase to the language." Dylan Thomas added a phrase to the language; I didn't. The book moved through this 3% and a phrase, a title, perhaps even an idea reached many more. But bear in mind that in book writing you're not dealing in mass media.

Conversations: Some gothic romances have sales in the millions. Of course, it's a different kind of writing, and it's a different audience.

Kahn: It's rare. Another thing which is complicated is that: books that sell and books that are good are two different things. Just eliminate *The New York Times Cookbook*; eliminate Kahlil Gibran—who has all the intellectual profundity of *The New York Times Cookbook*. You have just batches of these things that sell and sell and sell. Then you have *How We Made Jaws* which sells and sells and sells. I'm sure there's a book called *Star Wars* out now that sells and sells and sells. Just eliminate all of those.

Roger Kahn

Conversations: They're essentially doing that now with two paperback best-seller lists—the mass-market top-ten list, and the trade paperback list.

Kahn: But it is possible, once in awhile, for a book to be very good and also sell very well. That's what you're always trying to do. Frost's last book, *In the Clearing*, sold more than 100,000 books. How many people actually read it, I don't know, but it sold. It was the best book that he could do at that point in his life. Doctorow's *Ragtime* was a serious book; it sold very well. *Portnoy*. There are many cases of people sitting down and writing absolutely the best book they know how to write without a commercial thought—without saying I'm going to please the crowd—and then writing a book that becomes a number one best seller. All through the last five years or so there have been people coming to me, bearing real or imagined gold, to do something which they insist will sell great numbers.

And then there's the stuff that I feel I should do and that I want to do. Well, I won't get a great amount of gold for writing essays on the state of baseball in the United States. There is no way that *A Season in the Sun* will be a huge mass-market paperback book. You know art and cash are separate curves. But you can't aim for both, and one of the hard things of writing is discipline. Write well. Worry about sales some other time. If you're practicing surgery and you're pretty good, you're going to be very rich. If you're practicing corporate law and you work for major companies and do it well, you're going to be very rich. If you write books you want to write and you write them well, you may have to teach and do journalism all your life to make a living.

Conversations: Do you have a long-term career plan to move from this stage in your career to another stage? Or do you bother to think that far ahead?

Kahn: I bother to hope.

Conversations: What do you want to do?

Kahn: I would love just to do books. And I'd like to spend the next, I'd say, five to seven years working on these three books. That's about as far as I can see. I don't want to try to write at sixty what I wrote at forty. I think that one of the tragedies of American authors has been that they didn't know when to stop.

Conversations: Who in particular?

Kahn: Hemingway. I think Hemingway might have moved to journalism after *For Whom the Bell Tolls.* I don't think he ever approached that again, but he was able to do good journalism. Didn't Sinclair Lewis go on and on writing novels that fewer and fewer people read? I don't think that he was broke. He just kept writing, instead of *Arrowsmith, Kingsblood Royal.* Steinbeck kept trying. So what do you ultimately see in these lively and brilliant men? You see alcoholics with depressing endings— depressing even to read about. I'd like to write about three more, and then I don't feel that I'd have a compulsion continually to write books.

Conversations: You can quit?

Kahn: I would like to be able to quit and settle back into journalism. Red Smith is in his seventies, and look at Red Smith's seventies. I think that's a very nice way to spend your seventies— go to the World Series. . . . You're not writing about the most complicated issues and you're not doing the most demanding writing, but it's a damned sight better than doing nothing— trying to play shuffleboard at St. Pete. It brings you a certain income, and it keeps you in touch. So I would think after my books I would like to do some journalism. The effort of a book— the effort of making page 3 relate to page 393—is fierce, and I'd like to think that at a certain point I would have said what I have to say in books; I would have written my books, and then I'd like to go back to journalism.

Conversations: Are you encouraged about the state of American letters? Authors are being paid better than they've ever been paid, and the profession of authorship affords some promise for a young man.

Kahn: Being a violinist offers real promise, if you become Heifetz. Mostly your chances as a violinist end in the second-violin section of the Minneapolis Symphony, if that.

Conversations: Still, it pays better than it did fifteen years ago.

Roger Kahn

Kahn: It does. You can teach and such. Books pay much better than they did—to those anointed people who can get books published. The market that has vanished is the general magazine market. That was a wonderful transitional step from writing short stuff, which is easier than writing long stuff. You had a batch of magazines, but now you don't. The best magazine markets have been wiped out. I find that discouraging. What do you do if someone were to follow my pattern and work for a good paper for a while? You learn certain things from working on the paper and then say, "Well, I want to do books, but it's going to be awhile." It's an adjustment from newspaper rhythms to the rhythms of a book. Magazines were ideal for making that transition. There's no way to do that now. So I'm not that encouraged. The loss of the general magazine is disastrous.

More books are sold, but I have two minds on the damned thing. One is that Gerald Ford is getting $500,000 for his memoirs. A writer is going to make $100,000 typing this semi-book about a mediocre to awful politician whose memoirs are probably worthless to begin with—and under the way it's being put together are guaranteed to be worthless. A lot of what seems like big money for writing is not that at all—it's for packaging. The goddamn Watergate criminal books brought tremendous amounts of money. Is that good for writing or bad for writing? It's neither: it's confusion. Maybe it's bad for writing, as I think about it, because it takes editors away from doing serious work. I've heard a great deal about Haldeman's book: how Haldeman's book is going to name "Deep Throat" and is going to say who erased the eighteen minutes of tape. Ergo, it's a million-dollar book.

Baseball is not really an analogy for much of anything except baseball, but when a ball player becomes a $500,000-player or a $400,000-player, nobody writes about him as a ball player. Nobody. Specifically, there is Catfish Hunter's $3,000,000-contract and so the emphasis is on a contract, and not the way Catfish Hunter pitches. And in books—God, it would be awful if books became million-dollar books. Wouldn't that be awful if there were $500,000-books and $800,000-books, and the whole tone became with a book—as it is with ball players—the book is worth x; therefore, it's a good book? Hunter is a $3,000,000-pitcher—not a man who can use a slider very well.

118

There is, of course, a tremendous number of writers who get nothing. How does the first novelist benefit, or even relate to the fact that Haldeman gets $1,000,000? It doesn't help that writer at all. And if the Haldeman book is a bust, then there's one publisher who has lost $1,000,000. He's unlikely, then, to underwrite young writers.

Conversations: But the money that these Watergate criminal books make might allow publishers to take a chance on a first novelist.

Kahn: If they make money. But if they lose money—an example would be the Lyndon Johnson book, *The Vantage Point*: $1,500,000 was laid out for that book and nobody bought it. How many books were not published with the money that went to Lyndon Johnson? There is this kind of crap shoot with the public. The publishers look for a blockbuster. Maybe that's the nature of the publishing business from now on. But a lot of writers are outside of the dice game: a lot of writers are getting small advances and struggling and teaching, living poor. I've heard the idea that "Well, if we only did paperback firsts, you see, then we would reach great numbers of people with good books." I don't think that would work. If you did paperback firsts, we would all be doing the memoirs of Xaviera Hollander. That's another kind of snobbery—that's a belief in the cultural wisdom of the truck driver. Somehow things would be better, the Marxists say, if the great mass of people were to determine the kinds of books we get. The great mass of people give us *Penthouse*. The system now says you will be paid not on merit, but on popularity. Flawed, but still the only system that seems to work.

Conversations: Do you read much contemporary fiction and poetry, or do your interests lie in another generation of writing?

Kahn: The latter, another generation of writing.

Conversations: What generation?

Kahn: Well, I read—lately, I mean, different parts of time in my life—nineteenth century.

Conversations: Romantic poets?

Kahn: Poets, and then I've been rereading Hardy; the last thing I've been reading is Troyat's biography of Tolstoy. I read that with the sense that I should have 100 muzhiks, 1000 muzhiks taking care of the chores so I could contemplate man's fate. I don't read that much contemporary fiction. I've never read *Love Story*. I haven't read *The Thorn Birds*. I mean to read Walker Percy's *Lancelot*. I'll be reading *A Book of Common Prayer*. I go off, though, to read those things. I'm going to read a great batch of books by the shore in August. When I'm working a lot, as I have been, the pace is not congenial.

Conversations: Do you read while you're writing?

Kahn: Not much, no. Very minimal. Particularly to read fiction while I'm writing fiction is ominous. I've actually periods with nonfiction when I just stopped reading something which I thought was getting in my way—bad style, mannered style. Lord, I don't want to mess with that, because you start to see that style get into your own style. And then, at the end of that horrible little spiral, you say, "Well, do *I* really have any style at all?" I know writers who had the same problem. When I'm writing hard, I'm writing and then I'm reading over my stuff and revising it. That's about it. I have a good memory and I can just muse about poetry or books that I have read, and what I will do when I'm writing is just dip into some good poetry.

Conversations: The past four weeks must have underscored the fact that you're a celebrity of a certain type, and you have your influence. What do you want that influence to be, or what do you think it is?

Kahn: Well, I can see it now in certain kinds of sports writing.

Conversations: Must be gratifying.

Kahn: It is. Of course, you think two ways. You think, "Patent applied for; royalties cheerfully accepted." Somebody sent me a *Sport* magazine the other day and I saw four articles, and I thought, "Well, it's flattering to see certain things worked out"— the kind of technique that I was able to evolve was, again, to take the specific and to let the story unfold itself without too many mannerisms. The intelligent reader will be able to look at this specific and realize that although I am writing about a specific, I really mean to suggest general things—Blake says, "To see a World in a Grain of Sand"—the universe in a water drop. That's what I mean. Let characters talk, and then don't go use complicated transitions to get somebody from room A to room B, or from day A to day B. Just stop, skip four lines. Let the reader make that trip in his own mind. Change the weather; change the backdrop. The reader can fill in. And I see that a lot now; I think, "Well, that's fine."

The business of celebrity, I think, is a little—it's ominous in a way in that it's a semi-celebrity. If any of these people had to choose between one of Charlie's Angels and an author, they would immediately pick any one of Charlie's Angels. The best of writers is a minor celebrity. Johnny Carson is a barometer of celebrity standing in the United States. Where does the author go on the Johnny Carson show? First, the comedian; then the girl with the boobs; then somebody else. The author gets the last twelve minutes. That goes on toward one o'clock when people are going to sleep, or even making love. That's the state of it. You say something erotic.

Grimly, you can see where an author is threatened by celebrity best, in my lifetime, in Hemingway. A story is told of Hemingway being ushered into Toots Shor's restaurant by Jimmy Cannon and Leonard Lyons—a great coup going to Shor's with Hemingway. Cannon had one of Hemingway's big hands in both of his and Leonard Lyons was on the other side with the other of Hemingway's hands. A writer named Tom Meany sat at the bar, looked across his drink, and said, "There go three writers with varying abilities, but equal self-esteem." What happened with Hemingway, I think, with this celebrity status that he had, was that he began to confuse his public image with himself. That *macho* nonsense—he began to take that seriously. He had to fight—I wouldn't want to go any further into his life than he did; maybe he had a sense of great sexual prowess. Hemingway began to think of himself as a Hemingway character, even as the pseudo Hemingway character that Leonard Lyons wrote about. I think that confused him and made life and work more difficult for him: made it harder for him to write; made him drink more; made him unhappy. I think Hemingway's confusion between

121

Roger Kahn

the person that he was and the public image that he had was one
more factor that shoved him off the deep end. He couldn't just
simply be a writer.

You want to watch celebrity. Frost watched it.
Frost would go out into the world for little periods
and then go back. He had all of his rules by the time that I knew
him—and he was eighty—about how much he would go out into
the world, and how little he would go out into the world. You
know, it's possible now for me to spend my life on an endless
talk-show circuit. And it would be the end of me. Or I could
become, I suppose, a broadcaster of ball games—Red Barber
with a Northern accent. That's where that leads. No more real
books. So if you want to continue writing, you have to stop. You
have to pull back.

Though she characterizes herself as "just a girl out there trying to get a fast buck," Anita Loos has probably written more screenplays than any living writer. She had already written over 200 scripts when sound was introduced to motion pictures, and her contribution since that time has been no less extensive. Among her screen credits are Gentlemen Prefer Blondes (1928—from her novel), The Struggle (1931—D. W. Griffith's last film), Red-Headed Woman (1932), and The Women (1939). In addition, she has written for the stage; her most notable successes are Happy Birthday (1946) and Gigi (1951). Miss Loos has also found time for eleven books, including A Mouse is Born (1951), A Girl Like I (1966), Kiss Hollywood Good-by (1974), and Cast of Thousands (1977). Gentlemen Prefer Blondes (1925) was praised by William Faulkner, Aldous Huxley, George Santayana, James Joyce, and hailed by Edith Wharton as "the Great American novel (at last!)." Now in her sixty-fifth year as an active writer, Miss Loos continues to work every day.

Anita Loos

Anita Loos was interviewed by Matthew J. Bruccoli at her apartment near Carnegie Hall in July 1977. On display in the large living room are framed photographs of Miss Loos's Broadway and Hollywood friends and memorabilia from her shows. A tiny lady, she looked elegant in well-tailored slacks. It was four o'clock in the afternoon, and Miss Loos had been up since four a.m., the time she normally starts her working day.

Conversations: Your career has included marked successes as a novelist, screenwriter, playwright. Do you think of yourself as primarily any one of those things?

Loos: No, I just think of myself as a working girl because the reason I work is to earn a living; and whatever seems to come out best, that's what I do.

Conversations: Would you say that, in a way, Gentlemen Prefer Blondes *has tended to obscure the range of your other work because you're always associated with that book?*

Loos: I think *Gentlemen Prefer Blondes* is the range of my work. I think everything else I do is just earning a living.

Conversations: What you're indicating, then, is that you regard it as your most characteristic work.

Loos: Yes, I think so.

Conversations: Tell me how many screenplays you claim credit for. It's a staggering number, isn't it?

Loos: I did 200 before sound came in, that is, 200 that were produced. Then after sound came in—that was in 1931—I went back to Hollywood and I stayed eighteen years at MGM, and I've lost all track of how many films I did because in those days we worked on several films at a time. And Thalberg, who was the head of production, would pull me in on other people's films.

Conversations: As a troubleshooter?

Loos: Yes. Film doctor.

Conversations: Of your silent films, which one did you enjoy working on the most? Which one do you feel was the finest movie?

Loos: To tell you the truth, I never paid any attention to any of them. They were a job and I'd get them done.

Conversations: Did you go see them after the film was made?

Loos: No.

Conversations: Never?

Loos: No.

Conversations: What about the talkies?

Loos: I saw the talkies during the time that I was working on them, naturally. We saw the rushes. Yes, I did see the talkies because we previewed them, but after that I never saw them. I'm not a film buff at all. I'm a reader. I'd rather read a book than look at any film.

Conversations: In the days of silent movies you were identified with the giant, D. W. Griffith; in the era of talkies you were identified again with the giant, Irving Thalberg. Do you feel that working with these men enlarged your own capacities?

Loos: Well, working with them was a great experience, naturally. But I put that down to luck because I just fell in with great people from the time I was a child. I was always bumping into geniuses. And I just happened to be there.

Conversations: Remember the old joke about the harder I work the luckier I get? Do you think that's true in your case?

Loos: It is, indeed. I was a good worker—that I admit.

Conversations: Is there some quality required for screenwriting that you had—that you still have—that made you such a consistent producer?

Loos: Well, the writing of drama is a peculiar thing and some of the best writers in the world can't produce a theatrical job. We found that out at MGM where we had, at one time or another, every important writer in the world. Some of them made good, and most of them didn't. Scott Fitzgerald, for instance, had a very silly ambition that he wanted to write films. I don't know why a man of his quality wanted to be a movie writer, but he did. And he never succeeded at all.

Conversations: As a matter of fact, you were called in to take over one of his scripts, The Women.

Loos: Yes, that's true. So it is a knack, and I don't think it's any more to be explained than the fact that some faces are photogenic and others are not. Some of the prettiest girls I ever knew didn't photograph at all. Some girls who were not beauties at all came out on screen much better than the pretty ones. It's a mystery. That's one of the mysteries.

Conversations: Well, a minute ago, you referred to all of the important writers who passed through Hollywood—some of whom were able to meet the needs of the screen, most of whom weren't. Who were the most talented, the most gifted writers you were associated with in Hollywood?

Loos: Well, there was, first of all, Aldous Huxley who wrote beautiful dialogue in many films. And Christopher Isherwood, who throughout his whole career has written films. He's jumped back and forth from films to fiction or biography, and he's equally good at all of it. But on the old MGM lot most of the work was done by women. I hate to say this because I'm not a women's libber, but it's true. Most of the women writers took their jobs seriously and produced their scripts; and most of the men were at the racetrack, or playing with football scores, or doing that sort of thing around the studio.

Conversations: Some of these good, dependable women writers were Bess Meredyth and Sonya Levien.

127

Anita Loos

Loos: Yes.

Conversations: Who else?

Loos: Oh, now let me think. Wait a minute; I'll have to do a little thinking. Well, there was Zoe Akins who was very good and Jane Murfin was excellent. And well, anyway, there were about six of them at MGM. All of them were very excellent. These girls did the work, and I would say they did nine-tenths of the work of the studio—of the script department.

Conversations: Could you characterize D. W. Griffith for me?

Loos: D. W. Griffith was a poet above everything, and I think that comes through in his films. He wanted to be a writer. He started out to be a writer, and it was a disaster that he failed as a writer of plays. It took him a long time to appreciate the films. When he first started in the films his heart was on Broadway, and he never, never was happy about his work. But then when he got along into, well, *Birth of a Nation* and *Intolerance*, he began to take his work seriously. But he was a poet, and that comes through in any of his films, even the least successful. You find moments that are sheer poetry.

Conversations: Why did the industry turn on him and exile him in his last years? Was it just economics?

Loos: It was economics and it was the fact that he was a poor businessman, and they didn't take him seriously. He put all his own money into films, and when he died he was practically broke. He was just considered to be an odd fish that wasn't capable of handling business. With the producers—I mean the backers of films—that was the important thing.

Conversations: With few exceptions—the only exception that I can think of offhand is Singin' in the Rain—*Hollywood has been unable to make a great movie about Hollywood. Would you agree with my generalization?*

Loos: I certainly would. I've never seen anything about Hollywood that is any good at all.

Conversations: Perhaps the first version of A Star is Born *is an exception.*

Loos: Yes, that was sort of. . . . That was not 100% true by any means. No, there never has been a good film about Hollywood. I suppose they're too close to it, probably. They need somebody to come along from the outside.

Conversations: Let's go back to your favorite work. I recall the anecdote that James Joyce is supposed to have used his last days of eyesight reading Gentlemen Prefer Blondes.

Loos: That's true. Friends who knew Joyce told me about that, and it's even published in one of the books about him.

Conversations: Gentlemen Prefer Blondes *appeared in that magic year for American literature, 1925. Did you start out to write a book or was this a short story that grew into a book?*

Loos: I wrote it as a joke, because a great friend of mine was H. L. Mencken. I admired him enormously. I even had a mash on him, and he was wasting too much time with a silly blonde. So I wrote a sketch about this girl, saying to myself, "Well, I'll fix her." I only wrote it to make Mencken laugh. Then I forgot about it, and I think six months or more went by before I found it in an old suitcase. I sent it to Mencken and he read it. He was in Baltimore; I was in New York. He called me up and said, "I think this should be published." But he said, "I'm not going to use it in the *Mercury*"—which he was then publishing—"because we're just starting out on a new magazine. We don't want to shock our readers. Do you realize you are the first American writer ever to make fun of sex?" I didn't realize it, because I never thought of my writing at all. Anyway, he advised sending it to a fashion magazine. He said, "It can get lost among the fashion pictures, and it won't shock anybody." So I sent it to *Harper's Bazaar*. The editor at that time was Henry Sell, and he sent for me and said, "This is good, but you've started the girl on a tour. Why don't you continue?" I was just leaving for Europe anyway, and I said, "All right, I'll take her along wherever I go." And I went to London, Paris, Berlin, Munich. I never got her to Italy, though. That's too bad, because Italy in those days would have given her a lot of adventures.

Conversations: Is it too late for a sequel?

Loos: I think so, yes.

Anita Loos

Conversations: Do you feel that Ring Lardner was an influence on Gentlemen Prefer Blondes? Not on the subject matter but on the technique.

Loos: I don't think so because I never read him. I never did much reading of fiction—never have. That's one reason why I wasn't interested in movies, because I liked biography and essays and history. I don't think anybody influenced me at all. If anybody did it would have been the French. There is that novel called *Bouvard et Pecuchet* which is about two doddering old Frenchmen who once in awhile make very good sense. I think that impressed me. If anybody impressed me it was the French. Ludovic Halevy I adored, and that's the only thing I've ever been impressed with, personally, concerning my own work.

Conversations: You flourished in an era that was loaded with witty, brilliant, talented people. Why do you think the twenties generated so much good work—not just in literature, but in music as well as the other arts? What made the twenties this kind of magic decade?

Loos: I think magic made it because those phases have occurred all throughout history. Who knows why the Renaissance exploded? Who knows why the great British school of the Elizabethans or the school that produced Johnson and all of that group? That seems to come in groups. And I don't know why the twenties produced a group. They just suddenly did.

Conversations: But we haven't done it again.

Loos: No, it may be a long time before it happens again.

Conversations: Do you think that the reaction to World War I was an element?

Loos: Possibly, yes. Everybody started to kick up their heels and have fun, and we thought war had been finished for good. Everybody was getting rich in America with the stock market boom, and it just freed people's spirits. Today people are so bogged down by financial difficulties that it's hard to rise above them.

Conversations: Again, who do you remember from the twenties, with particular nostalgia?

Loos: Of course, I remember Mencken most of all. And then there are other people I remember that wouldn't mean anything. They were people who were not known.

Conversations: The young people of today resist Mencken.

Loos: Is that possible; is that true? Isn't that amazing!

Conversations: I'd like you to comment on that. Why do you think that Mencken is unfashionable now?

Loos: Well, most of the things he fought for, he won. So I suppose they don't mean anything anymore. They are a matter of daily life to these youngsters. He was against all sorts of hypocrisy and we live in an age where hypocrisy doesn't exist anymore.

Conversations: The battles may not seem important anymore, but yet there's the force of his writing, the exuberances and the humor of it. He was an extremely funny writer. His jokes don't go over nowadays.

Loos: That amazes me.

Conversations: Would you say there is a quality of irreverence in Mencken's work, a refusal to take certain things seriously, as well as his frank enjoyment of the right to be intolerant that scares off the young people of today who are afraid to be thought intolerant?

Loos: I somehow don't see that. The one young person I know is eighteen years old. She's the girl we've raised from a baby, and she has an intense devotion to Ogden Nash. Now that doesn't sound as if, in that particular case, she were afraid of being impudent. But, of course, she never reads Mencken. As you say, none of them do. I suppose the fact that he isn't read is the main thing. If you could get people to read him, maybe they'd like him. Who reads Trollope nowadays? Who reads even Thackeray?

Anita Loos

Conversations: When you ask who reads Thackeray, who reads Trollope, what you're really asking is who reads.

Loos: Yes, that's it exactly. But just the same, there's an explosion of paperbacks that is staggering. It's an awful lot of trash, I admit, but people must be reading it or they wouldn't get million-copy editions.

Conversations: We sit here and lament that no one is reading, but, of course, the paperbacks have made books more accessible.

Loos: Yes. And more trashy. Books have never been so cheaply available. Or in such quantities—such enormous quantities. I'll tell you what I just think at the moment. I think airplane travel has done a lot for books. People on planes read books. They get them in the airport, these paperbacks, and they gobble them up and read one of them on a trip and throw it out. I think that the airlines and the book trade have gone sort of into cooperation.

Conversations: What are you working on now?

Loos: I'm writing a story of the Talmadge sisters—Norma and Constance—and most of all their mother, Peg, who was a fabulous character. The reason I'm writing it is that people want to read about the movies. The publishers come at once with the big advance if I write about the movies, so I write about the movies.

Conversations: When you say a story, you mean you're writing a book about the Talmadge sisters?

Loos: A book, yes, a book, an entire book.

Conversations: Biography, or your recollections of them, or a combination of both?

Loos: I worked with Norma and Constance Talmadge for six years, so we had a lot of adventures. We traveled a great deal on location and led a very exciting life. We met everybody, went everywhere, and had a good time—so it makes a funny book. And, incidentally, it tells the story of the silent films. They primarily made silent films; they never really bridged that gap. So that's what I'm writing on at the moment.

Conversations: There is an explosion of interest in the movies which takes both the form of nostalgia and also a good deal of serious attention given to the movie as an art form. Why, after all these years, when Hollywood is now moribund should the movies suddenly be discovered as an American art form?

Loos: I think they were first discovered as a European art form, and then the Americans tried to get onto the bandwagon. I think that's what happened. I think the movies that are important as art were first of all done by Europeans. They were done in England, then France, and Italy, and in Germany; and then Hollywood, which was beginning to lose its standing, tried to get into the act. I don't think any important films have come out of Hollywood except for the films that Woody Allen has done. Not since—well, not since years. Of course, I think the best film writing is done by directors. I think that's where the films have finally found their status—with great directors.

Conversations: You share, then, the French auteur *theory, that the director is the creator of the movie?*

Loos: Yes, I do. And when the director is great the movie is great.

Conversations: I've heard it said that the big difference between Hollywood in the thirties and the movie of today is that in the thirties the producer had the most control over the movie, certainly more control than the director. But in Europe and then in America, after World War II, the producer simply became a glorified bookkeeper. The man in charge of the money, and the director—

Loos: The director took over.

Conversations: But is that statement true of Hollywood in the thirties?

Loos: I think that's true, yes. If there was a producer of taste, such as Thalberg and Sam Goldwyn, his good taste colored everything he did.

Conversations: Did you work for Goldwyn?

Loos: No, I never did, but I admired his films. He had an artistic ambition that was admirable. He would engage nobody but the

133

very best, and then he'd put things in their hands and let them take over.

Conversations: You're confirming what seems to be a revisionary theory of Goldwyn. Not so long ago there were all of those Goldwyn malapropism jokes, and Goldwyn was supposed to have been a vulgar, brutal man. But of late he is being reclassified as a man who had an honest compulsion to make the best possible movies.

Loos: He was an artistic snob, and that's what made him great. He was a vulgar and uneducated man. He was a clown, actually, but he had this driving ambition to engage the best of everybody.

Conversations: With his own money, too.

Loos: Yes, with his own money. And his output proves that he had something very important.

Conversations: You mentioned a moment ago the legendary Irving Thalberg. "Legendary" is an obligatory epithet because he has become the stuff of legend—"the last tycoon." Could you give an example of what it was like working for and with Thalberg, in terms of any one of the movies you did with him?

Loos: He was a perfectionist of such extremes that the average time spent on a script was five years. There was very seldom a script developed under five years. He would have ten, twenty, maybe, thirty scripts written on one single story by different writers. And out of the lot of them he achieved what he thought was perfection, and it was darn near perfection. But in his case it was a question of time—endless time, endless patience, and the fact that he engaged the greatest talents in the world in the way of writing and in the way of acting. Not only did he engage them, but he educated them. He would take an unknown actress like Myrna Loy or Jean Harlow and he would—like Pygmalion, he'd create a star. And he was a genius. When Irving died I was in the middle of a contract which I tried to get out of because I said to myself, "This is the end of the movies as being important." And I couldn't—they wouldn't let me go. But I think with the death of Thalberg the whole of that era collapsed, and it's never been found again. Now a movie that is a success is a haphazard thing. It just comes—it happens in spite of itself almost. And all of these movies that they pour millions and millions of dollars into and talents of all kinds, they just don't work out.

Conversations: I believe that you have said in print that of your Thalberg movies your favorite is San Francisco.

Loos: Yes, yes. I adored *San Francisco* because with me it was a personal thing, and I liked that and I liked *Red-Headed Woman,* which I did for Jean Harlow, and which, incidentally, brought on censorship. Not because of anything in the movie itself, but the fact that a very naughty girl achieved great success and never paid for her sins. And that's what brought the censors into Hollywood.

Conversations: Can you describe at this distance the actual process of working with Thalberg on either Red-Headed Woman *or* San Francisco? *For example, when you handed in the script how would he react—what kinds of advice or reactions would he give?*

Loos: What we did was—on *San Francisco* I worked with a collaborator. His name was Bob Hopkins. We were inseparable pals because we both came from San Francisco, and we both felt that we were strangers in an alien land in the south of California. One day we got an idea that right in the hotbed of Southern California we would glorify our old hometown. So we went to Thalberg with the idea, and he was very sympathetic. He liked it, too. And he said, "Well, go ahead and work out a plot, and we'll see how it comes along." The hero of that picture was an idol of both of us. He was an idol of San Francisco where he was a gambler on the Barbary Coast. His name was Wilson Mizner, and we both adored him. He had died about two years previous, and it was sort of a tribute to this town we were fond of and this man who epitomized the spirit of San Francisco. So we worked out a story line in which a gambler is regenerated by what else but the San Francisco earthquake. It was an invincible combination which Irving fastened onto at once. He said, "Gee, that's great." So we, Hoppy and I, would work out a certain block of material, and then we would take it to Irving and read it to him. He would criticize; he'd comment; he'd make suggestions. It just happened that he knew Wilson Mizner and was as fond of him as we were, and so little by little we worked out the plot. It was a fairly quick job for those days. I think we did it in a matter of about twelve months or maybe a little more. Just as we finished it, Irving died and we knew we were stuck with a very tough proposition because there was nobody on that lot who was knowledgeable enough about human nature to understand a man being an out-and-out reprobate and, at the same time, completely lovable. So we went through horrors getting that story onto film, fighting for every scrap of film that we made. But it came out all right and it's one of the big money-makers of MGM of all time. It still runs on the late late show.

Conversations: Do you watch it when it comes on?

Loos: No, because I go to bed at nine o'clock. I don't think I've ever seen it. But, anyway, it worked out fine.

Conversations: According to the current edition of Who's Who in America, *you were born in 1893.*

Loos: Yes. Don't let me figure out how old I am because I've always had a theory that as soon as I knew, I'd feel it. I've had a complete mental block against my age, and I can't add two and two, so being born in '93 doesn't mean anything to me. I couldn't possibly figure out my age.

Conversations: Neither can I, but it is nonetheless evident—

Loos: It's nonetheless true.

Conversations: . . . that you have been a successful pro for a long time, and you are still producing at a high level. Your recent book Cast of Thousands, *a pictorial history of Hollywood—of your Hollywood—was a splendid book. I'm not going to ask you what the secret of your non-geriatric career is, but instead I will ask you about your work habits. You regard yourself as a working girl; do you work every day?*

Loos: Yes, I work every day, and I start about four o'clock in the morning, and by ten o'clock I've done a whole day's work, and I can forget about it and go about my business. I work principally because—well, I look at work as a crossword puzzle fiend looks at crossword puzzles: to see if it works out. And I set myself a problem, perhaps, if I'm writing fiction. I set myself a problem as I did when I wrote a play for Helen Hayes called *Happy Birthday*. I set myself the problem of having a girl who is a complete hypocrite, a complete disaster, unattractive, and an old maid, achieve a complete changeover in twelve hours. That was my job, and I did it; and it ran for eighteen months. The way I worked it out, it was a sort of Cinderella with liquor: I had this old maid go into a bar and get tight, and in the process of getting tight she regenerates her whole life. So working with fiction I set myself a problem and then see if I can lick it, and in that case I did.

Conversations: We've been talking about your successes, your favorite projects. Is there one of your projects that didn't quite jell or didn't quite come off, but that, nonetheless, you have a special feeling about?

Loos: There are plenty of them, only I have no feeling about them except disgust. They were flops, so I had no feeling at all. I've never had any great, tremendous pride in work, so it doesn't matter. They don't work out—forget them.

Conversations: If you were replanning your career would you, with the advantages of hindsight, map a different kind of career?

Loos: I would map a career by which I could earn the greatest amount of money, and I don't know what it would be in today's market. As a matter of fact, I was an actress before I was a writer. I quit acting when I was about twelve. The reason I quit was because I made more money in half a day by writing than I could make in a whole week by acting in a show. So I can only look on my career as a matter of earning a living, but I just happened to earn a good one. I don't know whether you'll get anything out of all this, but I really never consider myself as a writer. I'm just a girl out there trying to get a fast buck.

Conversations: I can't help feeling you wouldn't have worked as hard as you have, as long as you have, if the work itself wasn't meaningful to you.

Loos: I worked to pay the dressmakers—and to get the clothes of Balenciaga and Mainbocher you had to have money. The easiest way to get money was, in my case, to write. That's really honest. I'm not being a hypocrite.

Conversations: I don't suggest hypocrisy at all. I think that many writers tend to play down their real dedication.

Loos: Yes.

Conversations: And I think, perhaps, you're doing that. Sure, the money is nice, but I hardly find it convincing that you have written steadily for more than fifty years to support a couple of dressmakers.

Loos: That's what I did. It may seem incongruous, but it's nevertheless true. Then another thing, I myself have such a great admiration for genius that, to me, any writer less than Shakespeare or Goethe or maybe Heinrich Heine isn't worth considering. And I certainly am not trying to vie with genius. To me it's genius or nothing; and I'm surrounded with nothings most of the time.

Conversations: Putting aside Shakespeare, Heine, and Goethe, who are the geniuses of twentieth-century American literature in your view? Do we have any? Have we had any?

Loos: I don't think so, not that I know of—maybe Auden. I don't share the admiration for Joyce, for instance, that the critics do. I have an all-out admiration for Auden—unqualified—and I can't think, at the moment, of anybody else.

Conversations: No American writer of the twentieth century? Not Hemingway, not Wolfe, not Faulkner?

Loos: Hemingway—I'll tell you I have one point in my—it may be a block: I cannot stand hysteria in writing. And I think Hemingway is a hysterical writer, and so I never had any admiration for him at all.

Conversations: That's interesting because the standard critical approaches to Hemingway are in terms of his control. . . .

Loos: Really?

Conversations: His emotional control and understatement, his refusal to let the emotion run wild. Will you expand on the hysteria comment?

Loos: I knew Hemingway.

Conversations: In Paris?

Loos: I knew him in Cuba; I knew him in Europe; I knew him in New York; and he wasn't my cup of tea, because we thought he was a big bluff. I know in the matter of his romantic life we knew he was a bluff. I believe his wife's biography—Mary's biography—rather indicates that, that he was a big bluff. He protested too much—his manhood and his male occupations. And I think that that last thing he wrote, *The Old Man and the Sea,* is just a scream of hysteria from beginning to end.

Conversations: How about Fitzgerald?

Loos: Fitzgerald I didn't like at all. I can't even read him. But you're talking to a very intolerant character.

Conversations: You've earned the privilege. Faulkner, Thomas Wolfe?

Loos: Thomas Wolfe is another hysteric. I wish I could think of somebody I have a kind word for. I love this critic named Wolfe who writes about modern art.

Conversations: Tom Wolfe.

Loos: Tom Wolfe, yes. I do enjoy his books very much.

Conversations: Have you ever written for television?

Loos: No, I've sold things to television, and I've seen one very good televised program. In Italy they did *Happy Birthday* with an Italian cast. It was awfully well done. They've done it in this country, too, with very good actors.

Conversations: A minute or so ago you said you write where the money is. Would you write for television?

Loos: I would write for television if it paid, but it doesn't pay big enough. It only pays when it buys the rights, the television rights of some other medium.

Anita Loos

Conversations: Have they adapted Gentlemen Prefer Blondes *for television?*

Loos: Oh, let me think—have they? I believe it's all tied up. I don't think they can. I don't think they have except to run the film.

Conversations: Did you like the movie version?

Loos: I did like the movie. I liked the musical movie version very much. It didn't have anything of my book in it at all; but it was done by somebody with my point of view, Charlie Lederer, and there wasn't a thing in it that I would have changed if I had written it myself. He just was completely right, but I haven't seen too many of my things on film. And *Happy Birthday* they wouldn't—the censors wouldn't pass it. Now, of course. . . .

Conversations: But, in your view, America is still waiting?

Loos: Is still waiting to get an education, and I don't know how it's going to do it with television in charge.

The date of James A. Michener's birth is unknown: he was a foundling raised by Edwin and Mabel Michener in Doylestown, Pennsylvania. After earning an M.A. in education, he worked as a teacher before establishing himself as a writer. Aside from a distinguished career as a best-selling author, Michener has served as a governmental advisor under various presidencies since 1957. His works include Tales of the South Pacific *(1947)*, *for which he won a* Pulitzer Prize, The Bridges at Toko-ri *(1953)*, Sayonara *(1954)*, Report of the County Chairman *(1961)*, *and* Sports in America *(1976)*.

James A. Michener

*In winter 1972 James A. Michener was interviewed over a two-day
period by John Hayes, who was beginning research on a biography
of the author. The interview took place in Pipersville, Pennsylvania,
at Michener's home, which sits atop a hill on his 80-acre estate. Kent
State had just been published, and on both days of the interview the
mail was delivered in 3' × 2' boxes.*

*Conversations: You were born in New York in 1907. What
section?*

Michener: That is right. I think Mount Vernon, New York.

Conversations: You're not sure yourself?

Michener: No, but I saw something to that effect once.

*Conversations: Did you have any sisters or brothers that you
know of?*

Michener: Mrs. Michener, my adopted mother, had a son, a very
fine man, named Robert who moved to California.

Conversations: Do you know what happened to your parents?

Michener: No, I know nothing really.

*Conversations: How would you describe your childhood? I
understand you were impoverished when you were young.*

Michener: Well, I think it was a two-fold childhood. I was raised
with a lot of love and affection and never wanted for that. But
there was economic hardship of a rather distressing kind
sometimes. I would suppose, of the two, it's better to be
deprived economically than emotionally. I have never felt that I
suffered from the latter.

James A. Michener

Conversations: Was it because you did well in high school that you got a scholarship to Swarthmore?

Michener: Yes. I not only did pretty well in high school, but I was also a pretty good athlete. Basketball and baseball and tennis. I'd also done a lot in student government and things like that.

Conversations: This was a four-year complete scholarship?

Michener: Yes, yes. Swarthmore had some very good scholarships in those days. They were called open scholarships and they were highly competitive, and I was very fortunate to get one of them.

Conversations: I read in your December article in Esquire *that you were expelled from college. Is that true?*

Michener: Yes, I was bounced twice, I think, for infractions of one kind or another. I was a considerable troublemaker and was, perhaps, ahead of my time in my attitudes toward education and so on.

Conversations: It was a liberal professor who helped get you back in.

Michener: Yes. I think Swarthmore deserves a tremendous amount of credit for not having taken away my scholarship, which they would have been entitled to do. But I always did well in class, so it was easy, perhaps, for them to make this concession.

Conversations: What other interests did you have when you were in high school and in college?

Michener: I edited the school paper; I was in student government; I was in dramatics—a fairly good cross section.

Conversations: Who were you reading at the time?

Michener: I had a very unusual high school career in that respect in that we had a lot of books around the house and I read. . . . Well, that row of books up there of Balzac—somehow our family · through some bizarre circumstance got hold of that; I don't remember the circumstance—and I read Balzac when I was in high school. I read Joseph Conrad, and Thackeray, and

144

Dickens—rather advanced reading, maybe, for a high school boy.

Conversations: Did you travel much before or during the time you were in college?

Michener: I had traveled a great deal before: as a high school boy I traveled pretty well across the country.

Conversations: There were only four states, I think it was, that you hadn't seen.

Michener: Yes, the Dakotas and Oregon and Washington. This was at age—oh, before the age of eighteen.

Conversations: How did you do it?

Michener: Hitchhiking. In the summers and on vacations and other things. I got around a good deal. Loved it.

Conversations: During this time families took you in and you stayed with them; so you didn't need much money, actually.

Michener: Yes. I have several times come pretty well across the country on a couple of dollars—never bothered me a bit.

Conversations: Did you start teaching long after your graduation?

Michener: No. Immediately upon graduating from Swarthmore I taught at a very good private school, boys school, where the fee was quite high and where I had a good time.

Conversations: Where was this located?

Michener: Hill School in Pottstown. It's a short distance from here.

Conversations: Didn't you run for Congress from this area?

Michener: Yes. I have been very active in politics here and probably will continue to be. I like it; it's a good feeling. I ran for Congress just a few years ago—'62, I think. I was an older man.

Conversations: What made you start writing? Was there something, all of a sudden, that made you write Tales of the South Pacific *or did it happen over a period of time?*

James A. Michener

Michener: No, I had . . . *Tales of the South Pacific* was the first thing I'd ever really written, but I'd had a pretty good training in this: I had been an editor at Macmillan Publishing Company; I knew what a sentence was; I knew what a paragraph was. I had a good background.

Conversations: The editorship at Macmillan came while you were teaching. Did they make you an offer?

Michener: Yes, that's right, yes. They had a gap in their chain of command. They didn't need me, but they needed someone around thirty-five years old and that often happens in a big organization.

Conversations: What made them look at you, if you hadn't written much?

Michener: I had been an editor for the History Teachers of America; I had done a lot of work with them. I had learned what editing was and the good use of words and so on. Their looking at me was quite logical. I think they circulated a questionnaire in the profession and my name surfaced a good deal. Quite often people do this, you know.

Conversations: How long had you been teaching before this?

Michener: On the order of eight years.

Conversations: At the boys school?

Michener: No, I'd had a rather broken experience. I taught two years at the boys school; then I went to Europe for two and a half years; then I taught three years in a little school, a Quaker school south of here; and then I taught in Colorado—about eight years, I guess.

Conversations: Did you only teach history?

Michener: No, I started out as an English teacher and then I taught history.

Conversations: Did you ever think when you started your editorship that you might someday end up a writer?

Michener: No. This came very late to me. I would make this point: I started later than almost anybody you know. I started very late, indeed. I was forty before I had anything published, which is unheard of. Therefore, I had a good head of steam up when I started.

Conversations: When the Macmillan job was over, you then went into the war?

Michener: Yes.

Conversations: Having served your time in the war, how did you get the idea for Tales of the South Pacific?

Michener: I wrote the book, *Tales of the South Pacific,* when I was on a little island during the war. I had a vivid experience myself but I was looking at the experiences of other people, also. I knew in my heart, I think, that when the war was over people would want a record of what had happened and how. I wrote from that felt need specifically. I knew that when the war was over people would want to recall what it was like to be in the South Pacific.

Conversations: How long were you there?

Michener: I don't really know, but on the order of three years. I had a very long tour of duty—'44, '45, '46.

Conversations: Did you marry before going to the South Pacific?

Michener: Yes. I married the daughter of a South Carolina Lutheran minister—marvelous family, a great girl—but we were separated for four years during the war. She served in Europe and I served in the Pacific; we never got together again afterwards.

Conversations: And you didn't marry again until 1955—

Michener: No, I married a very brilliant gal who was a researcher for *Time* magazine and other things. Then I went to Korea and that ended that way; so war has had a very powerful effect on my life—to my regret. I never wanted it that way, but that's the way things happen.

Conversations: Did you ever have any children? I read once that you have an adopted child.

147

James A. Michener

Michener: No. My second wife and I were going through the stages of adopting a child, but when we were divorced the courts gave the child to her, and the adoption did not go through. It's quite correct to say that we were in the process of adopting a child.

Conversations: How long have you been here in Pipersville and what brought you here?

Michener: Well, I've lived in Bucks County for sixty-five years. I've lived here on this hill since '49, which would be twenty-two years, so I was brought here by birth. It's always been my home. This particular area is a little way up from where we used to live, where I lived as a boy, and I think I just wanted a beautiful spot if I could find one.

Conversations: Is it true that the money you made from South Pacific *helped to build this house?*

Michener: Yes. It was very cheap land when we got it, about $60 an acre.

Conversations: How many acres do you have?

Michener: About seventy acres. I don't really know now since we've picked up a few small tracts, but it's on the order of seventy acres.

Conversations: We talked once about your complete self-employment; do you recall?

Michener: I'm one of the very few writers who has always been completely self-employed: I've never worked for anybody; I've never had any guarantees of that kind; I've never had a salary that way. There just aren't very many people who do this.' Even some of our greatest writers have had to have jobs teaching in schools and working at other things.

Conversations: You wrote once that you were a lucky man, publishing at such a late age. Do you still consider yourself a lucky man?

Michener: Yeah. I think it's remarkable that I've been able to do what I wanted to do so thoroughly and make a living at it.

Conversations: Was it shortly after Tales of the South Pacific *that you decided this was what you wanted to do?*

Michener: Yes. I published *Tales of the South Pacific*, I think, in '47, and in early '49 it was adapted as a musical comedy. So it was a year and a half later that I made the decision. It was a difficult one and I made my living in the first years by public speaking, which is the hardest way in the world to make a buck. I have scars all over me from long hours, bad food, poor railroad connections, murderous drives—but I recommend it for young artists when they're getting started. It's not an easy thing and it's not likable, but it is honest.

Conversations: How did you go about getting such engagements?

Michener: Well, there are many agents who are always looking for able speakers. I think there are more speaking jobs available than there are men to fill them.

Conversations: How old were you when you did this speaking?

Michener: Well, let me see, that must have been '48, so I was forty-one. And it's the hardest work that I have ever done.

Conversations: You've often said that you thought Tales of the South Pacific *would never make it: it was printed on cheap paper and the chapters didn't even start on separate pages.*

Michener: That is correct. If you saw an original copy of *Tales of the South Pacific*, you would be appalled at how poorly it had been put together. We thought it was a good, honest book and would serve a purpose, and that was about all.

Conversations: You never expected Rodgers and Hammerstein to come along.

Michener: No, no.

Conversations: What's in the future for you now?

Michener: I'm working on about eight projects. By that I mean I'm mulling them over and I really don't know what to do. It's an embarrassment of possibilities rather than the other way around. I haven't come to grips with what I want to do, but there are so many things that I would like to do that life is rather difficult right now for me. I'm trying to make up my mind what to do next and I don't know how to go about it.

Conversations: Does this involve the possibility of another book, the possibility of teaching?

Michener: Oh, yes. . . . No, all in the field of writing.

Conversations: It seems that your books are usually spaced apart.

Michener: Yes, I tend to have great difficulty reaching a commitment as to what I want to do next. Once I reach it I work with great directness and diligence, but I have a very anxious time trying to decide what to do.

Conversations: What do you do in your leisure time?

Michener: Well, I play tennis. I've always been very interested in music and art. I've done all the landscaping on this hill: all the trees that you see out there I planted, except the dogwood and the cedar, but everything you see I put in.

Conversations: Are you working for the government now?

Michener: Yes, but that's something of a misnomer in that the five of us on this committee get no salary. It's a job with some honor to it but no salary. So we can exercise only the leverage that our personalities or our commitments permit.

Conversations: Can you describe what you are doing for the government?

Michener: Yeah. I'm one of a five-member commission that oversees the news and public relations and propaganda efforts of our country overseas, strictly overseas. All the libraries, the television shows, the art exhibits, cultural exchanges, Radio Free Europe, Voice of America, Radio Liberty—we have a very broad area with a fairly large budget. It's a very hot area, very politically difficult. We seem to be in trouble all the time, but that's the nature of the work.

Conversations: Who are the other members?

Michener: A very distinguished group of men. Frank Shakespeare is the head of the area, but the commission consists of: Frank Stanton of CBS; Bill Buckley, the conservative columnist; Hobart Lewis, the president of *Reader's Digest*; and John Shaheen, an oil man with very powerful interests all over the world. So the five of us know the world pretty well.

Conversations: Were you appointed by Nixon?

Michener: I was appointed by Nixon because he is required by law to have one minority member, so that it isn't all from his own political party. He selected me. I've known President Nixon for sometime and I hold him in respect. He's a tough political operator. He's doing a great deal to keep the Republican Party strong and I feel exactly the same way about the Democratic Party, so it's fascinating from that point of view.

Conversations: What is the budget for?

Michener: Well, for all of our operations overseas: pay of radio and television people, pay of librarians, pay of public affairs officers—that sort of thing.

Conversations: You have other people working for you?

Michener: Oh, yes. We have probably 6000 or 7000, I would think.

Conversations: In Esquire *you wrote about what records the FBI has on you. How long have you known about that?*

Michener: Well, someone like me—I've been appointed to other government positions and whenever you're appointed you're told that this involves an FBI investigation. I've known it for twenty years, maybe.

Conversations: Does it make any difference to you?

Michener: Well, I mean, you can't do the things I want to do without it, so I have no strong feeling one way or the other on that. Everyone who appoints you to a commission or a job like this tells you that this presupposes you will pass an FBI examination. At that point, you can say: "Well, I don't want the job." But if you say you will take the job, then it's obligatory that

James A. Michener

you have the examination. And they always tell you; there's nothing secret about it. Now there are a lot of other exams that I've undoubtedly undergone that have been secret and I know nothing about. Quite a few employers in the United States, if they employ somebody, hire a private equivalent to the FBI, and they give you quite a stiff grilling. I've been through two of them that I know of—and undoubtedly others that I don't know about. I suppose that I know only a small portion of what has happened.

Conversations: Have you ever felt that your life was in danger in any way?

Michener: Well, I've had quite a few narrow escapes with death: I was in an airplane sometime ago that crash-landed in the middle of the Pacific Ocean and we could just barely get out; I was in two other airplanes that crashed—lives were lost and the planes a total wreck; I've seen a lot of wars. I've been in more than my share of close calls, but I wouldn't think that any of this had ever been directed at me. I have, unfortunately, in recent years developed a couple of areas in the world that I would not go back to because I might be in some trouble, but that's simply the result of a long and active life. I have been very close to death, and it's had a sobering effect upon me.

Conversations: No one has ever threatened you, though, because of your writing?

Michener: Yes, they have. My writings have been banned in a lot of places, and I've lived to see them unbanned, and it's not too encouraging.

Conversations: Do you have any superstitions?

Michener: No.

Conversations: How about pet peeves?

Michener: Well, I am very loyal to the United States and very much in touch with what we're trying to do—we don't always do it, but what we're trying to do. The only time I ever think that maybe we're doomed is when I see what the American consumer has allowed to happen to bread and cheese. I think we have the poorest bread in the world and some of the lousiest cheese. When the staples of life are corrupted this way, I get a little worried.

Conversations: Once you decide that you are going to write a book, how do you start and where do you begin?

Michener: Well, as I told you, I begin about four or five years in advance: I keep thinking about things and what I might want to do, and I make little outlines and so on; then I come to the moment of decision and I dig in. So we're talking now about when the moment of decision has been reached. I get up at 7:30 in the morning and work very diligently all morning and quit about noon—never work in the afternoon and almost never in the evening. I do this seven days a week, month in and month out, when I'm working. I would suppose that I've worked rather less than that. The other is germinating time and ruminating time.

Conversations: Do you think that your approach to writing has changed since the beginning?

Michener: No, I would think that I have remained fairly consistent. What has changed is the rather wide variety of subjects and types of books I've dealt with. I would think that that has been the escape, in my case: rather than shifting wildly in style and form, I've kept fairly consistent in that, but I've had a very wide scatter in interest and type of book.

Conversations: Why do you do all of your writing in the morning?

Michener: Well, I think people are divided between day people and night people. John O'Hara, who was my neighbor not too far to the east here, discussed this with me once. He did almost all of his writing from about 12:30 in the morning—that is, after midnight—till about dawn. For obvious reasons: he got no telephone calls and it was quiet and so on. He simply said that he thought better at night. By that time everything in his mind was clear and he was cleansed of irritations and passions that activated him at other times, and he was free to go ahead and write. I've known, maybe, more people who don't work in the morning than who do; I happen to be a morning worker.

153

James A. Michener

Conversations: Do you allow yourself to be bothered by telephone calls or visitors during the morning?

Michener: I can be quite disciplined on that, if I want to be. When I'm working I don't want interruptions of any kind. My wife is very good at handling that; she handles the phone calls and interruptions. She knows pretty well what state I'm in and protects me on that.

Conversations: When you are working do you travel or take time off?

Michener: No. By and large, I do one or the other. I have quite frequently worked for, maybe, six months without a single break and if you do that, you get a lot of work done. In that time I wouldn't travel.

Conversations: You don't mix them.

Michener: No, by and large, I don't. However, I have written when I was overseas; I've written about half my work when I was overseas.

Conversations: What book gave you the most trouble?

Michener: Well, I think of the books that I've published there would be no answer to that, but I have written a lot that I haven't published.

Conversations: A lot of books?

Michener: Yes.

Conversations: Are they finished?

Michener: In various stages of completion and, probably, I'll never go back to them because it didn't work.

Conversations: What made you give up?

Michener: Well, you see if I start to work on something it's about a two- or a three-year responsibility. Sometimes I break it and do a short thing in between—and the idea better be good, if you're going to do that. Sometimes the ideas are not as good in working them out as they were in prospect. In other words, I didn't do a good job and I knock it in the head.

James A. Michener

Conversations: How do you do your research for a book?

Michener: I have always in my life done a very wide degree of reading, and when I feel something coming on I may get as many as 150 to 200 books and browse through them and check things out.

Conversations: When do you know that you've had enough and that it's time to write?

Michener: That's a very difficult problem and I've never handled that well. What I do is I write, in the evenings I then sometimes move ahead: I may lay a certain thing aside, knowing that I will come back to that area in about three months, and then I do the substantive research.

Conversations: Does this research often lead you to other ideas and angles that you might take?

Michener: No, not in other subject matter, but it often is a digressive factor in the working out of this particular outline. Yes, it brings many changes and alterations in that. I mean, if I'm doing some research on the Jews in Russia and find something particularly exciting about Czar Alexander, it doesn't seduce me into thinking that I might want to write about Czar Alexander. I'd just file that as interesting material and forget it. But something might come up there which would have a vivid impact on me, so far as the book that I was working on was concerned.

Conversations: Do you keep files?

Michener: No, I don't take notes much; I keep it in my head. I make page references in the backs of books—the pages that I might conceivably want to consult later—and then, I just keep them all in my memory.

Conversations: How did the research for your book about Kent State differ from the research you had to do for Tales of the South Pacific, *or* The Drifters, *or* The Fires of Spring?

Michener: Well, I think it was much more difficult because it was dealing with specific situations and sometimes legal problems, and the material itself sort of determined the outline—the intellect of the writer didn't have a great deal of impact there. So that I would think it was more difficult.

155

James A. Michener

Conversations: How do you go about developing a character?

Michener: I have tended to have a theory in my writing of having the central character somewhat more bland and innocuous than the peripheral characters. I've been severely criticized for this by certain critics and I think, probably, justly so. But it's still a device I like and if I were doing a long book like this again, I think I would. . . . I like the more neutral central character and the stronger peripheral characters. I don't know why but I think I'm not good at plotting. It doesn't interest me at all; I'm not good at the well-rounded English novel—I've never really cared about that; that's for somebody else. I think that both of those things represent a deficiency in, maybe, dramatic structure.

The fact that my books have been so very widely read proves that at least in certain respects I wasn't wrong. But I wouldn't recommend what I do to any other beginning writer. I think it's better to have your central character strong—the focal character and the over-riding character.

Conversations: Do you usually model your characters on actual individuals?

Michener: That's a very difficult question. By and large, no. I want it to be bigger . . . I want the character to have more freedom than the man in life had. I want it to be more flexible, but you obviously have to start with some known experience or some known human being. And I do, but I sure don't stick close to it.

Conversations: If you decide to take notes, when do you take them?

Michener: Well, there are two cases. In a book like *Kent State*, I took copious notes: I think I have three notebooks full of specific notes, but that was on a specific point. Now in a book like *The Source*, which didn't have that problem, I don't believe I took any notes. I took some *aide-memoire*, maybe, but that I kept all germinating in my head. Now, I would take notes as to when something happened, or what the specific date of something was, or how old the characters were in a certain period—that sort of structural stuff. But notes, as college students think of them, I don't take.

James A. Michener

Conversations: Have you ever used a tape recorder?

Michener: No. I use it for dictation. I get a very heavy flood of mail here and I put the letters on tape, but I don't dictate an important letter. If it's important, I write it out in longhand.

Conversations: Do you work in a different way when you're writing an article than when you're writing a book?

Michener: Not much. About the same, I think.

Conversations: When do you decide on the title for your book?

Michener: Oh, I am very bad at that. I have usually allowed the publisher to recommend one from among a group of titles that I would submit. He has usually not liked any of them and has often come up with suggestions of his own, which I haven't liked. It's been a very tedious business. I'm not good at it and I don't write titles to magazine articles or anything else, really. I don't think that way.

Conversations: Do you think titles are important?

Michener: Very, very—and I wish I were better at it, but . . . . I think a title like *Streetcar Named Desire* is so brilliant that it really baffles me; it's just so perfect.

Conversations: Yours are usually simple: Hawaii, Iberia, The Source, The Drifters. *Would you like to see that change?*

Michener: Well, titles don't interest me. There's an awful lot in this world that just simply doesn't interest me, and doesn't concern me, and I slough it off—and titles are one.

Conversations: When do you do your rewriting?

Michener: I tend to work in big blocks. I will do a big block of, maybe, fifty pages or 100 pages, because I want to get it lined up and I won't go back to any of it until this is all finished. So that, if I were writing a short novel of, say, 60,000 words or a really short novel, I would write the whole thing I'm quite sure. And then, I would rewrite it; then I would rewrite it. I really do a great deal of rewriting.

Conversations: Is that morning work or evening work?

James A. Michener

Michener: I sometimes do it in the evening, the recasting of what I want to do, but, by and large, it's morning work. All my work is morning work.

Conversations: When you're rewriting do you ever have to add a character or take a character out?

Michener: Yes. More often, however, incident than character. I'm pretty well locked-in on my characters by the time I start. Pretty early. Well, I've been thinking about it for a long time. But ideas run away with every writer. It's just amazing how you can start out with something and introduce a supposedly minor character who catches your fancy as well as the reader's, and you find yourself grappling with him when you never intended to do so. This happens, yes.

Conversations: You've talked about thinking about books. Does this mean that sometimes you just sit and think about a book?

Michener: Oh, sure. Mostly, however, when I'm walking. I do a great deal of walking in the woods and I think, in the abstract, about the problem—particularly in the germinating period. And then once I start, every day I think about the next day's writing, hours at a time.

Conversations: Why did you elect to write novels? Why wasn't it something else?

Michener: Well, as you know, I graduated from college in English, but with a very strong history minor. After I had taught school for a while I went back to college all over again to make myself a history major, so I stopped in midstream and changed my whole life. My writing has oscillated between these two poles: when I'm writing fiction, I wish I were writing nonfiction; and when I'm writing nonfiction, I wish I were writing fiction.

Conversations: Please describe this second college career.

Michener: I graduated from Swarthmore, and then I had a traveling fellowship in Europe where I knocked around a group of colleges. Then I came back here and I took summer courses and some time out to do further studies. I still wish I could take time out and go back for a course in economics or the geography of Africa. In effect, actually since those days, what I do in my life

158

is more or less to give myself a seminar in advanced studies whenever I work on anything. My education has really taken place after college, not in college.

Conversations: Do you think, then, that the universities are responsible for some of today's writers?

Michener: Oh, yes. Oh, I think that four of the finest writers of my time, in my opinion, would be: Robert Penn Warren, Thornton Wilder, Saul Bellow, and Bernard Malamud—and they're all university people. I could go on and list another twenty—like Ralph Ellison and people like that—and they would all be university people, so I think that the relationship of the university and the writer is a very rich and rewarding one.

Conversations: Do you set up a quota in writing daily or monthly, that you make yourself meet?

Michener: No. I set up objectives. If I fell notoriously behind I would be worried—but not quotas. If I miss a day through nonproduction, it doesn't bother me much; I'm irritated, but not for that reason.

Conversations: Was there a time when you worked as a journalist?

Michener: No, I've never worked for anybody in the field of writing. Now, I have been on assignment sometimes for the New York Herald Tribune, Holiday, Reader's Digest, but they've been very flexible assignments and they really didn't mean a great deal. No, I've always been a free lance.

Conversations: Did you ever follow anyone's journalistic technique?

Michener: Journalistic, no, but I've been very deeply influenced by the writing of certain novelists, especially European novelists, that I studied as a young man and responded to remarkably. People like Balzac, Thackeray, Goncharov the Russian writer, Nexo the Danish writer. I feel a great debt to these writers; I responded to them tremendously.

Conversations: Would you think that a background in journalism is helpful, if not necessary, to be a free-lancer?

James A. Michener

Michener: Yes, because it establishes criteria and norms and also gives you a view of the operation of the industry, and the market, and what's happening.

Conversations: Who do you free-lance for the most, which magazine?

Michener: I would suppose the Reader's Digest, although, maybe, The New York Times would be almost as close.

Conversations: Did you go through a period of struggle to become a writer?

Michener: Oh, yes. As a younger man I wrote for eight years without ever earning a nickel, which is a long apprenticeship, but in that time I learned a lot about my trade.

Conversations: In 1947 you published Tales of the South Pacific; The Fires of Spring followed in 1949. What did you do in between, besides making speeches?

Michener: Well, you see I published in '47 and I got the Pulitzer Prize in '48, as I recall, and there was a flurry of interest then. A lot of invitations were offered, but I didn't have the skill to fill them. And so, I wasted a lot of time and heartache over invitations that I wasn't competent to fill. It was after that that I became. . . . So if you ask me what I did during those two years—I sweated; I really slugged it out.

Conversations: Did you ever dream that Tales of the South Pacific would become a play or a movie?

Michener: No, but I must say that when I first saw the rehearsal of the play that did result, I realized that it was something very special indeed. The whole magic was visible. I think I've only seen it twice: once in New York and once in Hawaii.

Conversations: Any regrets for not seeing it more?

Michener: No. I don't brood over what I've done.

Conversations: The movie was on TV about a month ago.

Michener: Yes. I thought it was a little dated—an entirely different war from the ones we're engaged in now.

Conversations: Have you ever written a book with the purpose of it being made into a movie?

Michener: No.

Conversations: How many of your works have been made into movies?

Michener: Oh, some eight or nine. *Hawaii, South Pacific,* several of my short stories. Others have been contracted for and the movie company saw no way of making them, because I don't write a tight dramatic line, as you probably know. I'm far more diffuse than that. And so if somebody buys one of my stories, they're buying a lot of headaches as to how they're going to handle it and so on.

Conversations: Has anyone ever tried to make a movie of The Fires of Spring?

Michener: There's been constant interest in this from all sorts of people. It goes on year after year, but nobody's ever figured out how to lick it. Primarily because of that defect I spoke of: my liking to have my central character somewhat subdued and my peripheral characters more interesting. I think Dickens did that in *Great Expectations,* which I think is one of his greatest books, but they've never been able to do much with *Great Expectations* for that very reason. The central character, Pip, is sort of diminished and the other characters are the interesting ones.

Conversations: The Fires of Spring *has such wonderful characters in it—*

Michener: I receive more mail on *The Fires of Spring* than anything I've ever written because it does affect a lot of people that way. It goes on and on and on; I'm just delighted. Such characters are the people who make a writer, of course. I'm sure that Hemingway had such people in his background and William Faulkner, Sinclair Lewis, because it is out of them that you establish your attitudes and sympathies.

Conversations: You must feel, then, that you owe a lot to people like Toothless Tom and Old Daniel—

James A. Michener

Michener: I have said that I am incredibly fortunate in the time that I came along, historically: in the fact that America was opening up and interested in things; that it was a vital period. I'm very lucky.

Conversations: What do you consider to be your best book?

Michener: I would think The Bridges at Toko-ri. In that I came closer to doing what I had in mind than I've come in anything else.

Conversations: I think you called that book your purest writing. Do you still think that?

Michener: Yes. I think that's a well-told, well-controlled story.

Conversations: Even better than The Fires of Spring?

Michener: The Fires of Spring is a lot more diffuse. It isn't as controlled as Toko-ri.

Conversations: What's been your best-selling book?

Michener: I suppose Hawaii; although over the years I suppose The Source will be.

Conversations: Do you have any idea of how many copies have been sold?

Michener: I think for Hawaii on the order of 5,000,000; The Source, somewhere around 3,000,000 or more.

Conversations: What have you found to be the makings of a good novel?

Michener: I think about this a great deal, because I love the form and I'm impressed with the good examples of it. I suppose, for me, the criterion for a really fine novel is the author has created a total world in which his people move credibly. The books that do this, I prize very much. Things like The Idiot of Dostoevski, it's just a total world. You have to accept it or not; you can't fight it. I think that's true of Thackeray's Vanity Fair which I like very much; I think it's true of Mark Twain's Huckleberry Finn. It's just a little cosmos there and you're prepared to accept it—that it's a real world. This is a great accomplishment.

Conversations: Isn't plotting involved in that?

Michener: I don't have much concern about plotting. I've never thought it was a major component. I respect people who can do it and I wish I did it better, but I think that's for somebody else; it's not for me. I am impressed with the plotting of some of the great French novels like *Les Miserables* and some of Dumas; they're awfully cleverly done. I don't denigrate it—even in Balzac, something like *Pere Goriot* is really beautifully plotted—but I don't have any envy of it. I respect it; I enjoy it. It's something somebody else can do and I can't do, and I'm not disturbed about it.

Conversations: How do you get around making a novel without a good plot?

·Michener: Because I spend so much time trying to create that world. I get thousands of letters from people who say how totally immersed they were in that world, and how sorry they were to see it end. So that, for me, it works; I don't know how it works for somebody else.

Conversations: Wasn't Kent State *something different for you to do?*

Michener: Well, no, if you remember I did *The Bridge at Andau*, which is the most widely circulated thing I've ever—it went into fifty-three languages, as I recall. But is was offbeat, yes.

Conversations: How did you receive this assignment? Whose ideas was it for you to write about Kent State?

Michener: Well, everybody in the publishing world was thinking about writing about Kent State, because it was really the major event of that period and an absolutely climactic one. I thought about it myself and, then, an editor at *Reader's Digest* who had wanted someone to do a book, on the spur of the moment, called me and found that I was already pretty deeply into my thinking on it. We went on from there, so that the proposal, as is so often the case with books like this, came from the publisher.

Conversations: How did you go about the investigation for Kent State?

James A. Michener

Michener: Well, Andy Jones, a *Digest* editor, and a friend of his had investigated the thing very thoroughly before I even knew about it. They had made contacts with all the officials and they had some pretty good dope there themselves. So I moved into a going concern, as it were. Then Andy and I set it up, laying out the general areas that we knew we would want to look into; then we broke it down by segments. I'm not sure that's the best way to do it, but that's the way we had to do it.

Conversations: How long were you in Kent before people started recognizing you?

Michener: I would think I was there two weeks before anybody really knew I was there. I worked in the library at the university every day for about two weeks before anybody really knew.

Conversations: They didn't recognize you there at the library?

Michener: No, no, because I was working with, you know, people who were part-time. I didn't meet any of the librarians; I met, you know, people who were filing and getting me newspapers and getting me books and things. That's one of the best things I did, that preliminary work; it gave me a respect for the operation.

Conversations: How many months were you there?

Michener: I was there from July to the middle of November, and then I came back for four days in December.

Conversations: Did you have the book written by November when you left Kent?

Michener: That's pretty difficult to say. For example, the essay about the trains coming in and out of Kent I wrote the first eight days I was there and changed it very little, except for some mistakes or improvements I wanted. The guts of the book was pretty well written by the time I left Kent, but none of the philosophical conclusions or parts had been. It's sort of a step process. Specific interviews which represented basic material were all done before I left, of course. I would say it was two-thirds done, I think.

Conversations: What reactions did you have to the Reader's Digest *selections, the two that they printed?*

Michener: I had received a very heavy flood of mail on *Kent State* all along. I think I had twelve pretty massive boxes of material. Included in that is a lot of mail which is as vituperative on the one hand and as scattered on the other hand as what you had in the newspaper. The bulk of the mail abused me for being too favorable to the students; and I've received another batch of this just within the last few days.

Conversations: You still receive mail about this?

Michener: Yeah. Well, I receive it when something new surfaces, let's say. They don't heckle me about it, but when something new surfaces they bang me. I think I sent it over to my secretary. I got a savage letter saying that we taxpayers pay good money for these buildings and these twenty-five students should go to jail and rot there—just as if nothing had happened; nobody had learned anything. I've received a good deal of that. People would say I was soft on Communism; others would say I had sold out to the hippies; and then, a lot of religious crank mail: "Don't you know that God is against the hippies?"—and all that bull. You realize that there's a subterranean nut basis in this country that just operates constantly and probably doesn't do a hell of a lot of damage. Now, that was the bulk of it; that was the bulk of it. The other, far less in comment, would be—maybe, one in ten— that I had sold out to the Establishment. Then in the middle there was a group of really splendid things which took me to task on specific points or elaborated and would go that way. I would say ten abusive letters about the students, maybe one abusive letter about selling out to the Establishment, and maybe five, in the middle, of really fine stuff.

Conversations: Did Reader's Digest *just want somebody to write something for them, and then it was your idea to write the book?*

Michener: Well, I've done this quite often. I've done it three times, as a matter of fact, and this is not unusual at all to me. In other words, you have to do so much work to do what is required to be done that you have a book when you're through anyway. I see nothing unusual in this at all.

James A. Michener

Conversations: Do you think that your book cleared up some of the points in the Digest *articles that seemed to confuse people or made people angry?*

Michener: Well, a lot of people say so. Two or three—no, maybe, four or five critics were quite abusive about it and said that it had not cleared up anything, but the bulk of them were quite favorable. I think that here you have exactly a case where anybody whose name appears in the book can honestly say that they told Michener a great deal more than he printed. That's the nature of communication: I'm going to tell you a great deal more this afternoon than what you will print. So with the problem of the *Digest* abbreviating a book: here is all this material and they take out some. They've got to offend somebody in doing that, but I think that's inherent in the process. I think all that you have to depend upon are reasonably honest editors and your own integrity.

You should see some of the things we left out. I mean for legal reasons, for reasons of propriety, for the fact that we liked certain people and didn't want to throw a hook into them.

Conversations: What did you say about the twenty-five cases that were recently dismissed?

Michener: I said from the beginning, even in the book, that I did not see how in a court of law with a jury there could be any convictions on the Sunday night and Monday indictments; I doubt it. I've always said that they ought to be dismissed and that I would testify on that behalf, if necessary. I thought there were certain actions on Saturday night that might well bring in **indictable counts. On Friday night I thought it was such a** melange that they ought to drop them all. So I specifically recommended it for Sunday and Monday; I was indifferent on Friday. I didn't think they would get convictions, but if they wanted to go ahead, okay.

Now sometime ago I wrote a very strong letter to *The New York Times* advocating, before the trial started, that the state of Ohio would be damn prudent if they dropped all these indictments right now. *The Times* did not publish that letter because they felt it might have impinged on the judicial process or something. The trial started and everything that I foresaw came to pass. So I sat down one Saturday night and drafted three or four versions of a very tough letter to the *Cleveland Plain Dealer*, saying that Governor Gilligan would serve society well if he would drop all of these indictments right now, because the state of Ohio was going to get into a hell of a hurricane if they didn't. It was then that I got this third flood of mail and I thought the matter rested there.

Then, to my great pleasure, the *Plain Dealer* came out with a front-page editorial adopting my policy completely. Two days later the governor—well, the legal process dropped all the indictments and this should have been done a long, long time ago. I've never deviated in my belief on that: I thought Ohio was running into trouble if they went on. So I was pleased to see them dropped; I've been in communication with some of the people.

Conversations: Do you often write letters to the editor?

Michener: Not very often. When I do it's on something I feel very strongly. They've had a lot of impact in certain places, but I think that goes to my attitude toward being a writer. I think that in America a writer doesn't enjoy a very exalted position; he's really a third-rate citizen in many respects. He doesn't enjoy anywhere near the position he does in countries like Russia and France, for example. So all he has left is his leverage and he better use his leverage as constructively as possible.

Conversations: Was The Drifters *written before you came to Kent?*

Michener: Yes.

Conversations: Was there any reason why it came out after the Kent State book?

Michener: Simply publishing convenience.

Conversations: This is about the first time you've ever had two books come out so close together.

Michener: Yes. It was unwise, I suppose, but it didn't do any damage.

James A. Michener

Conversations: Do you usually try to space your books out at two-year intervals?

Michener: Yeah. Contrary to what people think, I work pretty slowly; I really slave over it and I really hack it out very painfully. Now I have a certain skill in doing it so that, once I get started, I have a confidence that I can see it through, but I stop a lot that I start because it isn't good enough. I retype everything four, five, six times—critical passages more—and everything, say, three times. It takes me that long.

Conversations: Where did you get the idea for The Drifters?

Michener: Well, I had been knocking around Spain for a long time as evidenced by my book, *Iberia.* In doing so I had gotten to know the mob at Pamplona, an international group of absolutely splendid people, very lively, very lusty; I had known Torremolinos; I had traveled a little bit in North Africa. I'd seen this milieu rather close at hand; I'd been involved in it a good deal. My wife and I have always known a lot of young people in flight, as it were, and it happened that way I suppose. I didn't set out to write the book and then go there; it grew up the other way, which I think the best books do.

Conversations: How is the book selling?

Michener: Well, it's been a best seller for about a half a year, which means that everybody's breaking even on it. Actually, it's done very well.

Conversations: You still don't like it as much as Toko-ri *though?*

Michener: Well, *Toko-ri* is a small, compressed, artistic and intellectual problem. And just as it's easier to write a sonnet sometimes than an epic, it's easier to write *Toko-ri* than this. So far as intellectual content is concerned, I think *The Drifters* is way, way ahead of *Toko-ri*. A great many of the people who were writing to me say the same thing.

Conversations: Is that fan mail that you get?

Michener: In effect, yes. Although a lot of it is critical.

Conversations: Do you play a role in The Drifters?

Michener: No, I would think that I had observed all these people rather intimately. I knew a bunch of tech reps like that; I knew some people who were selling automobiles and insurance to Americans overseas—I would suppose that character came primarily from Japan, from experiences I'd had in Japan. But there is a whole international underworld, as you probably know. I mean, these cases of the GI PXs in Vietnam are illustrations. There is some pretty dirty ball being played. And also some very legitimate. . . . You know, a guy gets a hold of a good thing and he's selling the things abroad. I mean, a lot of airline pilots get into the import-export business simply because they're in the two worlds and they make contacts, and they do a good decent job. I would suppose many of these people that I saw abroad are quite legitimate.

Conversations: Can you give me any indication of what your next book might be?

Michener: Gee, I can't. I'm going to publish a book of essays and I probably will publish a book of short stories. But what my next big novel will be I really have not come to grips with yet. It presumably would be something about the United States.

Conversations: How many articles do you usually write in a month for publication?

Michener: I would say it's a matter of pressure: things that are happening; things that concern me; things that people know I'm concerned about. It's pretty obvious that I get invited about every six days. It's a strange world.

Conversations: Do you receive a lot of assignments?

Michener: Invitations to assignments, yes.

Conversations: How many of those do you usually accept?

Michener: I would say it depends on what I was into at the time. You know, if somebody was real keen to have a statement on rock music, I think I would stop what I was doing and do it. A lot of other things. . . . I think from my last batch of correspondence I turned down about four because, by and large, they could get somebody better to do it; that is, who would have a deeper commitment or more time.

James A. Michener

Conversations: What books have come out since The Source, *besides* The Drifters *and* Kent State What Happened and Why?

Michener: *Iberia* and the book on the presidential election, *Report of the County Chairman.* I guess that's it. So that's four books. See, there are two aspects of my writing that very few people know about or pay any attention to. One is my books on politics—I think the book on the presidential election will be a pretty important book next year, four years late. And also the books I've done on oriental art. I've often thought that if I were to die tomorrow, fifty years from now I would be more likely to be remembered for the books on oriental art than anything else because they're trailblazers; they really did a job. So that, you know, it's a mix and, for me, it's been an absolutely marvelously creative experience.

Conversations: Maybe the interest isn't that universal in your oriental pieces.

Michener: Yeah, it's a more limited field. But that it will be permanent, I have no doubt at all.

Conversations: Do you think that your writing style has changed since Tales of the South Pacific?

Michener: Yes. Maybe not for the better, but I became more adept in handling complex situations; maybe that was at the expense of psychological exploration, but I don't know.

Conversations: Does an individual book make you more money today than it did twenty years ago?

Michener: Well, the big difference is that twenty years ago you could count on a big movie sale. And a lot of people who wrote books and just got by made their living on these bonanzas in the movie sales. That's all gone. But, let me say, a young writer who was good and was well reviewed, and maybe had a Book-of-the-Month Club selection every five years and was picked up by the *Reader's Digest* Book Club would live quite well. It can be done and it's a marvelous living; and it's one that you're entitled to aspire to; and I would think that piecing it together that way could be done. But the easy money of fifty years ago—movie sales and publication in the magazines—that's all gone.

Conversations: When someone contracts to make a movie or a play from your work, what do you get in return? The rights, or do you sell them the work?

Michener: Those contracts are very intricate and almost indecipherable to the layman, and I would consider myself a layman. I remember that the contract with Rodgers and Hammerstein ran to some forty long foolscap pages of which I could understand very little. The merit of the contract was that it took absolutely everything into account and we've never had a day's argument about the contract. It was all spelled out there and it's very fair and it's very clear. By and large, what happens is that the dramatic purchaser gets all rights and he does with the thing pretty much as he wishes. Now I think there are clauses that if he doesn't produce within a certain number of years, then the rights revert—so that he just can't keep it on ice. But, by and large, he gets total rights.

Conversations: You were given part of the rights of South Pacific, *the play.*

Michener: That is right.

Conversations: And Rodgers and Hammerstein didn't have to do that—

Michener: That is correct.

Conversations: But they offered to. In Kent, when I interviewed you for the Plain Dealer, *you told me that from the rights of just that play you earn enough each year to pay for your house, clothing, and food.*

Michener: Yeah. I have been unusually lucky in that respect. I've had this slow, steady income and I have known that I could take risks—some of the books, well, you saw in Kent that research is very expensive. I wouldn't be able to do it just on my own and it makes a fantastic difference to have that assured income year after year because, at least, you know you're going to pay your mortgage; you're going to pay your life insurance. And so I have been able to take risks that the average writer might not be able to take.

James A. Michener

Conversations: You said once that you believe in giving the hardback publishers a return, or some of the rights, or returning some of the money you make on a book. Is that what the deal is?

Michener: Well, I think that—I have a very good contract with Random House; I'm quite satisfied with it. But, nevertheless, the contract does allow them to make a lot of money if a book is a best seller. And I'm quite happy to see them get it because I want to see the publishing house stay in business. I think they would tell you I've never held them up, and I believe other people have somewhat better contracts than I have. That doesn't worry me at all; I have a damn good one. But I believe as an acquaintance once said: all of us who succeed in this business are indebted to the business of publishing and agenting and representation, book reviewing, and everything else. It is one big interlocking business and I don't begrudge any of my money that has been plowed back into it.

Conversations: Do you think book critics are a helping aid in this business?

Michener: Well, let me say, I am very glad that they're not as powerful as the drama critics are. I think that would be dreadful. I've had great reviews and I've had bad reviews, and it really hasn't mattered very much. But in a thing like a drama, where the overhead is so high and so much is riding on it, the critics really determine—wow, I don't think I could live under that.

Conversations: You get along fairly well, then, with critics?

Michener: Yeah. I know some—a man like Orville Prescott was almost a determining force in my life. He spotted me early; he wrote a couple of splendid reviews; he attracted attention to me—and I'll be forever indebted to him. That's true of quite a few other people—people like Dave Appel of Cleveland and Philadelphia and others, also some of the radio reviewers and critics—boy, I owe them a real debt. They're real good guys.

Conversations: What role does Mrs. Michener play in the writing of your books?

Michener: Well, as you know from calling, she takes care of all my appointments. She pretty well determines whom I will see,

172

and where I will go, and what I will do. She is marvelous at entertaining people and sounding them out and getting her own ideas. She does none of the writing and none of the research, but I talk things over with her all the time. She's just a very, very savvy wife for a writer.

Conversations: Can you remember what you did last week or parts of last week?

Michener: Oh, gosh, yes. I carry a pretty long memory. It starts on Sunday morning, playing four sets of tennis with my regular partner. I played the usual tennis, which I do every Saturday and Sunday. Then I showered and drove over to Allentown and took an airplane to Washington for a meeting of the commission. We met with Dave Packard of the Defense Department, and Elmo Zumwalt, head of the Navy, Vice-President Agnew, and the head of a labor union that had a problem, and overseas representatives. And then I conducted a seminar on the Near East with the people involved. That evening we had dinner with the Yugoslavian ambassador because I have long been interested in the Muslim part of Yugoslavia and I may be going there.

And on Tuesday I came home and worked on an article which I am going to be publishing with *The New York Times*, an article on South Africa. Wednesday I had a meeting in town with some people who are concerned about a new library. And then Thursday I went to New York and had a meeting with the editors of the Sunday Magazine section of *The New York Times* on this article I'm doing. Then had a meeting with David Frost on some things he is concerned about. Friday I worked here all day on revisions that *The New York Times* wanted and the South African article corrections. I played tennis in the afternoon. And then Saturday—yesterday, I got up very early and finished the editorial work on *The New York Times* piece, played tennis, then watched the football game. In the evening, as so often we do, had a long sort of a skull session with Joe Livingston, the economics columnist for the *Philadelphia Bulletin* and a whole lot of other newspapers; we thrashed things out. That's the way a week runs.

Conversations: Is that typical?

James A. Michener

Michener: Going to Washington happens only once a month, but it's pretty typical.

Conversations: Do you spend much time socially with other writers?

Michener: No. Less, perhaps, than any writer who has ever operated—only because I live so far away. That's the penalty for living here. I have great respect for my peers and I would say that at least once every two weeks I am asked either to write an introduction to a book, or write a statement about a book that someone has written, or help on a book—and I do all that I can. I do rather more than most people. I would think that I may have done too much, but I feel it as a deep obligation. It works both ways: I think a lot of writers know me as somebody who will come through in a pinch always, but I don't do much socializing.

Conversations: When you write an introduction has the author submitted the book to you so that you've read the book before?

Michener: It would be more like—because I don't do that—I suppose I had three of those invitations last week. I don't do that too much. It would be more like five years from now I will someday get, out of the blue, a letter from you saying, "Well, I've finally done it. I've done this book and the publisher said that if you would do either of two things it would help: read it and give a blurb—" or, if it's a different kind, "Will you do an introduction?" And I would remember you and it's quite cold-blooded, tell you the truth. I'd think: well, what kind of guy was he; am I indebted to him; was he a good guy, you know—and it's a very easy solution. If I remember you as a good guy and a real pro and somebody wanted me to do it, I would stop what I was doing and do it. If it just comes through socially or through some publisher and I remember a guy who was a jerk when I knew him and he's still a jerk, I would find it very easy to say no. But it's more personal than that.

This is very onerous for me now, because I'm an older man and I know some of the people who are aspiring. I'm under rather heavy pressure—even under those circumstances I have suggested that I would do certain things; so it works both ways.

Conversations: What novels have you read recently?

174

Michener: This is a very difficult question, because I read so much that I have to read that I don't get a chance to read much short fiction—fiction. I wait until somebody tells me that I have to read something; and then when I get a vacation and I remember it, I read it.

So one of the two books I've read recently is *The Other* by Tryon, which is a delightful little psychological mystery that was very popular and merited every bit of it. And then I read a book, at the insistence of a very learned man in England, called *Unlawful Assembly* about a hilarious murder case in South Africa, a broad burlesque.

Conversations: Do you like poetry?

Michener: I do and wish that I wrote it, but I don't.

Conversations: Do you read it a lot?

Michener: I read it selectively, when I hear the word that I ought to read this. I've been reading a good deal of Sylvia Plath recently, who seems to me as good as Dylan Thomas. Hell of a good poet.

Conversations: How often do you take vacations?

Michener: Well, that's a sore point between me and my wife. I rather think of myself as being on vacation all the time and she feels that there ought to be a bigger switch. So the truth lies somewhere in the middle. But the fact is that, these days if I went anywhere on vacation, I would pretty soon be involved in something; I would be doing just what I would be doing if I weren't on vacation.

Conversations: Do you have any place special that you like to go on vacation when you do go?

Michener: Spain. Japan.

Conversations: What's so special about them?

Michener: It's just a nice society and, also, the fact that I know a lot of people there and it's like going home.

Conversations: What are you doing right now at home? What are you working on finally? Getting things cleared up, caught up?

175

James A. Michener

Michener: Yeah. Getting ready to make some big decisions. I probably will participate in the Presidential election one way or another and so on.

Conversations: Do you think you'd ever run for public office again?

Michener: Well, I would like to run for delegate to the Democratic National Convention right now. But the law in Pennsylvania is rather obscure and I don't know. That is, we're in the process of changing it so nobody knows what the law is. It isn't obscure; it's in total confusion. When they decide what they're going to do, then I'll have to decide. But I would like to, yes.

Conversations: What advice can you give for young writers? What should one do and who should one read; what rules should one follow?

Michener: I think you ought to find two or three writers in the great tradition—and let's say for ease of identification, in the last century—who, in one or two of their works, make you feel that they really knew what it was all about. Somebody like George Eliot or Samuel Butler, to name the writers that we haven't mentioned, or Hawthorne or Melville. Try to figure out how they did it. And then, so far as style is concerned, I would go to a lot of movies, a lot of plays, read the works of people who are experimenting.

I wouldn't bother much with Bellow or Roth or Michener or James Gould Cozzens, these are old-timers. I'd be looking at the new people to figure out what they were into. And then I would try to decide, intellectually, what I stood for and what my values were, and I'd go to work. But I would certainly look at the revolutionary and experimental forms in all fields: poetry, drama, painting, architecture, and the use of words. I would try to move into the twenty-first century, twenty years early.

Conversations: But what if one didn't like that? What if one liked your style?

Michener: If I were doing it again—if I were doing it right now—I would do just what I'm talking about, and then I might come back to my style.

176

Conversations: Then you're saying you have to make a name for yourself before you can do what you want to do?

Michener: No, I don't believe that's the problem. I think the problem is finding an intellectual world in which you are happy and in which you find a certain grace in what you're doing. I think if we talked a long, long time you would find me consistently saying, "Don't write the way I write—go beyond that—move into bold new areas."

Conversations: It's impressionistic what you do, though.

Michener: Yes. I am very hesitant about talking about these things because so often it sounds like bushwah. But the fact is that I have perfected a style which millions of people around the world will read. You ask me what I do. . . . I go into the kitchen every morning and I open letters from all over the world—from people who want to discuss things with me—a wide scatter of it, the inclusiveness of it. So that I am very happy with what I have devised, but I think it applies only to me.

Conversations: Are writers getting away from your style of creating a cast of memorable characters?

Michener: Yeah. I would say that I feel it is a duty to see as many movies as I can, because I love drama and I work in that field a lot. And I would say that some of the movies I've seen have been so lacking in form and what you're talking about that I've gotten nothing out of them at all.

Conversations: Do you have any regrets as a writer?

Michener: Gee, the things I've missed. Everything I ever started and was not able to finish hangs over me like a lead weight of regret.

Conversations: Are these books that you're talking about?

Michener: Primarily, yes. I can think of four, and I'd put one project in the arts, some articles I didn't write on pressing issues—and I think anyone, like me, who had had those frustrating experiences would have to feel regret. Now this is offset, obviously, by the fact that what I have done has got an awfully good track history; I'm grateful for that.

James A. Michener

Conversations: Do you think that it's possible for a man to earn a living by just free-lancing?

Michener: I think it's becoming so difficult that I couldn't recommend it for anybody. Now it may be that we're in a dark age right now. It may be that as television and CATV take over, there will be an equal number of jobs there to replace the jobs that used to be available in the newspapers and magazines. That's all very well for the nonfiction writer, but what is the fiction writer going to do? Where is he going to get his hearing? I had a seminar with a group of students, a large seminar, at some colleges near here and I advocated that they publish in the little journals of the universities. And since I made that statement, I've seen a report that some thirty or forty of these are going out of business.

So where the young man is going to get a chance to prove his writing ability I don't know. I suspect it will come through the universities, through off broadway drama, through underground movies, through kinds of publications that I never even knew about when I was a boy. But this country is going to be in perilous shape if it does not keep producing a group of writers like Bellow, and Malamud, and Cozzens, and the young men who are coming along. We're going to be in rough shape and we will have to make some way, to provide some way for them to learn their skills.

Conversations: Has this ever happened before?

Michener: Not to my knowledge. I think that we are going back, almost, to the days of Samuel Johnson in the late eighteenth century, where you had to glom on to somebody and ride with him. It may be that the writer is going to have to glom on to some corporation or some big operation, and keep alive that way. I don't rule out the possibility that writers of prose will pretty soon become like writers of poetry: they'll have to operate through the universities.

Conversations: Have you ever written confession stories?

Michener: When I was a young man I knew very well one of the men who was an editor at Street & Smith, the great confession publisher. Although I never wrote for him—it was only because I didn't have the skill. He wanted me to and he invited me to and I couldn't make it. But I learned a great, great deal about the profession from him, and I think this would be a completely legitimate training ground for the young writer.

Conversations: It's supposedly the largest market.

Michener: Yeah. Let me put it this way, a week ago I said if I were a young man I would hammer the little magazines with sophisticated, erudite, brilliant writing—if I could do that. But this week, having heard about the demise of so many little magazines, it seems to me that, maybe, what you're going to have to do is write the confession material, or write the pulp potboilers, and get them into pocketbooks and learn your trade that way. And, after eight or ten of these, do some stunning book that catches the eye of the general public. I would say this without qualification: if I were a young man with my attitudes and principles, I would not hesitate at writing anything to get into print—except hard-core pornography.

I would be very happy as a young man if I had written a book as good as *Candy*. I think it's a witty, brilliant book. It's not my style; I wouldn't write it now; it's one cycle beyond me. But, believe me, if I were the age of the fellows who did write it, I would be very proud and very pleased indeed. And so I would have a very wide limit as to what I would write: I would write advertising copy for Sears Roebuck and I would write the best they ever had; I would take a job in television; I would run the gamut—but I would write. I would be somewhere where I could write.

Conversations: How can a free-lance writer supplement his income?

Michener: I think if you looked at the books of all the writers who have made it—whatever that phrase means, I'm not sure I know—I think you would find that the bulk of their first three books, at least, was written while they held full-time jobs doing something else. They were written, like mine, at four o'clock in the morning; I wrote my first three books by getting up at four o'clock in the morning and doing it. And then having a full day at the office and working at night, sometimes when I hadn't done a good job in the morning. I was young then and I had a lot of energy—I couldn't possibly do it now.

I think that's what you have to do: you get a job doing public relations for a Cleveland bank and you learn every trick of the use of words; and then your wife, understanding ·what the problem is, helps you organize your life so that you have some spare time to club away at what you really want to do. I believe in this thoroughly. It may well be that fellows like that, who will spend their lives in universities, will get something out of it in the end. But it's how you do it. You just keep on writing and word gets around that here's an honest guy—and publish *anywhere*. I don't give a goddamn where. I've been through this and the job is to break through the barriers some way or other.

James Purdy's most recent book is A Day After the Fair: Three Plays and Seven Short Stories. *His other books include* 63: Dream Palace *(1957),* Malcolm *(1959),* Cabot Wright Begins *(1964), and* I Am Elijah Thrush *(1972).*

James Purdy

James Purdy was interviewed on 6 September 1977 at his home in Berkeley, California, by Cameron Northouse. The interview was conducted in the living room, which showed the evidence of Purdy's enormous correspondence.

Conversations: I've looked through any number of reference books on contemporary writers, and there is never a great deal of biographical information about you.

Purdy: I really wish now that I had printed my books anonymously or with a pen name.

Conversations: Why's that?

Purdy: I don't know. I just don't like publicity. I work best when I'm not under pressure. Also, I do not like the modern age, which is not interested in the writer but in his vices or foibles or whether he stabbed his wife. So I like to discuss my work, but I don't really like discussing my biography. Also, the other matter is that I never earned a living from my writing, that I'm kept afloat by working at other things. I used to get foundation grants. So, I really don't feel like sharing my life with a profession which is not giving me my bread.

Conversations: What do you think of people like Robert Lowell, or Sylvia Plath, or Anne Sexton, whose work is their life, at least to a certain extent?

Purdy: They're not writers that interest me in the least. I think we live in an age in which the writer has become, such as on television, a creature of publicity, a personality. Some of those writers you mentioned I think are totally trivial—all of them— but they found a way of constantly being on camera, and most of their energy went into that. But, in the end, the only thing I believe that keeps a writer living is his work, and not whether he stabbed his wife, or is an alcoholic. In the case of Dylan Thomas it would appear that what people were really interested in was that he was a drinker. They seemed to find an inexhaustible interest in that, which to me—having known so many alcoholics— they're the most boring people in the world, whether they are geniuses or not.

Conversations: Do you have any idea why people are so interested in these kinds of things?

Purdy: Well, I think in part they've been made interested. You know, it began with newspapers. In order to sell the newspapers they had to have shocking or disturbing headlines or people wouldn't buy them. And it has continued. Really, there is almost no important news in most newspapers. The really seminal events aren't in there and probably won't be known for twenty or thirty years. I think the same is true in literature: the writers who are toasted and made-over are really going to be forgotten, and their books not read.

Conversations: The characters in your novels almost live their entire lives at the present moment. Malcolm, for example. There is nothing behind him. There is no path, although there is a vague memory of his father.

Purdy: And his travels.

Conversations: But Malcolm really has no history. He has no biography.

Purdy: No biography. Of course, I'm not an existentialist but he sometimes is called an existential figure, because he is the here-and-now.

Conversations: You've said that you're really writing about the American spirit or the—

Purdy: Well, America. Or, one might say, I'm writing about here and now. When one uses grandiose words like "America," one then thinks that the writer is some sort of a propagandist or a patriot, you know. But, actually, I think one of the reasons my works have fallen into trouble from the beginning is that they are written in a real, colloquial American speech. And this has been pointed out by people like Paul Bowles and others, whose opinions count. But what other speech could I write? I would have to write speech that I grew up hearing in Ohio—and I lived in West Virginia and I've also lived in the South. What always interested me was using common speech to write my books. My books are very oral and aural.

So, in that sense, I think they are very American books. But when Whitman wrote *Leaves of Grass* his book was forbidden to be circulated through the U.S. Mail, and he was also considered unusual or abnormal and freakish—

Conversations: And pornographic.

Purdy: Pornographic, indecent—just all the things they have called my books from the beginning. So that I think the one thing that people don't like in a writer is that he.... The writer must be ordinary, because the critics are so ordinary and the newspapers are so ordinary. There are no serious book reviews. Occasionally a good reviewer appears, but he's usually gotten rid of for a stable of hacks. But there are no really serious literary newspapers, or magazines, or journals, at least that I know of— they're mostly trade magazines.

The books that are being pushed are being pushed by money with special influence and special political coteries. Actually, there is no literary establishment because there are no real literary figures involved. There are political hacks, monied spokesmen for special interests. The book business has become a kind of cartel. In the old days, you had gentlemen who were publishers. There are almost no gentlemen anywhere, and there are certainly no more than two or three among book publishers. So you have a kind of carnival of gross commercialism, burlesque, pornography, shoddy prose—all run by the conglomerate, the cartels, and the giant newspapers, television, and radio stations.

Conversations: This "presentness" of your work, is it because you feel history is not important or it drags the individual down? As with Malcolm?

185

James Purdy

Purdy: Well, actually *Malcolm*, if you look at it, has everything that is going on in America going on in the book. And I think Malcolm himself is nostalgic for a past that no longer exists. He's looking for his father, but in reality finds only confusion. People and events to which he has no key.

Conversations: Garnet Montrose in In a Shallow Grave *is very similar to Malcolm.*

Purdy: I suppose all one's characters are similar or related. Flaubert said that a real writer has only one story to tell and he tells it in different forms. So we may be born with one vision at birth and everything else is just a fugue event, one single vision.

Conversations: Is the disfigurement of Garnet representative of what we all have become?

Purdy: Of course, your question in a sense is making me rewrite my book, you see, because the book is the book and the meaning is in that. I find that when people ask me questions, even very good questions like yours, they are pulling me away from my own work as a novelist and making me write an essay on what my novel means. I can't always express in expository language what the novel means. I'm not sure that I know exactly what it means, but I know I had to write it and I wrote it in the way that I felt I should write it. Beyond that, I don't know that I am a guide to explain it. I think the reason art is art is because that is an explanation, insofar as there is any explanation.

Conversations: How did you start writing?

Purdy: Well, I always liked to write when I was growing up in Ohio. Even as a boy I used to like to write stories and so forth. I think I found life quite disturbing and painful and, perhaps, it was a way of not escaping from it but dealing with it. When I went to high school, too, I had several teachers that encouraged me. But that was the end of my encouragement, because I found not only was growing up and living in the world, as it is today, extremely disturbing and distracting; but also when I did begin writing stories, I found that there was no publication which would take them.

And I find that is still true today. Some of my best stories— recent stories, such as "Some of These Days" about the young man who was in prison and tries to find his landlord—languish without publication. People would not publish that story on the grounds that it was homosexual. Now from one point of view it is about homosexuality, but I think the real theme of this story transcends any kind of sexual orientation. It's about trying to find the man that he thinks he loves. But while magazines will accept rank pornography, they will not accept a story like "Some of These Days," because, I think, this story disturbs them. Pornography may nauseate people, but it doesn't really disturb them because it is simply an exhibition of organs and so forth.

Conversations: And it's also redundant.

Purdy: It's redundant. And then there really has not emerged a great pornographic writer, or a great pornographic filmmaker. They're totally unimaginative, like the so-called great novelists that are palmed off on us.

Conversations: Have you found a great deal of difficulty in getting your work accepted or published by New York publishers?

Purdy: Oh, yes. I was first published in England because my first stories, which no one would publish, were finally published by a friend of mine who had considerable money. He was also a writer himself and had written two books—one on Henry James and another on Joseph Conrad. He thought these stories were very important, so he published them. And then another friend of mine published my short novel, *63: Dream Palace.* I had a feeling that Edith Sitwell might like this, so I sent the books to her—though I did not know her. She read them and took them to her publisher, because she thought they were very important works of the imagination, and Victor Gollancz published those in England.

It was not until then that New Directions, who had rejected all these stories earlier, decided that they could publish them, after the British success. But even at this time they had to censor the book in England. They removed certain words which they thought would cause a lawsuit. That was in 1957. And then there were attacks on the book from what I call the V. S. Pritchett school. V. S. Pritchett is one of the worst influences on criticism today. I've always felt that one of the nasty reviews of my work, which appeared in *The Observer*, was really dictated by him. What they always do, if they don't like a writer and if the writer is a disturbing writer—they can no longer call you a nigger or a kike, but they can call you a homosexual and get away with it. And that is the word they tar you with.

So that when *Eustace Chisholm and the Works* was published, it received a disgraceful and totally unprofessional review by Wilfrid Sheed in *The New York Times*. Now Wilfrid Sheed is a paid hatchet man for the New York establishment, and he uses the word "homosexual" to mean that if you are a homosexual or if you write about homosexuality, you are *ipso facto* deprived of any basic true judgment or vision. Now no one would dare say because you're a Jew or a black your vision is impaired. They would not dare say that. So I am glad to see that gays are now marching against critics and newspapermen who **say, in effect, because you're gay your vision and your life-style are not correct and we cannot respect you.**

Actually, no artist is a homosexual or a heterosexual because man himself is not either heterosexual or homosexual. The components of his soul, if you wish to say that, are far more complex, and no writer ever worth his salt could merely write as a homosexual. He could not be an artist, you know. But to use that term to attack a work like *Color of Darkness* is the age-old philistine hate for art and really hate for humanity—certainly hate for literature—which is practiced by V. S. Pritchett, Wilfrid Sheed, and the rest of the New York establishment.

Conversations: Is it because they are afraid?

Purdy: Well, I think there is something wrong with them rather than with the homosexuals.

Conversations: No, I meant, is it because these critics are afraid of really innovative, new literature?

Purdy: I think they're men of very limited vision, judgment, and they have no real taste for literature. They are professional newspapermen who rush into print all the time. And yet men like this, and those in The Book-of-the-Month Club and The Literary Guild, and the great publishing empires are totally uninterested in serious writing, and they wouldn't know it if they saw it. They would not know it.

Conversations: You said that New Directions wouldn't publish the Color of Darkness *book until it was a success in England. Had they read all these stories before?*

Purdy: Someone there had read them.

Conversations: Is it just the old story that for someone in the United States to succeed, they have to be validated first outside of the United States?

Purdy: Well, I don't know that that's necessarily true, but I think the worse the book, the smoother the sailing. The worse the writer, the more popular, the more acclaimed by the so-called book reviews.

Conversations: Sort of an inverse equation.

Purdy: Yes. And I think it's always been that way and always will be that way, because if a talent is new and original, it is not too easy to appraise it. While an ordinary mediocre talent and an ordinary craftsmanship can immediately be understood by the type of mentality which is in charge of American publishing and reviewing. But I think things have gotten much worse since I began my official career in 1957—which is twenty years now. Things have gotten much worse. There are more bad writers than ever before; there are more dirty writers—when I was writing they fussed and fussed about my language, now they would like one to put in more dirty words. And the same people' are in charge. The ones who were in charge of purity are now in charge of filth, because the only reality in America is money, getting ahead, success, notoriety—and the whole of America is a giant pornographic workshop.

Conversations: Is there any way out of this?

Purdy: Yes, it's just being yourself and doing your own work and not worrying about whether you are rich or notorious. It is self-fulfillment and an interest in other people as human beings and accepting them as they are.

James Purdy

Conversations: Do you see any optimistic signs about American culture for the artist?

Purdy: I believe it was some of the early Christian writers who said that there's never any hope for the world. And there never is, because the world has the wrong set of values, so it can ónly end in disaster. But the individual need not have that set of values, so there is always hope for him. But there is never hope for the world in the sense that the world is bent on the pursuit of wealth and nonpersonal values.

Conversations: So then you would see most people who attempt to reform society as being either stupid, malicious or, at least, misguided.

Purdy: Well, I think the society is so corrupt. I don't know that you can reform it.

Conversations: People seem to be trying all the time.

Purdy: They try all the time, but I guess they just remedy one little frill and the roots are left the way they are. I think it's just another form of propaganda. I think it was Thoreau who denied that philanthropists were great men. He said they were merely great philanthropists, and I think that's true of reformers. Is the reformer himself reformed? Usually he's not. I know so many come to the door where I live promising me salvation, but I wonder about this promisor of salvation. Who appointed him to save me? And how does he know that I'm not saved?

Conversations: You've mentioned Whitman and Thoreau, and *I've read that you greatly admire Melville.*

Purdy: Yes.

Conversations: Do you see yourself in this type of tradition, the Romantic tradition?

Purdy: I admire Melville because he went his own way and was ignored by society. And yet I really think that the novels of Melville are almost, perhaps, the only literature that can still be read from either the nineteenth or twentieth century. At least I go on rereading them and finding new things about them.

190

Conversations: You don't feel the same way about Hawthorne?

Purdy: Less so, though I admire his short stories, and *The Scarlet Letter*, and *The House of the Seven Gables*. I think Melville is a much greater writer.

Conversations: Henry James?

Purdy: No, I don't admire Henry James. I find him interesting only as a gigantic exercise in rhetoric. I find that, to me, Henry James just doesn't know what or who his characters are. In his confusion in coming to terms with life, he invented a very fascinating kind of rhetoric. I don't think he's a great stylist or a great writer, but I don't know that one ever saw such an inflated and immense kind of rhetoric, such as *The Wings of the Dove*, which is an appalling work from one point of view. But I don't really learn very much from reading Henry James. I don't enjoy reading him; I enjoy reading Melville.

Conversations: Who else do you read?

Purdy: Well, there are very few writers today that I can read. I think Jean Genet is a very, very fine writer and some of Sartre's short stories. I admire Charles Doughty's *Travels in Arabia Deserta* which was written in 1870. I admire some of Sherwood Anderson's short stories and Stephen Crane's short novel, *George's Mother*, and then I have an admiration for Dreiser's *An American Tragedy*. And I like some of Faulkner.

Conversations: Which ones?

Purdy: Well, I like *Absalom, Absalom!* very much. And I like parts of *The Hamlet*.

Conversations: Do you read drama?

Purdy: Yes, I like Elizabethan and Jacobean drama very much and I like, of course, all of the Greeks tremendously.

Conversations: Your plays are almost revenge tragedies. I was thinking of A Day After the Fair *in particular.*

Purdy: Yes, it's been called a Jacobean play. I don't know how I came to write that play. I mean, where the subject came from. I had studied clowns, and I knew some clowns who were in a circus. And I knew street performers, you know, who did juggling and that—I knew them. But there was an actor who urged me to write plays, and I really wrote that to satisfy his belief that I could write plays.

Conversations: Are there any plans now for productions of A Day After the Fair?

Purdy: Well, there were, but again, like my fiction, this play is too much against the American stage to do. Tom O'Horgan wanted to do it but I don't think he really tried very hard to put it on, although he thought it a very remarkable work. And another man of the theatre, John Stix, thought it was a very unusual and original play. But they always find excuses not to do something original.

Conversations: You mentioned once that someone in Copenhagen was planning to do it.

Purdy: Yes, that was proposed too, but since then I've heard nothing. It's being translated into French by Monsieur Jaujard. He's translating it into French, but he's having trouble translating the title, because the title actually—though it has become an American proverbial expression: "He came a day after the fair," meaning he came late, or it's too late—goes way back to the Greek and the Latin.

Conversations: The colloquialism isn't in French?

Purdy: No, evidently they don't have any expression like that.

Conversations: You've written five plays.

Purdy: Yes. I've written some that I've never showed people— quite a few—one, a very long play. I'm still working on those.

Conversations: Of the five, am I correct that Cracks *is the only one that has been performed?*

Purdy: Well, *Children Is All* was performed in Yugoslavia, and I think it was done as a reading in Denmark. But, so far as I know, *Cracks* is the only one that was done—and that was done off-off-Broadway. I think in 1964 or 1963.

Conversations: There is a fairly large gap between your first two plays and the next three. A Day After the Fair, True, *and* Wedding Finger *are fairly recent.*

Purdy: They were going to do *Wedding Finger* at La Mama Experimental Theatre, but I really didn't feel that they were going to do it properly. They were going to do it very quickly, and I think that particular play requires music and also very good costumes, because it is, in a way, kind of a black opera and, of course, many of the characters are black. I felt if they just ran it through quickly, it would not be to the advantage of the play and that a great deal of thought was required before a production. Why do it, if you do it shoddily?

Conversations: Have you ever thought of writing an opera libretto?

Purdy: Yes, I have. Some of my poems, *The Running Sun*, were set to music by Robert Helps and those were performed in Alice Tully Hall in Lincoln Center. I have thought of writing an opera libretto.

Conversations: As a matter of fact, I would think A Day After the Fair *could be an opera.*

Purdy: Yes, I think so, too. And I think *Wedding Finger* could be easily set to music. In fact, there is a young composer in New York, Richard Hundley, who has set a great deal of it to music, but he can't get a grant because he, too, is not part of the establishment. Richard Hundley set some of my poems to music and they've been performed by Anna Moffo and Betty Allen and other famous singers.

Conversations: What's your reaction to seeing or hearing your works performed? Two of your novels have been adapted for the stage.

Purdy: Yes, actually Edward Albee did *Malcolm* in the Shubert Theatre on Broadway and *The Nephew* was done at the Knox Albright Theatre in Buffalo, New York.

Conversations: Didn't Stephen Varble and you and Hermione Gingold. . . .

Purdy: Yes. Hermione Gingold did *I Am Elijah Thrush* on radio. That was another of my books which was highly praised by Dr. Tony Tanner, but it was torn to shreds by *The New York Times*. Now, I think it's actually one of my best books, but, here again, a book has no chance because one or two powerful newspapers decide they don't like it and dismiss it. My publisher at that time was Doubleday. Doubleday was totally uninterested in that book so that, in a real sense, it was never published. But Hermione Gingold, who had admired *Malcolm* very much, gave very generously of her time, and a young black actor, Robert Christian, who has since played in O'Neill's *All God's Chillun*, read the young black narrator. It was done on Pacifica station, WBAI; it lasted an hour and a half. Hermione Gingold was very fine as the voracious Millicent De Frayne.

Conversations: Was Stephen Varble Elijah Thrush or were you?

Purdy: I had to play Elijah Thrush, though I couldn't throw my voice to make. . . . Cyril Ritchard was to have played it and then he decided at the last—I guess he had been reading *The New York Times*—that this work was too immoral and he would lose his reputation if he appeared in it. Since I have no reputation I couldn't fear losing mine.

Conversations: Did you write the script for Elijah Thrush?

Purdy: No, Stephen Varble adapted it with my assistance. But he did the actual cutting—it was very hard for me to know where to cut. It wasn't so much an adaptation as a reading.

Conversations: What's your reaction to hearing your works?

Purdy: Well, it's sort of annihilating. Actually, I think one is too close to it to have the proper judgment. When Edward Albee did *Malcolm* I was sort of numbed by the sight of seeing my own work done in public in another medium. Later, I could tell what might have been improved in it. But he, too, was very unfairly treated by the critics. They were the so-called antihomosexual young women's purity league, one might say, which includes all the big newspapers in New York. They decided to tar and feather him at that time, so that the play was condemned and burned at the stake. But actually, I think that *Malcolm* would do better as a film because it has so many shifts of scene, so many characters coming and going, such changes of mood—it really requires, I believe, the camera.

Conversations: Have you ever written a screenplay?

Purdy: No, I haven't.

Conversations: Would you, if you were asked?

Purdy: I wouldn't want to, unless I could do the whole film myself. I have quite a number of friends who write screenplays. Actually, *Cabot Wright Begins* was purchased for a film by Metro-Goldwyn-Mayer but it was never done.

Conversations: It seems that writing screenplays would be a very lucrative, but time-consuming job.

Purdy: I think so. I think it would have a bad influence on the writer to begin doing that. George Cukor was interested in my coming out there at one time. Edith Sitwell knew him. I believe she gave him my books, but I think he soon saw that I was not commercial caliber. I really don't think I have the talent. One has to have a certain talent to write that kind of thing. It's the same with trashy books, you know. It isn't that they're just trash, but they have a talent for writing trash. I don't think I have that kind of talent. It doesn't interest me. But one does have to study the market and study, I guess, crime in order to write that kind of book.

Conversations: Do you find writing for the theatre to be a greatly different challenge than writing a novel?

Purdy: I think if there were a real dynamic theatre I might want to write for it, but I don't think there is any in America. The theatre, like everything else, is a way of making money and really appealing to an audience that is not interested in the theatre. So the only theatre that seems vital is the off-off-off-Broadway, and one could probably write something for them. But I can't imagine bothering to write a play for modern American commercial theatre. And even if one wrote a good play, it would have no chance for success because there is no real critical approach to the theatre; everything, again, is just money and manipulation.

James Purdy

Conversations: You obviously admire Stephen Varble's work.

Purdy: Well, yes. I think he's very talented. I don't know that he will go on into the theatre—he's also a mime, you know, and does his own costumes. He's creating, I believe, a kind of art form of his own—where that will lead I don't know. But his one play which was done at La Mama, *Silent Prayer*, I thought was a very remarkable work.

Conversations: Did it remind you of Maeterlinck?

Purdy: Perhaps, yes. It did, yes. It's much more violent and ferocious.

Conversations: Do you feel that large-scale commercial publishing in the United States and large-scale theatrical businesses are deadening?

Purdy: If they were only buried it would be bad enough. They would stink even from a tomb, but they're above ground and they're hopeless.

Conversations: I imagine that in the theatre you especially mean people such as Merrick and Simon.

Purdy: Well, that's the only theatre there is left, almost.

Conversations: On the other hand, how about the very small theatres?

Purdy: The off-off-Broadway?

Conversations: That and regional theatre like, say, the Gutherie Theatre.

Purdy: Well, I think they've all been infected by the bacillus of the commercial. I think the repertory theatres are inclined to have a certain deadness.

Conversations: Because once they are partially accepted, they try and play to the crowd?

Purdy: Well, they, too, want to make money, you know, and want to be accepted by people who are really not interested in the theatre, but are interested in being entertained. I think the people that go to those small repertory theatres, spread

196

throughout the country, are really looking for a television program on a hot summer night. Most of the plays they perform are the same plays that were successful on Broadway. So I don't think they are any better.

Conversations: What about with publishing? I'd say there might be 3,000 little magazines in the United States. Is that really the center of activity or is it somewhere else?

Purdy: I don't know—I don't think you can tell where an important writer may rise from. He could even appear in New York or Alabama. You just don't know where lightning will strike. If he's a real writer, he's going to have a terrible time. And maybe that's why it has to be that way—because the worse the writer, the easier will be his rise to fame and notoriety and success; because people already know what he's writing about. Most of the successful novels, if you'll look at them, are really about fifty to eighty years out-of-date. They're dealing with things that are easily assimilated.

Conversations: What it means to me is that Harold Robbins and Irwin Shaw are still writing triple-decker Victorian novels.

Purdy: But they're not of the caliber of the Victorian novel. But it is true, they're long-winded.

Conversations: Young people, writers or people who think they ought to be or can be writers, what do you tell them?

Purdy: One thing that I try to warn them about is they really don't want to wait. They have no patience. They want to break into print at once—and many do—and they want to be famous overnight. You just can't do that, because writing takes a long incubation period. You have to be prepared to sacrifice, to wait, to be disappointed, and go through a long, long difficult stage, if you are going to be a really serious writer. You can't expect success or money or acclaim or notice. You have to really tend to your craft and study yourself and what it is you're trying to do.

Conversations: What do you think about university creative writing courses?

James Purdy

Purdy: I think they are a bad influence. Of course, they achieve one thing, perhaps, which is to teach people how to write decent English.

Conversations: Don't they teach them all the same thing, though?

Purdy: I think so and there are too many of them. There are too many writers, really—too many writers writing.

Conversations: Do people think that it is too easy to write?

Purdy: I think so. But that's because they really don't know what writing is. And certainly the critics don't know what it is—the so-called critics. They always praise the works that are not seminal, that are not creative, that are not original. The work that is seminal, original, and imaginative is almost always condemned. And it seems to have been that way all through history.

Conversations: Do you ever write criticism?

Purdy: No.

Conversations: Wouldn't you be a good critic?

Purdy: Well, my energies are all taken by writing, and that would be just another endeavor that isn't my prime purpose. I read a lot, of course, and I have my own views, but I only did one book review in my life, and that was for Life magazine. They personally asked me to review Edith Sitwell's autobiography and I did review that for Life magazine.

Conversations: Then it is primarily a matter of time?

Purdy: Yes, and it takes a long time for me to think through a book. I remember also that Life magazine asked me to write a book review of Willard Motley's last book—I believe it was his last book. Willard Motley had been a friend of mine. He was the black writer, you may remember, who wrote Knock on Any Door. They sent me the book but I didn't really like it, so I wouldn't write a review against a friend—especially when he was dead. Willard Motley was one of those young writers of that period who wrote a best seller, Knock on Any Door, but his tragedy was that he never wrote about himself. In other words, he didn't really find his own subject which was inside. He wrote outside and, though he made a lot of money, he could have been a much greater writer, I think, had he simply written about himself, instead of other people. He also wrote about white people when he was black.

Conversations: You write about blacks, even though you're white.

Purdy: Well, people really thought I was black when *Color of Darkness* appeared. That was a quite common assumption: Carl Van Vechten thought so, Edith Sitwell, Angus Wilson, and a number of other writers. I always thought that Langston Hughes, who liked that book, thought I was a black writer.

Conversations: Do you think there is a place for literary journalism—not necessarily written by you—but by other writers?

Purdy: You mean to appraise books?

Conversations: Well, either to appraise books or to write about literary subjects.

Purdy: Yes, I do.

Conversations: Why do you think that so very few writers do this?

Purdy: I think if one is a novelist. . . . It takes so much energy, for me anyhow, to write a book that I wouldn't want to be reading a lot of other novels and passing judgment on them. I just wouldn't care to do it. We've had terrible critics in this country who do that sort of thing, like William Lyon Phelps, who reviewed about 100 books a month. How you could even read that many, let alone pass a sensible judgment on them. . . . But the daily reviewers in the large New York papers do that, too. They pass these Olympian judgments on a book which you know very well they could not have read properly.

Conversations: And also the hyperboles—"the greatest book of the year—"

Purdy: Yes, and the arrogance of choosing the 250 or so best books of the year by a large New York newspaper—and you know very well that really the best books of the year probably weren't even reviewed by them, because they didn't fit their category.

Conversations: Would you comment on the interview you did for Penthouse *magazine, because the magazine itself would seem indicative of everything that you find distasteful?*

Purdy: That's true. But a young man of very great promise, Fred Barron, who has since written a screenplay which was produced called *Between the Lines*, took that interview to all the so-called respectable magazines. They wouldn't print it. The only place that would print it was an unrespectable magazine. So he said, "Would you be offended?" I said, "No." Because what do we care where it appears, if our point of view and our opinions can be heard? I feel the same way: if the only place they'll let you speak is a privy, why not speak in a privy? If the churches and other sacrosanct institutions are closed to you, as they usually are. So it created quite a sensation—that interview—and it offended many stuffed shirts and so on. Then there was also an interview with me in Andy Warhol's *Interview* magazine.

Conversations: In Jack Newfield's new book, The Abuse of Power, *he is content to generalize that New York is eating itself up from the inside. You've lived in New York for—*

Purdy: Since 1959.

Conversations: That would be eighteen years—

Purdy: Yes. I'm not there all the time, but I live there more or less permanently. I'm gone about half of the year, traveling.

Conversations: Do you think that New York is still the center for almost everything in the arts?

Purdy: In a number of ways it is, but there are different New Yorks, you know. The New York I like is that composed of nonconformists, unusual people. I don't think as many go to New York as used to, because New York used to be the great center for young people who were going to make something of themselves in the arts—actors, writers, painters. But today more doors are closing than opening for them, so I think New York may be dying so far as being a place for young talent.

Conversations: Do you think, then, people are just staying home or are they—

Purdy: Well, I think they're going, perhaps, to other cities—maybe San Francisco or maybe Europe. Of course, the Vietnam War had a terrible influence on New York.

Conversations: In what ways?

Purdy: Well, many of those young men who had to run off to Canada or Oslo would have settled, perhaps, in New York. So the Vietnam War has had a very bad influence on our culture in general. I think the media in New York is very dead. There are a number of new magazines trying to spring up, but I find San Francisco a more free city to live in, in many ways, than New York.

Conversations: Culturally?

Purdy: Yes, it's less oppressive.

Conversations: More people doing more things?

Purdy: Yes, I think so.

Conversations: Do you ever get involved in political events? Are you concerned with the community that you live in?

Purdy: No, I haven't been too much involved really. I was sort of involved in the protest about the Vietnam War, and I believe in things like gay rights, of course, and all that. But in the end my work seems to take so much out of me that it's about all that I can get done.

Conversations: Could you describe an average work day?

Purdy: Well, I get up quite early around 5:30 and I have most of my hard work done by ten o'clock. The rest of the day I have to spend looking up any material or checking on information and so forth—answering letters, and sometimes going through manuscripts, preparing them for publication. And then seeing people, of course, because a writer's life depends on people—people whom he knows—so I see lots of people.

James Purdy

Conversations: Do you think one of the problems for contemporary writers is that there is no longer any place where they can come together?

Purdy: I think that's true. Well, I found, though, in New York I have a lot of friends who have many friends—we do have circles where you can exchange views—but none of my friends are part of the establishment. We've been called counterculture, but I think even that is too pretentious a name. The people I enjoy being with are people who are different and unusual, sensitive, and who are not part of the media.

Conversations: What do you think of academics?

Purdy: I find, in general, universities are stultifying and oppressive, too. And I find that people who teach English in universities are apt to look to these essentially disreputable literary powers in New York. They should be looking to themselves, because the really good critical minds are not in New York and they're certainly not in the hire of the New York newspapers—at all.

Conversations: Who do you think are some good critics?

Purdy: Well, Dr. Tony Tanner is a very good critic; Irving Malin; James Martin, who writes for the *Los Angeles Times*; and Stephen Adams. There are very intelligent reviews appearing all over the United States.

Conversations: Is the main thing that separates Irving Malin, Stephen Adams, and James Martin from the other critics their seriousness about what they are doing?

Purdy: Yes, I think so, and they don't judge a book until they've read it thoroughly. Also they're not part of a political group which has already made up its mind who the important writers are and assume that there are no others.

Conversations: New York in the 1940s saw, when Jackson Pollock, Robert Motherwell, and the rest of the abstract expressionists came, a truly exciting period.

Purdy: Yes, that may have been—I didn't live there then, of course. But also, to take up a more practical matter, in the 1940s

202

and earlier and even into the 1950s, a young person could come to New York and find a very cheap apartment. Also food was not so expensive, so he could live more or less inexpensively until he had found himself in one of the arts. That's no longer possible because the big landlords and the outrageous cost of food and all other things—the expense of the subway—are discouraging really gifted young people from coming to New York.

Conversations: Now is it almost necessary for young writers to go to a university?

Purdy: I'm afraid so, and I don't think that's a good place to go for a writer: it's too safe; it's too sacrosanct; it's too dull.

Conversations: Did you do it?

Purdy: Well, I have taught, yes, from time to time. But I didn't find it too stimulating, though it's always nice to talk to young people, to students. And, of course, many of the faculty are very fine and dedicated people, but I just think for a writer or a painter that isn't the right place. I don't think the Macdowell Colony or the other colonies are conducive to really original work.

Conversations: Do you think it should be writers who teach these creative writing classes and workshops?

Purdy: I don't think they should be taught—at all. Because it's just turning out another conformist: a group of people that will probably end up writing for *The New Yorker* the same type of story which has been appearing for fifty years. We don't need any more of these stories. And I just don't think that's right.

Conversations: What would you suggest young writers do?

Purdy: I think it would be better if they worked in a hospital or almost any place—in a restaurant as a waiter—and try to write in their leisure hours. I think if they go to a university, they're just not in the thick of things and they will learn to make concessions and to be respectable. A writer should not be respectable in the sense that he is a conformist—we have too many conformists-writers.

Conversations: Should he deal with disreputable—

203

James Purdy

Purdy: He should deal with life, I think.

Conversations: You once said that you were interested in blacks until they became respectable.

Purdy: Oh, yes. Well, as soon, I think, as people become a power group and begin to be conventional and wear nice clothes and so forth, to me, personally, they're just not as interesting. I find that the minorities that finally become power groups are—when they deal with the arts—just as hidebound and respectable and shortsighted as their WASP slave masters forty or fifty years ago.

Conversations: But should one deal with a subject that is not commonly dealt with?

Purdy: I think the writer has to choose his own subject. That's what is probably wrong with going to a university and becoming a teacher of creative writing. You become timid and fearful and you want to keep your job—and then you become interested in money. But, of course, it's very hard to keep afloat economically today. It's a very hard thing to be a writer; it always has been. But I think it's harder today, because there are too many temptations to become respectable and conventional—ordinary—to become a V. S. Pritchett type of writer.

Conversations: You avoid that by challenging yourself?

Purdy: Yes.

Conversations: To avoid among other things, I suspect, repeating yourself.

Purdy: Yes, that's death.

Conversations: How do you see yourself? Do you see yourself as undermining the illusions of other people?

Purdy: No, I don't have any such purpose at all. Each new book is, to me, a new subject which presents itself to me as though it were a spirit or . . . and I have to deal with that. But I've never written a book to shock people or to horrify people—I think it would be a huckster who would do that.

Conversations: When you get a feeling to write a book, what occurs? Let's take Narrow Rooms. *How do you work it out? Where do you begin?*

Purdy: Well, I get interested in, perhaps, a person or a story that I've heard, or a group of people. Suddenly I see that as a story that I can work with. It may be a short story like "Some of These Days," which is about a young man who came out of prison. Usually, however, the only stories I can work with are the ones that, at first blush, I think are totally impossible and I think I can never write because they just bristle with all kinds of impossibilities. And those, in the end, are the only stories that I can write. The story that I think I can't write, because it has so many hidden difficulties and obvious difficulties, that's the story I work with particularly well.

Conversations: Are you, in a sense, driven to write?

Purdy: I think so, yes. Well, I think writers are divided into two categories: there's the called writer; and then there's the writer who really is a professional—a pro who has no real inner compulsion to tell his own story, or tell the story of someone who's very close to him.

Conversations: When you began, for example, Narrow Rooms *did you know how the novel was going to work itself out?*

Purdy: No, I didn't. I rewrote it four times. The first time I realized I was on the wrong track and I didn't think I would ever be able to finish this book. Then I rewrote it, and it was still not right; and then with the third writing I really began to get into the subject, and now I'm rewriting that.

Conversations: From scratch each time?

Purdy: Well, the second time it was really from scratch, but I kept the first part—so it's been a very difficult book to write.

Conversations: How long a time are we talking about?

Purdy: About three years.

Conversations: With the publication of Narrow Rooms *what sort of response do you expect to receive—not from the critics—*

Purdy: Oh, from the people who've read it, they were bowled over by it. It's an extremely violent book about murder. It's one of those violent love-hate relationships, the hero-slave relationship between two men who can't admit that they really love one another. One is a football player and the other is a boy whose father was a renderer—do you know what that is?

Conversations: At a meat packing plant?

Purdy: Well, it's worse. It's someone who goes and picks up old bones and renders them into lard. So he came from a family which had that profession, and he was looked down upon in a small West Virginia town. These two boys actually admired one another but they couldn't admit it, and partly through this misunderstanding the one boy kills another boy and is sent to prison. When he comes out of prison this same terrible psychological situation is still in progress. It's a very delicate subject. It has shocked everyone who has read it, but they think it is one of my best books. It's based on a real story. It's always fascinated me but, of course, when one writes the story is changed—the characters are changed. As in a painting: if it's really a good painting, it never looks quite like the sitter.

Conversations: When you get feedback from readers do you learn anything from that? Does it modify your attitudes?

Purdy: I learn about them, I think. And I learn about how explosive these books are, which, perhaps, I've lived with so long that I don't realize how they are to someone who is not prepared to read them. But rather than be successful or popular, I would rather fail than choose a subject that isn't what I really like.

Conversations: I didn't mean that you would tone things down or change—

Purdy: No, no, I understood. Yes, you do learn a lot from your readers—provided, you know, they are with you because you learn nothing from someone who is against you, except that he's against you. Because what that means is he's unwilling to enter into your world and he's unwilling to stand up and see what you're trying to do. In other words, he closes the door on you and then describes you when he can't see you. And that is the typical, middle-class, philistine critic.

Conversations: Do you think your new novel, Narrow Rooms, *is more brutal than, say, your earlier works?*

206

Purdy: That's what the readers say; that it's more violent and more upsetting.

Conversations: *You don't think so?*

Purdy: Well, it's hard for me to judge, you know, at this stage, but I guess I would agree with them. It is an extremely violent book.

Conversations: *In your works hasn't there been escalating violence?*

Purdy: I believe so. I don't know what that comes from. For instance, this book is said to be more violent than *A Day After the Fair* which is, in a way, the most violent work I've written— wouldn't you say so? But whatever presents itself to me, I have to act on that. I think, "Well, this is a very violent subject but it seems to be the one that I can work with." So one has to work with what he can work with and not try to choose a subject that might please other people. Or please your publisher. But I think each of my publishers has always been somewhat astounded at the next work, because he hadn't foreseen it would be quite that way. And what they're looking for, I believe, is that you just repeat yourself.

Conversations: *That way they can get used to you.*

Purdy: Yes. They complain that with each new work out by me they have to get new spectacles to look at it, because it's totally unforeseen.

Conversations: *I think that is much to be preferred.*

Purdy: Well, one would get very bored writing the same book all the time. *I Am Elijah Thrush* was very different from *Jeremy's Version. Jeremy's Version* was sort of . . . well, you know, they half liked it—I am speaking now of the so-called critical establishment. But *I Am Elijah Thrush* they thought was trivial and frivolous, until Dr. Tony Tanner wrote a very perceptive essay on it in *Partisan Review* of all places—that old-guard, left-wing establishment of the thirties which still hangs on somehow.

Conversations: *Do you think that now we are experiencing a cultural renaissance?*

James Purdy

Purdy: No, I don't feel that. No. I think we're slipping into another very dead period like the 1950s. I think things are getting very conservative again and people like creature comforts, television, and so forth. I don't feel any vitality in the world of art.

Conversations: Do you think the average intelligent reader is confused?

Purdy: I think they're lazy, which leads to confusion. I don't think people are interested in reading. I think it's a very small group of people who are, and I think that's always been true. And I think there's a very fine perceptive intelligence among a minority in America that are very receptive to real writing, but they're a minority without a voice, without power. They are essentially underground.

Conversations: Has that not been the case all along?

Purdy: I think so, yes, but I think that today it's even more pronounced, because there is such loud noise about trivial writers and the writers that are original are apt to be totally overlooked. Certainly no great noise is made about them.

Conversations: Do you feel that over the long haul your work will stand up?

Purdy: I just don't know because—

Conversations: Do you care?

Purdy: I don't know whether I care or not. It's been such a long battle and struggle with so much disillusionment. I mean, what you gain with one hand is taken away with the other—it's that simple—and, perhaps, people won't even read in times to come. They may not read books anymore. It's quite possible. And, after all, in the Middle Ages how many people read? I think we are more or less like the Middle Ages in that there are millions reading nothing, one might say. Actually the amount of really literate readers is very small. The number of real books that are fit to read is also diminishing so that, though we publish so many books, how many are even worth reading at all?

Conversations: Do publishers have an obligation to see that good writing is published, regardless of the fact that it may or may not make money?

Purdy: Yes, but they refuse to do that. You see each magazine like—well, why mention any by name—you know what the names are. All the magazines that publish fiction will not publish serious fiction unless it can be put on the procrustean bed of their rules. They have more rules than Queen Victoria. *The New Yorker* has more taboos, rules, regulations—no one can write serious fiction with all those rules; you can not.

Conversations: It almost seems like a grand conspiracy.

Purdy: Well, it is in the sense that the fiction in those slick magazines has to go along with the ads—what's really important in the magazines are the ads. And the copy on the ads is really better written than the fiction, and more interesting often. But then there have been very bad influences on the American short story such as Martha Foley—she's one of the worst influences—and Whit Burnett. The "best short stories of the year" are always just frauds because there are no best short stories anymore. The best short stories have to be privately published. You get a formula-story that's turned out like a donut. But the short story has been especially harmed by the slick magazines because they'll only publish one story.

Conversations: What's your opinion of government support of the arts, particularly to writers?

Purdy: I think it's evil and I really suspect that many of the writers one sees on the front page of these literary reviews are, one might say, CIA-approved writers.

Conversations: You mean that metaphorically, I assume.

Purdy: Yes. But I think our government is a very oppressive government in many ways.

Conversations: Do you think the government should give money to writers?

Purdy: No. I think they would try to control them. Even as it is there are no breaks given to writers, you know, on their income tax: they don't give a writer the break that they give a businessman. And now they're not even allowing you to deduct your living quarters where you do your writing. Governments never like artists and writers, unless they are propagandists for them. So I think the government has a bad influence on the arts. The media and the government have agreed, for instance, that a composer like Aaron Copland is a great composer. Is he or not, you know? But it is shoved down our throats that certain composers and certain writers are great.

And when you read over the list of the Nobel Prize winners and Pulitzer Prize winners, when you go back years and years, you see that many of them were not the seminal figures. For instance, the greatest novelists of the twentieth century never won the Nobel Prize: Marcel Proust never won it; Unamuno didn't win it; Theodore Dreiser didn't win it; Joyce didn't win it. They go to these second-string people very often. The award is given for political reasons or sociological reasons. It's not given on merit very often. And then, of course, that's true of the Pulitzer Prize in fiction. I don't think it's ever really gone to a distinguished book of fiction. The same is true of these large newspaper book reviews which recommend certain books. You can always tell that those have political overtones. It's who is respectable politically, not who is really a good writer. So we already have too much government—too much government influence. If the government began to support the arts it would ostracize the real artists, and it already does that, I think, in the grants it gives to certain writers. The government won't give grants to other writers.

Conversations: Are we in a desperate situation?

Purdy: Well, I'm right back where I started when I began my career: I am now publishing my own book privately, *A Day After the Fair*, which I think contains some of my best work. But no publisher was interested in publishing it and so my friends published it for me. So I think the lesson—if there is one—is that one has to depend on himself and on those who understand his work, which will be a very small number of people. And you shouldn't expect too much. You should expect everything from yourself, and not very much from other people, and nothing from society. Because if you do, you're going to be very disillusioned.

Ishmael Reed teaches English and composition at the University of California, Berkeley, and is very active in small press publication and distribution. His writings have earned him the National Institute of Arts and Letters Award for the best noncommercial writing (1974) and the Guggenheim Foundation Award for fiction (1975). His works include The Free-Lance Pallbearers *(1967),* Yellow Back Radio Broke-Down *(1969),* Mumbo-Jumbo *(1972),* Conjure *(1972),* Chattanooga *(1973),* The Last Days of Louisiana Red *(1974), and* Flight to Canada *(1976).*

Ishmael Reed

Ishmael Reed and Cameron Northouse met at the Claremont Hotel in Berkeley, California, on 5 September 1977 for this interview. The Claremont is a charming hotel which figures occasionally in Reed's fiction.

Conversations: The biographical comment on the back of Chattanooga *says, "Ishmael Reed was born in Chattanooga, Tennessee, grew up in Buffalo, New York, learned to write in New York City, and wised up in Berkeley." The title poem deals with Chattanooga. How long did you live there?*

Reed: Oh, I was just a child when I lived there. My mother moved to Buffalo and then she sent for me—I think I was four years old when that happened. I went back a number of summers. We'd usually go back. When northern blacks want to show off their finery, you know, they always go back to the South in a Cadillac. That was always a joke: Go to the North; make it; go back in a Cadillac.

Conversations: And you stayed in Buffalo then for—

Reed: I grew up in Buffalo. I left Buffalo when I was twenty-two.

Conversations: And moved to New York City?

Reed: Yes.

Conversations: Where did you learn to write?

Reed: Well, I started writing very early. I just seemed to be able to put words together, had a good style very early when I was in school. In high school I wrote columns in the newspapers. I had a jazz column, and I guess I was about thirteen or fourteen. I tried some creative stuff in college, my first year in college. That's how

Ishmael Reed

I got going. Then I started writing for newspapers again, the same newspaper I worked for when I was a kid. I was writing journalism.

Conversations: Did you keep writing for newspapers?

Reed: Yes, when I went to New York I was writing for newspapers. I had my own newspaper in Jersey. I was in on the founding of the *East Village Other*—as a matter of fact, I named the *East Village Other*. And that was the first time you had painters, the first time you had collage newspapers. That was the first New Journalism, too. It was poets and writers. But then the term got co-opted by the Uptown. Well, the Uptown came down to the lower East Side, and they were tourists, really. They didn't know really what was going on, but they devoted hardly a thing to nonwhite bohemia. Even though it was a big black population downtown with 60,000 people—60,000 blacks, I think. About 30,000 Puerto Ricans or even more. When people write up what's happening in culture they usually talk about whilte culture— what's happening among white artists—and they leave everything else out.

Conversations: What do you think?

Reed: It's very difficult to relate to groups that you're not acquainted with or to alien groups. You want them to go away, to move off some place. We hear this now, like Benny Goodman the King of Swing, Mick Jagger the King of Rock, and Elvis Presley the King of Rock 'n' Roll. Well, this is obviously omitting the experience of an entire culture. It's not an accurate picture. I used to be very worried about it, but now we are beginning to do our own things, such as publishing books. I have Reed, Cannon and Johnson—that's an outfit I run, Reed, Cannon and Johnson—and magazines. We did four *Yardbird Readers* in an anthology which we called *Survival*. Then we do an audio magazine called Steve Cannon Show.

Conversations: What's that?

Reed: That's just a phenomenon. It's a cassette magazine kind of like the *Black Box*, the same idea.

Conversations: Was it poets?

Reed: Poets, and interviews, and jazz concerts, and also a regular feature which we would call "personal column"—soap opera—which would give us an opportunity to have Afro-American writers, other writers, Hispanic authors, and native American writers contribute scripts. The television and movie media are closed up to them. These are still Johannesburgs—they say that blacks can't write. Norman Lear says that black writers are not qualified.

Conversations: Can't write for television?

Reed: Right.

Conversations: Or can't write?

Reed: Can't write for television—well, can't write. And I heard recently that they are doing a Latino series and feel that Chicano writers can't write. I've read a lot of Chicano writers and they write pretty well in my opinion. Writing is still the only power we have, but we're still trying—we use that as an ancient way of influencing. It's like a czar getting upset about some anonymous cartoons somebody's cranked out. We are still in the nineteenth century. We just don't have access to these people. We're trying to get into television though. We are left out of it. We used to complain about people not letting us in, and then found that we could do it. Now it's cheaper; it's becoming cheaper to make the use of television and radio available now with video cassettes, computer editing, and all of this. So we are going to go on to that.

Conversations: You're going to start producing television shows?

Reed: Yes.

Conversations: On video cassettes?

Reed: That's right, and maybe explore cable television. There's a great deal of resentment against this. I mean, they would rather see you as some kind of revolutionary hero than to have you build things. I'm writing a whole novel about this now. That is the kind of difficulty an exceptional nonwhite person has in this country. In my research I found that exceptional people get it from both sides. It happened to Douglass; it happened to

Ishmael Reed

Booker T. Washington; it happened to DuBois; and it happened to Marcus Garvey. They got it from both sides. But the whites like situations they can control, like seeing you as a mugger or a so-called revolutionary hero who entertains them. They like that. So we get a lot of resentment because we actually are going off and attempting to build things, and this has always been a phobia. The role of the nonwhite person in this country is always supposed to be dependent on other people. When you try to build something of yourself, they feel that you are getting out of line.

Conversations: Because it is unpredictable?

Reed: Yes, it's unpredictable in a sense.

Conversations: In a white culture?

Reed: Sure, sure, and they have what I call "the black auxiliary." For example, I just had a major article turned down by a magazine because they didn't like my conclusion. But what I've done is to convert this into a novel about them—

Conversations: Turning down the article.

Reed: Turning down the article because they wanted me to start a race war with them. Or to write a sensational article about race war. Then I went out and gave them 10,000 words more than they asked for, because I thought it was a serious subject. And I went around the country and interviewed people and interviewed intellectuals and they said, "Well, you interviewed so many intellectuals." So I interviewed grass-roots people: I stood on the corner, put up a stand and interviewed people. All of these people said they were satisfied, that they couldn't relate to South Africa, and they didn't feel that anything that happened in South Africa would affect them. They thought that people were educated and too sophisticated for race. That was the majority opinion. So I said, "Well, people said that there was not going to be a race war." So they said that they didn't like my conclusions.

Conversations: Was it sort of a Louisiana Red *type of attitude, promoting dissension?*

Reed: Oh, yes, sure. In my research for this article that I was doing for them, I found that a lot of the difficulty and conflict

216

between the races is promoted by inflammatory press. So you can't knock them, you see, since they have more power than politicians. They can get Nixon or somebody like that because he is obvious, but what I said in that article was that Nixon destroyed his own administration. But the inflammatory media that we have in this country is quite likely to destroy civilization, if it continues on the path that it's on.

Time magazine for the last three or four months showed blacks as looters, and bums, and muggers, and people on welfare. That's the typical image. Whenever they cite welfare on the television networks, it's always black examples—when the majority of the people on welfare are white. So you can see why we have to be propagandists. Sometimes there is no way to avoid this. Somehow, we have to be a rival to the television networks. Somebody said that a great writer is like a rival government; well, my new book is going to be a rival television network, a rival medium to them. It is a conceptional novel in which I'm going to go all over the country and have people join the novel. I'm going to have people sign up and join. Because I'm sure that somebody is going to come out with a big article on race war, I'm going to do mine to counterpose that. So that's what we're into now.

We are into projects that we are creating ourselves and promoting ourselves. Of course, this arouses a resentment, especially from the liberal establishment, which usually sees itself as the guardian for nonwhite people who have never made it.

Conversations: Is this "liberal" attitude a throwback to racial superiority?

Reed: Well, I read in an article the other day—I'm using a lot of newspaper material in this book—that the old-fashioned racism was that blacks were inferior. Now I don't think . . . well, you know, there may be some people who believe that—maybe millions of people believe that—but I don't think that's the standard, the modern approach to it. Now there is something called "symbolic racism." And that means that they think that blacks are getting away with everything, which is crazy.

Conversations: Well, it's equally destructive.

Ishmael Reed

Reed: It's equally destructive, but it's more sophisticated and, therefore, probably more of a threat to Afro-American gains. We see these gains being wiped out. As a matter of fact, in the article—I'm going to give away the novel—I talk about the kind of cyclical things that are happening. They wanted me to blame everything on South Africa. Well, I had a line about people in white houses shouldn't throw stones. But I just see resentment against Africa, but it's always been there—I mean, at least for 100 years. There were a whole lot of lynchings, burnings at the stake, and dismemberment, and all this—it's really like Nazism, you know.

People talk about Germany and Hitler, when we have a very fine tradition of American Nazism. As a matter of fact, I understand, from a new book from Doubleday by Toland on Hitler, that the Germans derived their notions of mass extermination from the way the Indians were treated when they were put on reservations. So there's a tradition of American Nazism.

Conversations: What do you think is the best training ground for young writers?

Reed: Well, I don't know. I just think the best training ground is to write and to read.

Conversations: But write for whom? For themselves—

Reed: I don't know who you write for—that question doesn't occur to me. Because we are in a situation now where we can't really appeal to fellow nationals. I get better reviews in Japan. The best review on *Flight to Canada* just came out in Nigeria. That's really weird, because I have always been accused by black critics in the United States of not abiding by the black aesthetic. When it comes to the mother country, Lagos, Nigeria, I think it's great that they did my book along with Alex Haley's *Roots*. They said that Alex Haley's book was taking one myth and substituting it with another myth: that all was correct in Eden or Africa was some kind of Eden—that this is not the case; it's an illusion. And they pointed to my book, *Flight to Canada*, as one that sees the histories as simultaneous. I guess maybe there's some connection between that and the idea of African time.

218

But I think, probably, my material is more within the classical Afro-American tradition than some of the critics who accuse my characters of being pathological—like this person, Addison Gayle, Jr., whom the liberal establishment has made the black aesthetic czar. You see, there was a fight there in the sixties where somebody said that he didn't feel he was qualified to judge Eldridge Cleaver's work. I don't feel that I'm qualified to listen to Duke Ellington, you know—it's just absurd. They had been intimidated by these fascist types, you know.

Conversations: On both sides.

Reed: Right. And they felt that they wanted to bow out. So then these black opportunists in the English departments, who really didn't care that much about Afro-American culture—as a matter of fact, had contempt for it—people like Houston Baker, Jr. and Addison Gayle, Jr.—both juniors, incidentally—were the ones that they set up to arbitrate taste. Not Gayle as much as Baker. Baker and I had an exchange where it got really personal. It's always been that kind of attack which people have made.

There was a nonaggression pact signed where liberal whites said, "Well, you guys do it. You be the guardians of the Afro-American experience. Check them, you know." They had a lot in common. They both were against any kind of experimentation in form or content. So they wanted to keep Afro-American writers in their place. To the novel of nightmare and pain that Roger Rosenblatt and Irving Howe. . . . They are all together; they all publish in the same magazines. I was naughty enough to call Harold Courlander a tourist for the *Washington Post*, because his material on Afro-American culture was not substantial. For example, he did a book on the Afro-American culture, Afro-American folklore, in which he didn't use many of the writings of the Afro-Americans and natives, not many Haitian writers, not any writers from the country. They used white nineteenth-century tourists to describe the kind of dances that the Africans were doing in New Orleans, which is not very accurate when there were a lot of other sources they could have used. So I said that. So the next thing I know, they're jumping on *Flight to Canada*. It's predictable.

Rosenblatt and Irving Howe, I understand they have some kind of relationship with *The New Republic.* I had *The New*

Republic in the book, you know. And then McPherson is connected with *The New Republic*. I guess white writers have the same problem, but it just seems like some kind of assassination thing: "You don't fit in." If you're not giving them some kind of decorative prose—what they call elegance and eloquence—then you're a bad boy; you're a heathen, you know. When it comes between heathens and the kind of writers they promote—the tokens they got back in the East, dependent upon them—I'd rather be on the side of the heathens. That's why I've been more around Alaska among Eskimos and the Indians in the Southwest. I get along with people like that; I'm influenced by their cultures. But this is a transition. I think some of the people I'm working with and I have to take credit for this, we have changed the whole way of Afro-American writing in that there's been a revolt. We came to the West Coast instead of going to Europe, as was the practice in the forties and the fifties, and others went South and to the Midwest. And so this machine that they tried to create has crumbled.

Matter of fact, Addison Gayle, Jr.—one of the lucky things they have going for them and that they profit from is that the followers of these leaders don't read any books. Addison Gayle, Jr. has come out with a book from Doubleday, *The Wayward Child*, which is an appropriate title because he's crawling back into the literary establishment. He's given up this black aesthetic in this book. At the end he becomes a hippie-born-again-flower-child; he's always ten years behind. But he's still going around the country lecturing on the black aesthetic, and hitting me, and talking about blueprints. I mean, I've never heard of a white critic come up with a blueprint for white writers. But they always put us in these slave pens, and, when it's not a white overseer, they have a black overseer.

So, I think because of the efforts we have made on both coasts, there is probably more freedom available to the Afro-American artist than ever before in history. Because we've broken up these traditional machines: the liberal machine and the nationalist machine, that packed considerable power over what happened in Afro-American culture.

Conversations: Do you think this has a lot to do with small presses?

Reed: I think so.

Conversations: Particularly in California.

Reed: Oh, sure. We're able to publish books that don't fit in with the political idea of what they think black writers should be doing in the East. We've published Victor Cruz's book which was rejected by a big company; we published Calvin Hernton's book. The major new black poets—I mean, the people who created a new black poetry. They gave LeRoi Jones credit for it, because he had strong ties with Allen Ginsberg and that was a powerful lobby, a powerful machine, with a great deal of influence. They were able to select who was going to be the head of the blacks. There again, there are all these different groups and interests selecting their own black.

I can see it right now: they're always selecting which one, who's going to be favored, and it's traditional. I mean the liberals selected Douglass. The abolitionists, the fathers of the liberals, were responsible for the kind of hassles the Afro-American avant-garde has to go through, because they are the ones who went down to the South after the Civil War and tried to Victorianize all the niggers. So we have those kind of critics on our back, who have no idea of the avant-garde as such. They are very conservative and very much like in *A Wayward Child.* What one of the big, aggressive, combative proponents of the black aesthetic, Addison Gayle, talks about when he's thinking about jumping off a bridge is how Keats comes to mind. Not Claude McKay, you know, it's Keats he's thinking about. They all have their different leaders.

Booker T. Washington was created by the same liberals and philanthropists, and they've got them now. Jesse Jackson has a very powerful media trying to get him over. They haven't been successful, I think, because that charismatic leader whom people have just accepted indiscriminately in the past is over, that period is over. So they are having a difficult time getting those people over.

Conversations: Then, what's the explanation for your novels coming out of Random House?

Reed: Well, I like to think that they are good novels and—

Ishmael Reed

Conversations: I mean, how did The Free-Lance Pallbearers *first—*

Reed: I really don't know; I really don't know. That was strange for Doubleday to publish a book like that. And it's almost running out its advance after ten years and *Yellow Back*, too. I don't know—I think that sometimes they have good editors and books like that can get through, and the same with Random House. They are not commercial novels, although they sell pretty well in paperback. I understand *Louisiana Red* sold well and *Yellow Back*.

Conversations: Isn't there some sort of incongruity, though, with your own books coming out of New York while you are in Berkeley publishing other people's books?

Reed: I don't think so. I don't think there is any incongruity in that.

Conversations: What I mean is, it seems as if you have made it—

Reed: Well, I haven't made it really. See, I still have a very difficult time raising the rent. Maybe I'm overly generous in giving to different projects, and you can't be that way all the time. I'm going through a court case right now where I was used by some blacks in Berkeley—nonliterary types who hate writers—to work for them in establishing a company and building it up. As soon as it looked as if it was going to be successful, they destroyed it; they destroyed it. And that's a novel right there. Life is very easy when you can blame everything on white people. It induces a real laziness, I think, intellectual laziness and a lack of sophistication. I find that there are black slave masters, too. I mean I was used by these people as black slave masters. Hobos and degenerates, I tried to help them out, and they turned on me.

Just like the old story about somebody who picks up a snake, a wounded snake, and holds it to his breast—the same thing happened to me, but I think this is a very important experience for me. It was a profound experience for me and I will take advantage of it. I mean, I'm losing right now. It's been very bad. I've had a situation where my company is going bankrupt because a person, who was supposed to be the fiscal manager,

222

wasn't taking care of business. You see? So when I went to the board and we all removed him, he went out and got some other disgruntled shareholders. People that hadn't done any work and believed that the world owes them a soft life because they are black—you get this kind of mentality in Berkeley. You get these bums, hobos, and their liberal patrons. Their liberal patrons hate me, because I tell the niggers to stand up and do something for themselves. I'm removing their favorite charities.

So it's been a very interesting experience, and that's why I think, maybe, the Africans are able to see my work better than Afro-Americans, who think it is incoherent or crazy. When I go to Haiti or some place like that, I see a cultural tradition which is right in line with what I'm doing. I mean, it's not social realism, the kind of Marxism these people learn. It's kind of like a surrealism. It looks like surrealism and is abstract. See, so I'm able to get along very well in Haiti. As a matter of fact, I just published a book by the Haitian ambassador, Dr. Mars, on voodoo. It's one of the first of these works to be translated. So while people are going around the country calling me pathological and gossiping about me and putting down my works as nuts, I'm bringing a whole tradition to them.

A lot of the young kids are interested in it, white and black. I go up to Colorado Springs and find that *Mumbo-Jumbo* is a cult book up there, and they want to know more information about other realities and other cultural forms. I think that, maybe, when it comes to blacks and black critics, I'll probably in the future get a better break in Africa—which is really filled with ironies because I would be the last one to talk about Pan-Africanism. Although I'd never really considered it that much, in my art I'm apparently doing what a lot of the Africans are doing.

Conversations: You seem to be considerably more indepen-dent. One thing that strikes me all the way through is your concentration on work: that if you don't work in one way or another you are lost.

Reed: Oh, yes, I think that's true. I think that's true. I look at the Haitians: they don't have anything and they get put down all the time and people call them "savages" and "cannibals" and all this sort of thing, and I see much idleness down there. And I think that we're dealing with people that have been really crushed psychically and every other way. It's going to be hard to put that back together. I think maybe that you can save some of them—a few. It has always been a tradition in my family to do something, to build something, and to begin something, and I think I probably got it from that. But I found that things are upside-down so that people who work are the ones who are despised. They get a great deal of criticism. They're called reactionary, you know, and all this. I'm not political. I am trying to build something, to publish people. The idea is that the more acceptable people are those who do a lot of talking about radical things, talk radically.

Conversations: It seems the more political you are—

Reed: Well, they like that; they like that. We did receive some grants. We received a few grants from the National Endowment, and the Coordinating Council of Literary Magazines. But the majority of the value and the assets is our labor, like working for nothing. Al Young and I have not been paid since 1971, since we started these projects. As a matter of fact, we had to put up our own money to bail the company out. This guy went out there and then the judge voted for them. The last hearing we had. . . . Well, we had agreed to issue people stock on the basis of the labor they did. Well, I had put out a big volume by myself single-handedly, *Yardbird Five*, and so I issued stock for this guy because we hadn't been paid in six months. They totally confused the judge, so he voted with them, these rascals. So we have got to take them to court for misconduct. Maybe he'll vote for that. I mean, he probably will take their side on this because we found the judicial system is as much against black enterprise as anybody else.

That's how Garvey went to jail, and that's how Booker T. Washington was almost killed by a white man in New York and the white guy was acquitted. They like bums—you go to court with some bums and they're going to go for them. There's another kind of justice and these bums know that. There is a more ancient justice and that is beyond the walls of these courts. I happen to believe that.

Conversations: You mean a spiritual justice.

Reed: Well, there's a justice that's very real. And I don't know if it's all that spiritual, but I think it's real. These people we're fighting with know that.

Conversations: Everybody gets their due in the end.

Reed: Oh, yeah, sure. I mean you look at the Egyptians. That is where we all come from, man. There's another kind of judgment and I don't care if we win in court or not, but I know that after all the work we've done—of course, with bums and hobos—that they're not going to get away with it.

Conversations: Do you think people who are involved in small press publishing are more concerned with the emotional, rather than the practical, aspects of what they call "the word"?

Reed: We're concerned with that, too. We've begun a coalition called Before Columbus, and we have worked for a year on a $5,000 budget. We had nineteen magazines—some of the people cooperated, some didn't, and some ripped us off. We sent them money to set up book fairs, and they didn't send us reports or anything. It was like a gravy train. So we hobble along. Now we're going to open up a warehouse and have a catalogue and a reading program—poetry. Everywhere—where we will send poets to the jails and to hospitals and to schools, if these institutions put up matching funds. We'll have readings around the West, and the first Alameda County High School Poetry Contest. I was the judge for the New York high school contest when I was a professor, and I thought we'd do it here.

You know, it's made up of Asian-Americans, Irish-Americans, Jewish-Americans, Afro-Americans—we all wrote for it. Not because it's some kind of brotherhood thing. It's very important that we all get together because all of our literatures are suppressed, I believe. And I believe that it is some of the best writing in this country. You know, the United States has a tradition of eclecticism. Like in Los Angeles you might get like a regency, ranch-style, gothic house. It happened to architecture; it happened to fashion; it happened to cuisine. We are not beating a drum saying that this is the best literature, because enough people are doing that. You know, you go around the country and everybody thinks that their own place is the center of American culture. We completely puzzle people, because they feel very left out and provincial—because they are. I mean, if you look at what goes for the standard of poetry in this country, like Ashbery, O'Hara, Brownstein, Lowell—all of them. They come from the same tradition, and the same images and similar allusions, and it's not mixed up enough.

We think there's a new art that is emerging, where it is going to be mixed up. It's going to get into writing, and music—well, music has always been that way. So I think that is what's happening to the kind of writing that you like and the kind of stuff that we support, because we believe that America has many cultures not just one. You know, it's not just one crop. So we have these genteel academic poets that still reign, whether it is the Black Mountain poets or the Lowell-style—they have gotten together now.

There was a typical *New York Times* article, you might even call it "the Aryan"—if we were in Germany you would call it "the Aryan editorial," where they say, "Well, what's happening is like in white males." It begins with the north beach people and the people in the academy got together. . . . Robert Lowell was reading at St. Mark's Church and they're all together. All the other groups are like women and blacks, and we are all in guerrillas out there, standing in line for food stamps, I guess, or something like that. I don't see it that way. I really don't see it that way, and, if I say that, I mean, you'd think that any normal person would say, "Well, that's true." We should have as many poets as we can—there are Latino poets all over the West, so many that you almost have to speak Spanish to get along out there.

We should include all that, but just because of some kind of paranoia—I don't know, John Wayne and that Alamo thing, you know, which applied to culture—they don't want to view it that way. They still have to go on and see themselves as a "super people," you know. I've been really trying to think of a polite way to describe this, and the only thing I could think of is Nazism—that's the only parallel in the West that I know, historical parallel, and probably in Africa and all this. Fascism— we have a fascist culture where fascism is not only in politics, but is in culture: you have one elite class, which seems to be the only gifted group,· and everybody else is subhuman or patronized. You know, this kind of thing. So I think if we see it that way—with no holds barred, just see it as Nazism—as a continuation of American Nazism, there's the problem.

I get in trouble because these are their gods. I get into very emotional arguments, and people say, "Well, you don't know what you're talking about." That's the whole trouble because—the stuff is so unreadable. Know what I mean? And it is shrouded so much with pseudo-academic terminology that it is very easy to be dismissed as a Philistine if you say, "Well, look, I can't read this stuff. I mean, this is bullshit!" You're not supposed to say that. So they have all these poor people intimidated, and they are followers. It's like a religion. It is threatening, because suppose it enters politics—which it could—and we have to deal with it in the streets. So I think the Before Columbus Organization is anti-Nazi. We are Nazi fighters and Nazi hunters in culture.

Like somebody says, for example, of the King Tut exhibit—they see a piece from 3000 years ago: "Is it art or is it archeology?" Or "200 Years of Black Painting" at the Brooklyn Museum, Hilton Kramer says, "Is it art or social documentary?" In other words, only white men can create art—a notion which I find white men don't even agree with. Why do they write these things as if there's some kind of agreement on this? I mean, it's foolish of them to believe that. But if we write letters, they say we are cranks. So the best thing for us to do is get our own organizations. We can influence whites as well as other people, because I see that we have whites with us, working with us. It would be foolish to, say, dismiss Ed Dorn or Shakespeare or Bertolt Brecht—I mean, that's the kind of position they put us in, in the sixties. Where, you know, we started imitating them saying, "Well, we can whip them!"—and all these super races were going around fighting each other.

So we're in a very sensible, rational position, and I can't understand why we're still getting resentment. We're still getting resentment from people who think we're getting away with murder or that we're spending the grant money. Some of the grant money we received—we get criticized for actually spending it for what it is supposed to be intended for: putting out magazines and books. You are not supposed to do that. You are supposed to rip it off and spend it on Ripple, or dope, or something. Then they will give you more—well, you know, they are trying bribes, bribes!

Conversations: It is the same thing as what Tom Wolfe called "Mau-Mauing the Flak Catchers."

Reed: Yes, I know. Well, they like that; they like that. But I never have indulged in that. Maybe when I was younger—I flirted with it when I was twenty-two or something like that—we were all militant. But I've always felt that an appeal to guilt was not a strategy that I wanted to be associated with, because I have felt guilt and it's a very terrible feeling. All of us have felt this: growing up in this culture you feel guilt, and it is an agonizing and depressing feeling. I wouldn't want to put that on anybody, and I think it should be abandoned as a strategy.

Conversations: What do you think would happen when what you are doing becomes acceptable?

Reed: Well, I think we will behave better. That's what I said before. I mean when we become the establishment, we will behave better.

Conversations: Better than the current establishment?

Reed: Oh, sure. It's like the philosopher-king. Remember the old longing for the philosopher-king? That one-man rule, or an establishment is okay, if they act right. So that's the only thing we could hope for—and I think we have been pretty fair. See, the problem is that we are going to start taking over some institutions. I see that already. They are worried that we are going to be as selfish and as narrow as they are—we're not. I'm the vice-chairman of the Coordinating Council of Literary Magazines, and I've always advocated that women be on the board, that women be in the clusters, but I get flack. I don't know—it's a crazy time, but I think it would be fair just, as I insist, to be fair—if we would just be fair. We may lose, but now we are gaining.

I think by the eighties it will be our time. I think I said in 1969 that the Afro-American establishment in the early seventies would be Afro-American, and that happened. All the people that were screaming in the 1960s were getting awards from the

President's daughter on television and all this—so it happened. Now the Asian-Americans have a very strong movement going on. Chicanos and the rest of the people—I just hope that we don't behave like the people who try to block us, and try to block them. Although there are blacks who are against that attitude. That was one of the big fights we had with the *Yardbird Reader*, which Al and I singlehandedly put out—obtained all the grant money, and went around and sold it. There were some of those very narrow people that didn't want other people to be included.

Conversations: How are the sales and the distribution?

Reed: Well, it has been terrible. I mean, we've done the best we could, but the person that we dismissed kept most of our inventory in his basement—he's still got it there and that's what we went to court for. He is a spiteful person, who hated writers—that's all. He really blew it. After I did *Yardbird Five*, he tried to prevent the magazine from coming out. And when that got around to the artistic community, of course, he lost allies. I mean, he just didn't know, because he's not a writer. So he has kept all the stuff—all the stuff, all the work that I contributed to, gave up vacations to put out—it's all in his basement. He and his cronies are trying to sell it as theirs—and these are blacks. These are blacks—they are not Simon Legree—they are black people doing this to us.

Conversations: It seems that no one, not just those in literature but in the other arts as well, can really bring things into focus. Now, I think this bothers most people.

Reed: I think the linear novel is finished. I find it boring now. I think if you'd write one of them for television and movies, in order to entertain, that's fine. But novels are going to have to do much more. As a matter of fact, I don't even think we're going to call them "novels" anymore—that is a term that is imposed upon us.

Conversations: What would you call it?

Reed: I would call mine "a work." I just find myself restless and anxious about the novel as it has been done: just page after page

Ishmael Reed

of this dry type—predictable—I mean, the formula, the scenery, the characterization, and everything. I just can't put a handle on it anymore. I don't know where my books are going, but I think they are going in other directions even more than ever before.

Conversations: Do you ever write for the stage?

Reed: I'm doing something for the stage right now. I don't know if it's going to happen—I've done two scripts already that I think are terrific. *Yellow Back*, I made that into a script, and I wrote a screenplay of *Pallbearers*. I spent about eight months on that. The people who were buying this said they thought it was too arty. So I mean, you know, well, okay—so that's that. But I'm doing something now with Carman Moore for the stage and I hope it works out, a new version of *The Beggar's Opera*. We've done the outline and worked on everything; now I think we can go ahead with the script. I think it's a lot of fun. I did one piece for the stage—*Flight to Canada*, the first chapter of that was adapted for the stage, but it never went off. It was supposed to be in an American series over in San Francisco. But they wanted to cut mine up—as a matter of fact, they cut it down to 300 words, after all the work I did, and wanted to use it to precede Amiri Baraka's play which is about Marxism. I just withdrew it.

Conversations: I asked about the stage because it seems to me that, at least in New York, the really first-rate things are to some extent, breakthroughs, such as Robert Wilson—

Reed: Yes, I know, *Einstein on the Beach*, and all that. My wife was doing that ten years ago; she was doing that kind of Dada stuff a long time ago.

Conversations: The sort of heavily choreographed theatre production—

Reed: More related to the theatre than dance, you know. She was doing that in 1965. She's in Japan right now, performing in four cities with a group over there called Carla Blank and Suzushi Hanayagi. I am influenced by her and she is influenced by my work. She's taught me a lot about motion and dance. I used this in my work, *Mumbo-Jumbo* especially. But I think I know what you are saying, and I like to write for the stage. The thing I'm

230

doing is not as avant-garde. I'm doing a stage play, and I have a lot of fun with it. It's based on John Gay. I really feel at home with John Gay's sensibility.

Conversations: Will it be an opera?

Reed: Well, yeah, it's going to be operalike. I'm very excited about it. I've been disappointed a lot, because, in the sixties, I was accused of being reactionary and everything, but I always wanted to go along with what was right. There were whites who wanted to buy my works and I wanted blacks to do them, because they had expressed interest in them—although nothing ever came of that: people backed out of deals and nothing was ever done. But now I'm going to be going ahead and giving it some more tries.

Conversations: Well, in a sense, don't you think you're a reactionary?

Reed: I don't think so. I think in the sense that I believe in history, tradition, and the fact that they mean something—I am reactionary. In a world where everybody thinks that history began yesterday, I am reactionary.

Conversations: You seem to have a really distinct historical point of view.

Reed: I think it's very important and it's helped me a lot. Sometimes when I felt alone, such as in this fight that I'm having now, I felt that my viewpoint was my own and I had nobody to talk to about it who had gone through this. And then, just as a blessing, I got this assignment from this magazine. There were some advantages to getting this assignment. I read about DuBois and Douglass and Booker T. Washington, and they had the same problems. So that is voodoo—that is necromancy, which is a big part of those, and that has helped me a lot. You know, voodoo says that the past is contemporary, in that you don't really have to relate to your contemporaries; you can relate to other contemporaries, let's put it that way. And if a person's book is around, you can communicate or evaluate the book, and reflect upon it. So that helped me out a lot.

I was really down when I went to Alaska and I heard that the judge—this idiot judge. I mean, you should have seen the courtroom. They were too chickenshit to show up. I was there. All the whites in the room, all the lawyers, they thought it was a big laugh—what these niggers were going through—they laughed, and they thought it was a joke. And the judge thought it was a real big joke. You know, that's our lives out there. Niggers trying to set up a corporation and—what did he say—he said I was trying to unilaterally issue stock—which I didn't—and that I was trying to have a power play. As a matter of fact, they felt that it was probably somebody making $100,000 a year—when that was the only way we were getting paid, with stock. So I just sat there watching it, and when I heard that they had won, I went up to Alaska very depressed. But I started reading Douglass and all these people, and they had the same problems. It is the same pattern. So when you know that, there's less anxiety. It's just something that is a pattern.

Maybe we can break the pattern. That is possible. If things could go the same for 100 years, 1000 years, and all of a sudden something happens: a Christian figure—which we're all interested in now—comes along, like Christ, or Lao-tzu, or some institution, or some force—which I was trying to get into *Mumbo-Jumbo*—comes along and offers a way out. So you don't have to go through this rut. I think we're in a rut; Afro-Americans are in a rut. If you look at history you find that it is cyclical. The white settlers give you a little, and then they take it away; then they give you a little. That is the way it has been. There is a possibility that some dynamic force will come along and change that. The world was going along for thousands of years when all of a sudden the glaciers started moving, and changed the world—it made the Great Lakes.

Something like that can happen, and I think we are approaching that: we are in a transition. Well, it is a cliche to say that we are in a transitional period—morality, values, ethics, and the state of the world. There's the possibility that something will change, and I think that something dynamic will happen here. So we're going to have to go through this over and over again.

Conversations: Right. Things seem to be in chaos and no one can stand it, but I think it is tremendously exciting.

Reed: Oh sure, I mean most generations are born and they die with the same values. But things are changing in the way the

232

novel is moving, for example, or the arts; we see that things are in flux, and that we're going into a new period. It might be a very good period.

Conversations: In your classes at Berkeley do you teach creative writing?

Reed: Well, I thought I'd teach creative writing, but then they had a tenure meeting and they said I couldn't write. So that really lowered morale up there. It was difficult to stand up before students and teach when your colleagues say you can't teach and you can't write. But I'm trying to show through works that writing for students is worthwhile. I do a lot of work off campus; some of the students work with me in my private enterprises. Like this kid came in this morning with his novel, and I am going to help him with it. I like the novel. I'm giving advice year round, because I'm not only up there to get along with the English department. But the way they came on against me—I still haven't recovered from that. It was really a bad two years. These things happen when people feel that they have to cover for themselves. They start lying and Watergate types of things happen. I just didn't press it, because I don't have time for a big black power rally every day with thousands of students at an Angela Davis meeting.

I don't think another black person in any department at the University of California is the issue. I think that American liberal arts is the issue. Are you going to train people—like Nixon—to be devoted to one culture, to one experience? Or is it going to open up, so people will be capable of living enriched lives by being exposed to many cultures? That is how you live a rich life.

Conversations: Well, it sounds like the culture of most English departments.

Reed: Yes, but they are not going to last. I think I will last longer than they will. I don't think that they are going to last.

Conversations: It isn't a force-out situation that you're in— where they deny you tenure, and you are forced out?

Reed: No.

Conversations: What kind of courses do you teach?

Ishmael Reed

Reed: I taught an American literature course there last quarter. I used some good books.

Conversations: Auden would only teach literature courses, because he said it was the historical distance that was important. Are creative writing courses destructive?

Reed: No, I don't think so; not for me, because I learn a lot by doing it.

Conversations: From the students?

Reed: Oh, sure, from the students. I can learn from them because they don't know what the rules are. They're not writing with like all of history over their shoulders, like others are. I'm not only teaching them writing but also about the trade. I teach a writing factory. We have actually been putting books out. You know, like the *National Student Anthology*. They raised $5 for every student and needed some more money, and the English department turned them down. They wanted $125 and the English department had a big meeting and said they couldn't give it to them. So, the students got a grant. They received more money, and now they have a magazine coming out. The people in the class raised the money and chose the editors.

Conversations: And they actually go through the physical production of the book?

Reed: Oh, sure. I have the galleys at home. It's going to be the first *Student Anthology* and what we are going to do is get material from writers who teach—there are writers all over the country who teach, and have manuscripts. This is going to be an annual. We are going to have the best student writings—

Conversations: Nationwide?

Reed: Yes, because students can write, and they are discriminated against. People want them shot at; they don't want them to write. They don't take their writing seriously. I do.

Conversations: When you walk into class the first day, what do you say?

Reed: I just tell them how I am going to run the class.

234

Conversations: How do you run it?

Reed: Workshop. We Xerox the stories, and we all comment on them and make notes in the margins.

Conversations: I assume you don't act as the arbiter over what is good and what is bad.

Reed: No, no. I don't think so. Nobody can do that. That is stupid.

Conversations: Since creative writing students are like everyone else, how do you keep them from knifing each other in the back?

Reed: Well, you don't. You just mediate in the class. My role is to keep things going. You keep peace in the classroom. We are pretty successful. I tell a joke or something to relieve things. It has been successful.

Conversations: With all of the things that you do, do you have input from the community?

Reed: What do you mean by community?

Conversations: Just the community of the Bay area.

Reed: Well, I don't know—

Conversations: Not necessarily the black community.

Reed: I get people calling me up asking me to publish their stuff. My office, which is a studio office, is in the black neighborhood while most of the people who criticize me live in apartments in white districts. I call them the "Afro-American elitist class." They like good wines and good clothes. They have their Gucci rucksacks and the latest styles. They sit back and just throw darts at people, and see themselves as revolutionaries, which is strange—I mean, because all they'd have to do is like take a photo of their lives and they'd see. But it's some kind of illusion. I don't know where it comes from. They will talk about the community and all that kind of scene—right now it's the black women. I don't socialize very much. That's how I get work done. I don't socialize very much, and I don't go out very much to parties, and all that.

Ishmael Reed

Conversations: But do people from the area come in and ask you how to write?

Reed: Oh, yes, sure. I go out and talk to people. I'll see people in the streets and I will say, "Gee, I've got this thing I'm working on. . . ." I saw a kid the other day and said, "I've got this thing I'm working on," he was a black kid, "it's about Jimi Hendrix. Do you recognize him?" He said, "No." So I told him to give me a call, and I had coffee with him one Sunday to talk to him. I do things like that.

We are sending poets into the community, and I'm working with high school kids on a radio show. We did our first radio show a few months ago and talked about film and music. The people that were listening said that it was the first time they thought that black teenagers had thoughts. It's always been just sociologists telling what they believe.

Conversations: The last poem in Chattanooga, *"Jacket Notes," begins: "Being a colored poet / Is like going over / Niagara Falls in a / Barrel / An 8 year old could do what / You do unaided. . . ."*

Reed: An eight-year-old went over there once and survived.

Conversations: So it's literal?

Reed: Yes. Also, the fact that children still have their imaginative quality intact. But mainly it's about that—about this kid going over and surviving.

Conversations: With contemporary poetry, a number of people seem to be locked into a particular set of ideologies. How can one create a bridge between one ideology and another?

Reed: I don't know. I'm becoming more and more non-ideological in that I believe work is an ideology; building things is an ideology. That is my ideology. But I write mostly out of the heart. A long time ago I used to write stuff that was academic: that was where I was coming from; I had just left the university. But now I write by ear and the heart. I'm not really interested in making a big fuss about some Italian glassmaker of the sixteenth century. My own time is becoming more and more interesting to me. I am influenced very much by African sculpture, and more and more of my form has come out of that nonwhite, non-

236

Western sculpture. I am also influenced by Western art. In the new book I'm writing I have a character named Michelangelo—that appeals to me. So, I think we have a lot going for us, because we know more than one culture.

I'm doing a magazine article on the poetry business for *Oui* magazine. I went to Boulder, Colorado, and interviewed Ron Sukenick and Michael Brownstein and some other good people. The high point for them, I think, was the 1920s when all those people were in Paris—the expatriate movement. I mean, we know about that; we went to school, and we know about Hemingway and Shakespeare & Company. I was in Paris in March and somebody asked, "Don't you want to go see Shakespeare & Company? Do you want to take a picture of that?" We have enough poses of that in the United States already—Pound, Eliot, and the whole legend. At the same time there are writers, there are black writers in the United States, like Langston Hughes, who might, in the end, have been more influential in the sense that they influenced Caribbean literature, African literature. You know, we not only know about Shakespeare & Company and the Pound movement, we also know about the Afro-American movement, the international movement, which gives us kind of like an edge, I think. That is becoming more and more apparent: the more cultures you move in and out of, the better the work you do. It really enriches your work.

When I wrote *Flight to Canada* I had an Alaskan Indian myth of the raven in mind, although you don't have to know that. And a hereditary chief read *Flight to Canada*, read some of my work, and sent for me. I went up to Alaska and went out to the totems, and he was there and they provided me with their crest—they rarely do that. The raven crest and all that, so, you know, that helped me out.

Conversations: Then is that the way this stagnation will resolve itself?

Reed: They ought to get out of New York. Writers, poets—all should travel around the country and see what's going on. It is best to get out of American culture. We are still dealing with people who see themselves as an extension of European civilization. It's a white settler idea, and I don't have to look at it that way. When Jimmy Carter said that England is the mother country and went over there taking pictures like a tourist, you know—I don't particularly see anyone as my mother country. I don't see Ghana as my mother country. I was born here. I was born in Chattanooga. This is what I have to use.

Just as transitions in European culture occurred when you had a number of writers working at one time, I think that's what's happening—happening here. Maybe it takes twenty years, not two centuries, to realize this. In twenty years, the way things are going, people will have forgotten the Fiction Collective and all the stuff you see in *The New York Times Book Review*, because they are completely out of contact. They don't know. I've tried to talk to Harvey Shapiro: "Why don't you get somebody to do something on the Chicano movement now?" But they only look at the same stuff over and over again in a very political, very much self-interested way, and it is not going to change. You are not going to make them change.

Ron Sukenick is starting something called *The American Book Review*, and I am one of the advisory editors. We'll just publish something for people who are not interested in just one thing and that we could get into. So things are going to change. I mean, they are changing already. As a matter of fact, I think the multicultural thing is the next wave. You had the black thing in the sixties, which was narrow and parochial. You had the white thing, counterculture: counterculture propaganda, counter-culture politics, counterculture machines. They had everything but the Houston plan—and they were so much like the people that they were combating. You know, we did a reading out at the poetry festival—a benefit for KPFA.

Conversations: When was that?

Reed: That was in May, in the stadium—4,000 people.

Conversations: Four thousand people came to a poetry festival?

Reed: That's right. And it was like Third World. See, if they come to Berkeley, they have to have Third World, you know: I was on there; David Henderson was on there; Simon Ortez was on there; Robert Bly; Allen Ginsberg; Janette Harris; Lewis

MacAdams; and Alison Dobson arranged the whole thing. But in the reviews it came off as counterculture—they emphasized the counterculture poets, Allen Ginsberg and Robert Bly, and made it seem as if we weren't even there. So you are going to have to have new critics and multicultural critics, who can see everything and don't have blind spots. But it happens all the time between whites and blacks, and I'm putting this in my book about the race war and communications.

I had an experience the other day where a feminist woman told me to shut up about six times. I said it really made me discouraged to hear her say that, and the other feminists in the room said that they didn't want to hear it. See, I would never pay any attention to these things, but I'm trying to really get into the psychology of this stuff—of racism—because I think that it probably impairs your sense of perception. You know what I mean? Some kind of wound like this, some kind of blind spot like that—that is what I'm saying in my class. On the final day of class they said, "Well, do you want to talk about race now?" I said, "Well, I think that's a problem for a psychologist now, at this point." And, see, like when I went into a store the other day and I asked this guy, "Is this line closed?"—the shopping line—he said, "Yes." When I moved away, he said, "Where are you going?" I said, "You said the thing was closed." He said, "No, I said it was open." And the woman next to me there said, "No, he said it was closed." This happens every day in everyday life. There are blind spots. Blacks and whites calling each other paranoid because they don't see with the right vision.

I'm getting more and more into this. The whites saw Elvis Presley as a great hero. *Jet*, the black magazine, came out and said they remembered the remark he made about the only thing niggers could do for him was shine his shoes and buy his records. So we have different heroes; we have different humor. So I really think that, ultimately, the multicultural thing might improve the American perception of things, because there are blind spots where people can't see. And I'm sure this damages sensory equipment—it probably affects other areas. If you have got this perception of race, you can't hear and you can't see and your information is blocked off. This is a problem for psychologists and, maybe, it has spilled over into other areas of perception.

239

Ishmael Reed

Conversations: It seems like The New York Times *seldom praises anything that is different, or don't you find that to be true?*

Reed: Well, when John Leonard ran it, it was different. I think he's a little more open, but now they've got him doing things like shooting Berkeley. *The New York Times* has to stomp on California twice a year. The last words of *The New York Times* talked about Al Young and all the problems we were having, saying that we weren't getting over with our publishing concern. The powerful *New York Times* against us, man. We're nothing; we don't have any money; we can barely make the rent every month. We're doing all right, but them saying that will mess us up with our creditors. They recently got John Leonard to go and talk about the people in Berkeley not being smart or something like that. That's not true. I mean, there are independent presses here; there's literature here; people are writing. Where else could you get 4,000 people to a poetry reading? He didn't say anything about that. He talked about people not reading Nabokov. And I said, "Why is he wasting his talents doing that?" If there's nothing going on here, why do they have to spend so much time knocking it twice a year?

I went to see a Woody Allen movie—you can't escape it— and a character says, "The only cultural advantage of California is that you can turn right on a red light." I just did a 350-page book of poetry. I was awarded a grant from the California Arts Council and I've been spending the money on getting the book out— although all these people who read Nabokov think, when they get the smell of grant money: "Bums. They take grant money and spend it on themselves." You know, I've been working under a rush trying to get the thing out, but in the course of it I've covered 200 years of multicultural poetry. I've got Afro-American and European-American advisory editors and all these people, and I have found that there is an interesting tradition—a good book. So I can't understand why. . . . I don't feel that that's the only cultural advantage. The ice cream parlor shaped like an ice cream cone, that's not the only thing out here; people lining up for movie stars at the Chinese Theatre are stupid. I think the public is going to start demanding this, and we're going to do something about it with Before Columbus.

Powerful media, which say that blacks can't write and Chicanos can't write, fill up hour after hour with British television on the taxpayers' money and bring the Russian ballet over here on the taxpayers' money. They are going to have to start looking around here. I talked to a woman I know named Karen Bacon, who arranged this festival. She knows more about it than I do. She goes all over the country looking at the festivals that Americans arrange. It's something else. That's what I try to do in my enterprises. We are here and we should talk about building our own civilization. I mean, people who are dependent on other cultures grow lazy and lose something. I believe that.

Conversations: It seems like the grant-making agencies and other organizations have a tendency to support anything that is not American.

Reed: Yeah, well, some do; some don't. I think the government's policy on small presses. . .

Conversations: I was thinking of NEH.

Reed: Yeah. The National Literature Panel, for example, their policy on small presses is pretty good. It's not the best, but they are supporting a lot of magazines which would not ordinarily work, small presses which are necessary. These outfits are usually run by writers. They know what they're doing. I talked to the publisher of one of my books, and the art designer wanted to know what to put on the jacket before they went to press. I said, "Did it occur to you to read the book?" Well, the people who do our covers read the books. They actually read them.

Conversations: Did you write the biographical comments on the jackets of your books?

Reed: I do that, and I design the covers. I designed the cover for *Mumbo-Jumbo* and influenced the design for the cover on *Louisiana Red*. I did the cover on *Chattanooga*; I designed that one. And I write the jacket notes, and get something tantamount to editorial control on this, because I have a good lawyer and the clause where it says it has to be satisfactory to them was struck out. That can be done.

Ishmael Reed

Conversations: Do you deal through an agent?

Reed: I have a lawyer. He gets insulted when I call him an agent. He comes from the old English tradition of law practice. But he deals with publishers.

Conversations: Big commercial publishers really don't seem too interested in publishing fiction, or poetry and drama—

Reed: Yes, they want the blockbuster.

Conversations: Is there any possibility for small press people to bring out books in hardcover and for major publishers to do them in paperback?

Reed: Well, that might happen—I don't know. I haven't been too successful. I'd send books to them. We brought out our first in hardcover with the book we did last week.

Conversations: Oh, you usually bring them out as paperbacks?

Reed: Yes, but we are going to start bringing them out in hardcovers. I don't know, for some people it works; some people it doesn't. We did a book called *Changing All These Changes*. I met Jim Girard in Lawrence, Kansas, when I was out there doing an artist-in-residency. I read his manuscript and it was a good novel. I wished I could help, but, you know, who could publish a sixty-page novel and call it a novel? I understand that the first English manuscript novel was seventy-eight pages long. So I sent it to an agent, who sat on it for a year, and I got a call from Jim in 1975, saying that he had not found anybody to publish it. I said that I would raise money to publish it. So I went in with the wrong guy, and last week the book came out and I designed the cover. A big publisher is interested in that now.

First of all, we are competing with them and they don't want to give us revenue. They are not going to support their own demise, although we are doing them a favor. Doubleday published a fantastic book by Calvin Hernton called *Scarecrow* and we bought 300 copies of that. You know, I think that we can move books like that better than they can. I'm not against big publishers; I'm against conglomerates. I do believe that things are better when things are handmade or when things are a little slower. I tried to say that in the article, but the magazine didn't go for that. You know, the idea of all those people standing on the corner waiting for their welfare checks—I can use those people. I've seen these people in *Time* magazine and they seem to have a bum every week on there: some blacks hanging around, laying on the sidewalk. I can use those people; I can use twenty-five of those people right now. That's what I think, and this is a very unpopular view among Afro-Americans and whites.

The Afro-Americans' intellectual class is a Buddhist class, which is not the way that people should participate in the real world. They work at universities, and they have cultural occupations which afford them leisure, sabbaticals, and all that sort of thing. But for the rest of us, they don't believe that we should be in the real world. Then we have the white banks and banking policy. They don't want to give us any money because niggers are not good in business. You're caught between these two different things. So my argument—a very lonely argument—is: instead of Jesse Jackson and these civil rights leaders going to ask the government for thirty billion dollars, or Vernon Jordan asking to give General Motors and these conglomerates money, with the hopes that maybe—just possibly—they will give some blacks jobs, they should directly fund young black people who are interested in unboarding those stores in the ghetto and starting up. They could do it. It's absurd to say they could not do it. With three million people unemployed there are ways, but we are tied to old industries: B1-Bombers and these ludicrous building trades. Look what building trades have done to this country.

The people I'm talking to are the minority now, but it's going to change. And a lot of the young people are coming around to our point of view—even though we are considered rascals and outlaws and all kinds of terrible things have been said about us. But I believe that's what can happen. It's just ridiculous. No culture, no people can survive with all that lawless idleness: all these people standing on the corner when they could be doing something. So I said, "Why don't we try to go back to the pre-Industrial period when people made things, like the beautiful things that you see in the museums?" Things that one person made all the way through—there are no markets for that. They don't want that, and you can't say it. I'm against these big conglomerates because: they are stupid; they are dinosaurs without imagination; and they are selling us crap in books and movies and everything else.

But I can understand. I'm not in a quarrel with Random House. Those people started their company, and they published me, and they can publish what they want. I have no way of influencing their list, and Doubleday is the same way. So it is not people on the outside. I'm handling this the same way I handled my tenure case: not somebody on the outside knocking to get in, and they get in there and then the same old cycle begins again; we're building on other institutions. It's not the university, but I think by fall we will have our own school. Before Columbus will have its own school. Booker T. Washington built his own school and he was a slave. Why can't we? He got money from philanthropists, but the basic building and all was built by students and Washington. Then he comes down through history as being an "Uncle Tom," because he did something. And the people who were just talking against him come out as heroes—it's crazy.

Conversations: It is safer to have people that don't do anything.

Reed: Right. So Washington told them that a person having something in his stomach and having some chickens is just as important as having two tickets to the opera. People couldn't stand that because they would then be able to say, "Well, I'm just as good as you. I know about Verdi. I know about the Italian opera. Why don't you accept me? You see me wearing a suit!"—ah, hell, it's ridiculous.

Conversations: Do you think President Carter has got the right idea?

Reed: I don't think so. I don't think any president has got the right idea. Politics might have meant something a long time ago, but now we have ceremonial heads all over the world. Sometimes they wear khakis and smoke cigars, and sometimes they wear business suits. But they are still representing big interests, multinational interests, which are beyond government and beyond ideologies. You hear these kids trying to get corporations to change their minds about South Africa, and

244

some corporate spokesman says something like, "Well, we have to go along with the customs and the traditions of a different country." So if they were in the Soviet Union, they would go along with that. You know, the people who represent Boeing aircraft in the Soviet Union or another large corporation would come up with some Lenin buttons. I mean that is what we are up against. This country is very lucky because they have the blacks to use as scapegoats and as a buffer.

Conversations: Well, the blacks and all the rest of the minorities.

Reed: They say, "Look at these people! Niggers standing on the corner taking lamps off the stores." Then the whites say, "Well, isn't that awful." And so every white person thinks that his basement is a true first floor, that there is somebody underneath him. So that's what I mean, it's ridiculous. And Jimmy Carter saying that he's the last hope of blacks; blacks are his last hope. That's what I was trying to say in this article: Blacks are his last hope, because they wanted a revolution a long time ago in this country. I think blacks were the idealists but the whites wanted scapegoats. I mean, just like the average white person—millions and millions of them are starving. See, they say that the blacks and Hispanics looted New York because of their suppressed rage and a lack of economic opportunity, which happens to be true. But up in the Bronx the whites were looting; I have pictures of white looters. The blacks are used to diminish the widespread discontent in this country. They say, "The only people bitching are niggers. Ain't you sick of them bitching all the time?"

Conversations: Some groups are moving back to small businesses which are almost feudal-like—

Reed: Yes, right.

Conversations: Yet the things we hear about in the news are moving us toward a situation that is controlled by international corporations.

Reed: Oh, sure, I think ultimately. . . . I read this book called *Contours of American History,* and they talk about the Taft administration as being the last time that it could have been stopped. When you hear about Taft, it's that he was a fat guy and stupid, but he was trying to stop this. That ultimately a few people on a board are going to run this country is possible as these things get larger and larger, and people get swallowed up. That might happen to the world. We might have one board running the world, a corporate board. That is dangerous, really dangerous, because they don't have imagination. They do not have the input of other cultures in the society, like poets and artists and other people, intellectuals. It's just profits. That is the problem, and I call it a "New Feudalism" in *Flight to Canada*. They use the rest of us as slaves. We are their slaves.

Conversations: It seems like the seeds for the destruction of this international corporate control are already extant.

Reed: I think it could change. I really do. I really think it could change.

Conversations: Do you think it will change by violence?

Reed: I don't know how it is going to change, but it might change through an interdynastic fight. That's what happened with this government. Everybody thought that the big changes that would happen would be through a revolution in the 1960s. Can you imagine Tom Hayden and the Cleaver people running the government? I mean, it's ridiculous. I think I'd prefer Nixon. And then what happened was an interdynastic fight—a very complex interdynastic thing: the Kennedys versus Nixon; the old grievances and Watergate—that's what happened. The people were for Nixon—you remember those polls—they were all the way through. He had 70%, 60%, you know, a great deal of support. But it was Congress that got him.

I told a friend of mine when the Watergate thing happened—I'd been following Nixon all my life—that that was it; he had to be behind it. And the night that the break-in happened, I said it was all over for them. But they got him—I mean Kennedy and the liberal establishment. They are going to be going back and forth. The next thing there is going to be a big fight. . . . The liberal establishment is going to be under attack. It is going to go back and forth that way for a while. They're going to get them on Korea. You know, that's what's happening. Watergate did more to change things in the sixties and early seventies than anything in the streets did. So it might happen like that, where you get some big benevolent corporation that will fight some of these others. Something like that is going to happen.

Conversations: Where they just beat themselves to death.

Reed: Yes, beat themselves, and then you have the ants taking over—like us, you know. We'll take over or something—I don't know. I am optimistic, because it is very easy to be the other way. You don't have to do anything, just let things go to hell.

Conversations: You know, as soon as everyone says something then you can assume that it's not going to happen.

Reed: That's the American tradition. We've got the same thing happening now we had in the 1960s—the great awakening—very similar to what's happening now. I think that we are going to get a syncretic religion like they have in the rest of the hemisphere. That Christianity is not going to happen; this is the last gasp and it's going to be all mixed up with Buddhism and African ideas. Some kind of new spiritual form is emerging.

Conversations: Aren't there problems with that though, when people start relying—

Reed: Well, not relying, but I think that man has spirit and it has to be exercised. That doesn't mean you rely on it; I don't rely on these things. I think they are very interesting. I think there are things we don't know that we will soon know, probably in our lifetime. We know now things we dismissed twenty years ago. Now we find they are commonplace.

Conversations: In general, what do you think is the role of a writer or an artist?

Reed: I don't know. I've thought about that a lot and I still haven't figured it out. I like to write; I know that. And I like for people to read my work. I like to feel that I tell the truth.

Conversations: You seem to be very interested in undermining people's illusions, whether it's through satire or just straight-out.

Reed: Yes. It is always necessary to have somebody to say, "This is stupid. What are you doing?" That's part of my nature. I didn't sit down and say, "Well, I'll be this kind of writer since everything is ridiculous"—I mean, it's just me. Maybe I've been too lighthearted in life or something like that. I'm in the classical Afro-American tradition, the pre-1940s tradition, before we got all these existentialist and Marxist critics on our asses. When these people say I am incoherent; I don't know what I'm talking about; I should write a novel about somebody brooding over Camus's *The Stranger*, I say, "Well, you know, I've got my own tradition. That's your stuff." I like Camus and Sartre. You know, their work is okay; I've read that stuff. But I don't like cultural imperialism where somebody is trying to pull this on me. So that's the big fight we have right now.

We're all having this fight with that last big machine that can control our culture, attempting to keep their people in power. They bring Baldwin back here. He's got a new book out, you know, bringing him back here—just like when Douglass decided to start his own newspaper, they brought William Wells Brown in from Europe: "Come home," you know, "we need somebody to run this stuff." I would hate to be in a role like that—I like his writing and everything, but Baldwin and a few others, I think, are used as spokesmen by the same historical establishment. Why can't they leave us alone? They can't leave us alone—they called me names. Irving Howe calls me names. I read his new book, *World of Our Fathers*. I liked the book—a lot of typos in there, misspellings, but it's okay. Why can't they just be cool? They can't.

Conversations: What do you think of literary criticism?

Reed: Some of it is okay. You know, if somebody jumps all over me and goes crazy, I resent that. But I don't deal with that anymore.

Conversations: You read your reviews?

Reed: I think earlier, when you're a kid and you start off . . . everybody starts fighting for liberal attention: I want to be The One. But when you start controlling the means of production, I don't care about those things anymore. They can have their tokens. They've got their tokens lined up. You know it is always going to be one guy or two guys, and they are going to have to say, "Well, this is *the* guy." And they've got their counterculture tokens, establishment tokens, *Village Voice* tokens—there are even *Playboy* tokens.

Conversations: It's more of a whipping boy. Whenever they need to bring somebody out, there he is.

Reed: Yes, right. It is usually somebody messing up or cutting up, in trouble because he is raising a ruckus.

Conversations: Aside from what you are involved in, do you think there is any definable movement in the arts?

Reed: I don't think so, not anymore.

Conversations: It's more splintered?

Reed: Yes.

Conversations: It is not Pound or Eliot.

Reed: No, no, that's old. Camelot has fallen.

Conversations: But there is no equivalent?

Reed: No. The press is trying to make Boulder, Colorado into the place, but that's not going to work. It is not one place anymore.

Conversations: Do you think the thing is now regional literature and regional publishing?

Reed: Individuals and families and different kinds of groupings which are regional and ethnic.

Conversations: Is the problem that there is really very little communication between writers?

Reed: Well, that is because we don't have any intelligent national book review.

Conversations: I mean just conversation.

Reed: Oh, sure. I think there's a lot of back and forth stuff going on. Like I'm in contact with the Boulder group, although I don't particularly admire their style. And they're in contact with the Third World and multicultural groups. And the poets are all in contact with each other. Although the novelists . . . I think the novelists are pretty much isolated. You know, novelists are not very gregarious. It is just one guy with a typewriter. Poets have readings and they get together—they have a community. Poets have more of a community than novelists. Novelists I know talk about money—if they're drinking, they talk about money and irritating the hell out of their families.

Conversations: Why don't poets buy other poets' books?

Reed: They do; they do. Oh, sure. I think the really serious poets are people who are elite craftsmen and professional poets, and they read other poets.

Conversations: There are all kinds of stories about magazines receiving 2,000 poems a month that are submitted for publication.

Reed: But there are about 500, 600 magazines and about 25,000 little magazines. I read stuff that comes across my desk from the mail, and it's a lot of poetry. There is probably more poetry being written now than ever before in the history of this country. It almost seems as if everybody is writing it and a lot of it is very good. But we have no mediators to bring this to the reader, because the book reviews haven't done their job. All the places that you could go to, except for reviews of the small presses— you can go to places like that—but all the places you read for information do not give it. From *The Saturday Review of Literature. . . .* You're not going to get it in *Publishers Weekly.* You're not going to get that much from *Library Journal*—maybe a column once in awhile. They have really failed. The place where you want to go to find out what's going on would take a huge book every month, or a periodical, to tell what's going on—it is that rich.

Conversations: But everyone assumes that if you publish a book of poems, you can expect to be wiped out.

Reed: Yes, well, publishers don't promote them now. In fact, they don't know how to sell them, and the booksellers don't want to carry them. There has to be a new means for distribution. That's what Before Columbus is all about.

Conversations: What sort of new means do you have in mind?

Reed: We're going to set up our own warehouse. We're going to actually go into the distribution business.

Conversations: How are you going to get the books from the warehouse to the reader?

Reed: Well, we're going to have to work on it, and we've got some ideas about that. One of the ideas is sending professional writers out as salesmen. We'll see how that works.

Conversations: To bookstores?

Reed: That's right, everywhere—schools, all over the place. I think that distribution is the number one political problem. I think that if people have more information, they act better. It seems obvious, but, I don't know, it's hard to convince people of that. If you didn't put all that crap on television. . . . Television is really where the movies were in the thirties. It's like a whorehouse, man, where you jack off or something. Art movies, that's where they're at now, but the creative people are going to change that; cable television is going to change that. Just like the underground newspaper changed the establishment press. Half the people who write the editorial page in *The New York Times* worked on the *East Village Other*. You know, like those graphics in there by Mary Wagner and people like that, they are all from the underground. Closed-cable television will change that. And so that will all change, even though they have tremendous influence over the psychology of the United States. TV's directing us; it's bad candy; it's slop—and you're going to react that way. People are going to behave like that.

If you give people alternatives, maybe, they will behave better; or else, you can just say that man is born in sin and leave it at that, and only a few of us is going to get out of there. I hope I'm on the bus, you know; I want to get out of all of it. But I don't happen to believe that we are born wretched. I think we can change. I have seen a lot of people change. I have seen societies change in my lifetime.

Conversations: Which are the best literary magazines, the best literary presses?

Reed: I don't know. I don't know about all those things. It's difficult to say at this point, but I think, maybe, in five years they all won't be there.

Conversations: You mean the bad ones will drop out?

Reed: Yes, of course. They have to drop out. Nobody is going to be able to read that anymore. There's a hunger for something that's not from the establishment. Like with the Fiction Collective, like what we are doing. I like a lot of Blue Wind Press and Turtle Island press and Black Sparrow, you know, and some of the black presses, like Broadside. Broadside did a great job. I read like a whole bunch of things. I like to get the whole picture, but a lot of people don't have that much time. Usually people have to go to work from nine to five. But, I mean, I am in the business, and publishing books gives me a lot of opportunity to look at this stuff. I can't think of any one place, but I think *The American Book Review* is probably going to have a lot of—

Conversations: When is that going to start?

Reed: The first issue should be out in October. That might be something.

Conversations: Is it being published in Berkeley?

Reed: New York. See, I read more than anything else. My house is full of magazines and newspapers. I treat them as seriously as I treat books, because all the information is in there. I like to have Andy Warhol's *Interview* in there—I buy that every once in awhile. I buy *Time*, and I buy *Newsweek*, and *The Rolling Stone*, and *Jet* magazine. I read the *Chronicle*, and I read *The New York Times* every day. I just read a lot of stuff, a lot of different stuff, a lot of periodicals. And every once in awhile I'll get a novel. I bought *Public Burning*, Robert Coover's book.

Conversations: What did you think of it?

Reed: Well, they put us together in *The Times*. They said, "Reed, Doctorow, and Coover." I have to get through it. I haven't read all of it. I met Coover in Paris and liked him very much. I bought Sara Davidson's book, *Loose Change*, which I thought was interesting sociology. And Kate Millett's book, *Sita*, which I thought was a very brilliant and a very excellent book.

Conversations: That was one book The New York Times *damned. The first sentence was, "This is an awful book."*

Reed: Well, that's just patriarchal—they are just showing their patriarchal bent. We all have it. The culture made us that way. It's hard to get rid of it, you know. You can't flirt with women anymore. They can get uptight. It's just difficult to say things— you don't even know what to say to them anymore. So all of us are going through this and I think *The Times* just reflects it. They don't want a woman . . . they figure a woman writer is a whore, like in the nineteenth century. All those people have trouble because you're considered, you know, trash if you write novels, and some of those ideas are still around.

Conversations: Tell me about The American Book Review.

Reed: Well, I think Sukenick could tell it better, but it came out of conversations that he and I had about the need for a new national book review. And I was going to go in with him, but I had all this other stuff. I couldn't possibly get into it. But he went on and did it. They raised money. It's his magazine, and he's going to call it *The American Book Review*. It's going to represent all the cultures, instead of just one.

Conversations: Will you write for it?

Reed: Oh, yes. I've got an article coming out in the first issue on Richard Wright.

Conversations: I assume it will concentrate on books that aren't going to be reviewed in the major periodicals.

Reed: Oh, sure. Which is easy. They want the blockbusters now. They review the blockbusters, and the bookstores go along like sheep. All of them have the same thing in the windows. In the East Village, West Village, and Uptown, they have the same books in the window. They feature the same books. But I think change is in the air. I think we will have some decent things to look at in a few years.

Conversations: What is the potential for new writers? It's obviously not in the universities.

Ishmael Reed

Reed: I think it's on the streets and in the enclaves around the country, different writers surrounding literary magazines and newspapers. That's what it's going to be.

Conversations: Working in conventional jobs.

Reed: Yes. I really think eventually we will take our operation out of the university. I mean, they're not going to let us in there, if they aren't even going to give us a department, which would be a gradual thing until we get a budget. We're probably going to have to take it out on the streets and take it to warehouses or some place, and start a new school. Let them be just a front for things like the neutron bomb.

William Styron was born in Newport News, Virginia, on 11 June 1925. He graduated from Duke University in 1947 after serving in the Marines during World War II. His first novel, Lie Down in Darkness *(1951), received the American Academy of Arts and Letters Prix de Rome. After publication of* The Long March *(1952) and* Set This House on Fire *(1960), Styron was widely considered to be among the most gifted contemporary writers. His position was officially acknowledged in 1968 when he was awarded the Pulitzer Prize for* The Confessions of Nat Turner, *published the previous year. Styron is presently in the last stages of revising his new novel.*

William Styron

In April 1977 John Baker visited William Styron for this interview at the author's house in Roxbury, Connecticut, where he has lived for over twenty years. The Styrons live in a large, yellow house on a wooded hillside, facing a quiet country road, nearly two hours from New York by car. There is a large guest house on the grounds where Styron does his writing and frequently puts up fellow writers.

Conversations: Can you remember the first time you felt you wanted to be a writer? Is it something that you've wanted to be ever since you were a small boy, or did it come to you later?

Styron: I think it stole up on me. In a curious way, I think I always was fascinated by the printed word. I remember I was brought up in a family which, like a lot of Southern families, treasured the written word. There was a great deal of reading in the house.

Conversations: Were stories told to you as a child?

Styron: Yes. It was, generally speaking, a Southern environment, where storytelling is valued anyway. There was an enormous amount of reading. My mother was quite ill most of her life that I remember and was bedridden, and she read incessantly. I remember one of my chores as a little kid was to go to the lending library—this, of course, was in the thirties—and pick up books. They weren't just your ordinary best sellers; she cared what she read. I think that's how I got started. I was quite simply awed by the idea of the writing in books.

Conversations: Do you remember any of the things that you read at that time as a child? Do they linger in your mind?

Styron: Yeah, some of them—a whole lot of them, really. They were the standard children's books. The Christopher Robin books, of course—I'm starting with the early ones—and the Oz

books enchanted me. I had the—I guess you'd call it privilege—
of reading the Oz books, which had been dedicated to one of my
classmates who was the nephew of L. Frank Baum, the author. So
all of these Oz books were dedicated to "My Nephew Bobby." I
always got a big thrill out of that. Then as I got older I read, of
course, *Tom Sawyer* and *Huckleberry Finn*. I remember reading
kind of an abridged version of *Moby-Dick*, one that was made
for kids, quite early on. Then I read the whole thing when I was
about eleven or twelve, I think.

*Conversations: Did you grasp any of the metaphysical range of
the book at that time? Or did you just read it for the story?*

Styron: No. I read it for the whaling part, mainly, and I think,
perhaps, I skipped around the other parts. But nonetheless, it
was a very exciting sort of thing to do at that time. Then there was
a big gap in my adolescence where I didn't read a whole lot.
Because I was in prep school, I sort of disdained reading as a
chore. But when I got into college, when I was about seventeen,
again this whole idea of books swept over me. I began then—I
suppose you'd call it a standard older reading. By this time I was
beginning to read, well, everything you can name from Thomas
Wolfe to—I'm talking about contemporary—Fitzgerald, Hemingway. And then I began immersing myself, in college, in just about
everything that I could lay my hands on. I was getting into
Faulkner in college. Of course, by this time I was majoring in
literature and reading the curriculum: I was reading Chaucer,
Elizabethan poets, and so on.

Conversations: Did your curriculum go as far as Joyce?

Styron: I was reading a great deal of—I suppose you'd call it
clandestine stuff by this time. Joyce would have been not strictly
clandestine. He was not on the reading list, though he was in the
library, so you read him because someone said you must read
Joyce. As I recollect, he was not taught in the forties. And at that
time you found your Henry Miller in a clandestine way. And, of
course, Miller was considered pornographic, so you really had to
get him "under the shelf," so to speak. Fortunately, I was at that
time at Duke University, which has a remarkably good library,
and so I was just reading voraciously anyone you can name, quite

without any direction. But I'm rather glad I read that way—sort of indiscriminately.

Conversations: Were you swept off your feet by Thomas Wolfe at the time, as a lot of young men were?

Styron: Certainly. I was just absolutely bowled over by Wolfe. In fact, he was almost my Vergil in a sense. Without Wolfe. . . . I can't conceive of any other, almost. He was an absolutely overwhelming experience, which I've described, actually, in a couple of essays. And again, alas, you have to make that final judgment: He no longer does the same thing to you as an adult, but he's almost a perfect writer for an adolescent.

Conversations: At this point you went off into the Marines. Was your college career actually interrupted, or did you graduate and then go in?

Styron: Well, it was interrupted. It was a very complicated education because I was at a little college in North Carolina called Davidson, a little Presbyterian school—a rather good school. But it was right in the middle of the war, and I was yanked away from Davidson. I joined something called the Marine V-12 program, which was the U.S. Marine Corps college program in which you were sent to a university to sort of mature—getting an education while reaching the age to become a Marine officer. The academic side figured rather prominently in the whole deal, so that you were getting what passed for a standard education at the same time you were learning to be a Marine. As a result, I did not have, by any means, a normal educational process. It was splintered. But nonetheless, maybe because of the pressure or the fact that war was very close, I think I felt a kind of urgency about reading and considering the possibility, maybe, of becoming a writer.

Conversations: Now was The Long March *born at a time when you were actually in the Marines?*

Styron: Yes, it came later, because one of the major traumas of my life was to have been called back into the Marine Corps only five or six years after having served in one war. That was for the

William Styron

Korean War, of course. I was called back, and that experience there more or less gave birth to *The Long March.*

Conversations: I've always assumed that The Long March *was the first thing that you actually wrote, although it was your second published novel.*

Styron: No, *Lie Down in Darkness* was the first that I really claim. *The Long March* came very rapidly after that, only a year or so after.

Conversations: I seem to remember it was printed originally as a story in a magazine, a long story, and then printed in book form as a sort of novelette.

Styron: That's right. *The Long March* came out in a little semi-experimental journal called *Discovery,* which Pocket Books published, and then, of course, it more or less gained a life of its own because people began to read it and liked it. So Random House brought it out in their paperback series.

Conversations: How long had Lie Down in Darkness *been in gestation? Had you been pondering it for a long time before you actually started to write it, or did it accumulate over a long time?*

Styron: Well, it caused me a lot of trouble. It's one of those vainglorious things, really: I was determined to have a book out by the time I was twenty-five, I think. It was really one of those very youthful ambitions that had to do with getting the book out while I was young. Very vain, as I said, but I wanted it to be of some quality. It was agony putting it together because I was under so many influences—Faulkner, Hemingway, Fitzgerald— and I was trying desperately to find a voice of my own. I went through a lot of anguish, really, putting it together. The first chapter I wrote, I remember, was in the winter of 1947. I was only, I think, twenty-two years old, something like that. I realized then that it was pretty good, but I didn't know where to go from there.

Conversations: How did you begin? What was the first chapter you wrote?

Styron: My main influence at the time was Faulkner, and certainly, as Malcolm Cowley pointed out, my book was influenced by such books as *The Sound and the Fury* and *As I Lay Dying*. I just conceived the idea of writing about a girl I had once known; really it was three girls—a combination of certain girls I have known, one or two who had come to sticky ends, really. One had committed suicide. It was quite a trauma to me; although I didn't know her very well, I had grown up with her. It seemed to me a very dramatic way to tell a story: to begin with a funeral of the girl coming down from New York, and then, through an interlocking series of flashbacks, trying to use her as the sort of vantage point to examine a middle-class life in Virginia of a certain period, a certain time; to see her through other people's eyes, her parents' eyes; in a sense, to get a kind of vision of a way of life in the society.

Conversations: But it was she who came first, rather than Milton and Helen, her parents.

Styron: Yes. I realized that I would be making an awful mistake if I merely stuck with her—it would be your standard youthful outpouring, you know. I had to sort of withdraw myself in order, I realized, to give the story some functional validity. I realize now, in the end, that a lot of what I was writing I was not aware of. A lot of people now describe the book, because it's still very much around, as a kind of novel of alienation. There's a book called *The Fifties* in which the authors use *Lie Down in Darkness* as a kind of touchstone for the fifties, saying that it was the classical example of the literature of alienation. Whether this is true or not, I don't know. But I was unconscious of that aspect. I really was writing about the total disaffection of human beings, I think, in certain circumstances. In this case, about this girl who was violently at odds with her family and with society.

Conversations: Was the fact that she went to New York an essential element? Was this basically the notion of contemporary culture corrupting somebody from a more ancient culture?

Styron: I think so, yes. Because even then, I think to a degree it does not at the moment have, the South—any place south of the Mason-Dixon Line—did have a kind of sense of identity of itself. It was considered a little outrageous if youthful members of society went north, especially to New York, and embarked on the hairy life of the Bohemian, which Peyton did. Now, of course, everybody is having that life in Atlanta.

Conversations: At what stage did you decide on Peyton's long stream-of-consciousness towards the end?

Styron: I had that in mind throughout the whole book. I realized that I had a kind of strategy, which, I think, helps make the book as effective as it is: nowhere in the early part of the book do you go into her mind at all. She is seen from every point of view; she's seen from her mother's point of view, her father's point of view, her father's mistress's point of view, the whole thing. I think I was gambling on the idea that unconsciously this would create a certain curiosity, a certain tension, so that at the very end to suddenly plunge totally into her consciousness would have some sort of effect. And I think probably it did. I think it's probably because I did keep my distance from her during all that time.

Conversations: It's also been said that landscape, weather, the physical surroundings of people are enormously important to you. I think that somebody has said that in Lie Down in Darkness *particularly, and to a lesser extent in* The Confessions of Nat Turner, *the physical setting and the interrelations of the characters with the physical setting were very important to you. Somebody even said that they were too important, as if all the weather took place on cue. You know, a shadow would pass across the sun at an appropriate moment, and so on.*

Styron: Yeah. I think that this is an element of narrative prose which I find not only valid, but often necessary, perhaps because I just have an unconscious or semiconscious belief that we are constantly responding to our environment in one way or another—at least I am, and I'm sensitive to it. I feel that people behave almost in counterpoint to nature, to the fact of nature, even if it's a very mild and harmless day in Connecticut, with shadows of light, etc. Another sensibility might not feel the same way. I think it's perfectly valid to write without this sensibility, but it's the way I respond and that's the way I've got to write.

You were talking about someone criticizing me, I think in *Nat Turner,* for overresponding to nature. I may be wrong, but I remember that there was a long essay on the book by Richard Gilman. It was very critical of the book, put it down rather harshly. He said that the book seemed to be a set piece for natural descriptions. My response to that is simply that only a twentieth-century, very urban critic could make that criticism about a book involving a nineteenth-century slave boy whose entire world was nature. I remember that distinctly, not because I bridle too much at criticism—I'm quite used to it by now—but because it was a very stupid, I think, misreading of the book which was, after all, about a black boy living in the deepest part of rural Virginia 170 years ago, and whose whole universe was nature. Understand, I'm not taking umbrage about criticism, and I don't intend to.

Conversations: Connecticut is mild compared to the fierce weather of Virginia and even further south, which is such an important element in Nat Turner *and* Lie Down in Darkness. *Is living up here cutting yourself off to a certain extent from important roots?*

Styron: I don't think so. I don't honestly think so, because I think, largely, your responses to things are formed very early in your life; I don't know when exactly, but the first two decades, two and a half decades. I'm hazarding the guess that by the time you are twenty-five you have more or less absorbed everything you're going to absorb from your environment. If you have any kind of sensitive memory, this is going to constantly reverberate throughout the rest of your life. You don't really cut yourself off as long as you have that early well. The well is filled up.

Conversations: The sense of the physical atmosphere of the place would remain with you always thereafter?

Styron: Yeah, and, therefore, I hardly see that it's necessary to artificially root yourself to someplace where you don't belong. I'm saying that only because I still feel very attached emotionally to the South as an idea, but I don't feel the necessity for living there, largely because I'm not constitutionally desirous of living there at the moment and haven't been throughout most of my life. I feel just as happy up here as I do in the South, which has become quite homogenized, really, and in many respects resembles the North.

William Styron

Conversations: Well, you foreshadow that in a lot of Lie Down in Darkness, *the country club life and all.*

Styron: Yeah, yeah, right.

Conversations: I remember seeing you quoted once to the effect that you thought one day you would retire and go back to the South and open up a peanut farm or something like that.

Styron: Yeah. Still, if I went back to Virginia, I'd like to start a peanut farm. It's a great crop. And the part of Virginia where I originate is "a rich peanut area." I could easily consider going for peanuts. You make a lot of money for one thing; it's a very popular crop.

Conversations: You went back quite a lot, I believe, while you were researching and writing Nat Turner. *I seem to remember a long piece you did for the* Atlantic *or* Harper's *in which you actually revisited the scenes and meditated upon them.*

Styron: Yeah. I did that piece in *Harper's* for their Civil War Anniversary Issue in 1965. I felt, I guess, a sort of nostalgia. I wanted to go back. I still feel very, very tied to the South, in a curious way, emotionally, but not to the degree that I want to live there. I'm just not constitutionally put together that way.

Conversations: How did you feel about the reception of Lie Down in Darkness? *Did it meet with your expectations? It was widely admired and extravagantly praised.*

Styron: I was very excited. It got largely very favorable criticism. And being so young, to see it on the best-seller list, which is quite unusual for a first novel, was exciting. And I think it just got the right amount of excitement for a book of this sort. It never achieved, let's say, the titanic success of *From Here to Eternity* by my good friend Jim Jones, which was on the best-seller list at the same time—number one.

Conversations: Did you coincide on the list?

Styron: Yeah, we did. Quite interestingly, still another prodigiously famous book was on the list at the same time, several rungs higher than me, and that was *The Catcher in the*

Rye. Those three books were all on the best-seller list at the same time.

Conversations: That was a vintage year, wasn't it?

Styron: Yeah. It always tickles me when I remember that at the end of the year *Time* magazine in its usual roundup—at that time it was so pontifical—said this had been another mediocre year for fiction.

Conversations: The Long March appeared so shortly thereafter and was such a different sort of narrative—much sparer and leaner and more concentrated. That probably gave a lot of people quite a shock.

Styron: I don't know if it was a mistake or not, but my editor— he's dead now—Hiram Haydn, did not see it as being a book which should come out in hardback. I realize now that this might have been a mistake, because though it is a short novel, it could easily have been published as a hardback. But, as a result, it never got any reviews. It's been examined critically since then, but it never blossomed as a book. And I don't care any longer. But in that respect I've often wondered if it might not have been interesting to see what kind of reviews it might have gotten had it been published as a hardback.

Conversations: In what way was The Long March *related to the play you did,* In the Clap Shack?

Styron: It was really not directly connected chronologically. *In the Clap Shack* was roughly based on an experience I had in World War II when I was a so-called "boot" at Parris Island— semiautobiographical. It nonetheless obviously is connected to my other work in the sense that I've always been fascinated by the military and the way it has affected me and people in our time, but that's about all I can say for it.

Conversations: After Lie Down in Darkness *you went off to live for a number of years in Italy, I believe.*

Styron: Right. I lived there for about a year and a half. I was in Paris for a year and then in Italy for a year and a half. I got married in Rome and lived in Ravello all during the year of 1953, and came back. I finally said, "I've had it with Europe." I loved it, but I had to get back, so I came back here in '54 and just lived briefly in New York and then moved up here. I have been here ever since.

Conversations: Were you at all part of the writers' world of American expatriates at that time—Tennessee Williams and Vidal and people who were living in Rome in the early fifties?

Styron: I didn't see many of them, no. I was at the American Academy in Rome and I did see a few writers from time to time. But if there was any kind of expatriate life that I felt, in that sense of the word "expatriate," I felt it more when I was in Paris earlier, as soon as I came to Europe, where I really did feel myself a part. I helped start *The Paris Review*, with George Plimpton and Peter Matthiessen and Harold Humes. I was not in any direct sense a founder. I don't claim that, but I was very much on the scene when it started. I wrote the preface to the first issue, which I've always been proud of in a curious way. I feel myself very much a part of that group. It was great fun in those days, and that, to me, was almost the best time I had in Europe—my Paris days; down-and-out in Paris, so to speak.

Conversations: Set This House on Fire *was the legacy of that time, wasn't it?*

Styron: Yeah, right.

Conversations: People are inclined to read that book now, I think, as a sort of examination of the destructive effect of the American temperament upon the European temperament, shall we say. Is that a fair statement of what you had in mind—the ruthlessness and the self-centeredness of American materialism?

Styron: I think possibly so, yes. I think I was reflecting, if it was at all valid, a kind of new American imperialism. After all, most of the earlier work of Henry James and his contemporaries on Europe—well, even dating back further than that, to Hawthorne—was about the innocence of America and an old, wise, and corrupt Europe. Certainly this was one of James's most persistent themes. I don't think in any conscious way in *Set This House on Fire* I was doing the opposite, but I certainly was aware that after World War II we had emerged as the major power in the world, and that was not all to the good. The tables had turned in a curious way. No longer would we be innocents. We were developing and exploiting our own capacity for corruption. I certainly didn't program the book to say that, but I think the element is there.

Conversations: The first sixty pages of Set This House on Fire, *the account of the driving out of Rome and then the crash, seem to me one of your single most remarkable pieces of sustained narrative. It was published separately somewhere, wasn't it?*

Styron: I think it was; it may have been in *Esquire.* It's based on a similar accident I had in Italy. Everything worked out all right, fortunately, but I did have a similar experience. Of course, again symbolic "Knock him down—dumb Italian," so to speak.

Conversations: To what extent is Set This House on Fire *also the study of the ruthlessness of the artistic temperament, the self-centeredness of it and the riding roughshod over other people it involves?*

Styron: I think it's a component in the book. To what extent I really can't pin down, but it's there. This particular aspect was much dwelt upon when the book came out in France, where it was a big hit, a huge success. And they mentioned over and over again just what you said.

Conversations: For all sorts of reasons in America it wasn't nearly as well received as your previous books had been.

Styron: No.

Conversations: Have you any feeling for why that should be? A lot of people complained that it was overly melodramatic, that the elements didn't cohere.

Styron: Yeah. There were very, very violent reactions against it. I really don't know; I don't think they were ready for it. I myself would change a lot of things in it if I were rewriting it, though I don't think I'd make major changes. But it's curiously had a very big and constant life in Europe; it's sort of essential to my work through European eyes. And in Russia, I know, although it has not been published, it's the one that they read in English the most, I've been told. So it's amazing. You never know what kind of effect your work is going to have.

Conversations: Possibly it's because you see the Americans and Europe in the same way that Europeans do. Maybe that's also the thing that American critics resent about it.

Styron: I think possibly so.

Conversations: It is also the furthest of your works from your roots; critics love to place people with their roots.

Styron: Yeah, that's quite true. "What's he doing there after all these years? He should be back where he belongs." Exactly. That pigeonholing desire is very strong in critics. And I think that has legislated against the reception of the book to a large degree, although even it wasn't universally put down. It had some very glowing reviews, but, you're right; it was a book that puzzled people. And then, of course, about two and a half years later I had this wonderful sort of bonus, which was having it beautifully translated into French by Maurice-Edgar Coindreau, who translated Faulkner, and having it become for France an incredible success, a best seller. It was a nice thing to get after being put down so harshly here.

Conversations: Curiously enough, Set This House on Fire *is the only one of your books that is out of print today. I mean all the others are in print one way or another; even* The Long March *remains in print.*

Styron: Random House has just run off a fresh printing. I think when this book that I am working on now is finished they definitely plan to do a whole edition of all my work. For instance, *Lie Down in Darkness* needs nothing, because a guy who keeps track of my work I saw in Virginia a few days ago said that the Viking Press edition is now in the fourteenth printing and the New American Library is in the eleventh printing or something like that. So it's very much alive. And I'm glad to see that Random House has brought *Set This House on Fire* back, because you feel a little lost when people can't get hold of your work. I'm happy about this.

Conversations: I read somewhere that you said you'd always been thinking of doing the story of Nat Turner, but it wasn't until quite far along that you felt you could handle it. Was this because of your Southern background and sort of ingrained feelings about blacks?

Styron: That might have been part of it; I think that that was certainly part of it. It was very complicated. I think I had the instinctual feeling that one could not tackle anything having to do with slavery unless one had a kind of—pardon the expression, but I can't think of another word—*overview* of what slavery was, what it meant, what its entire meaning was as a historical actuality. And when I was quite young, even in my teens, it seized me as an idea. It's incredible. A mysterious, black, sort of hero-demon; this mystery. . . .

Conversations: Was the story of Nat Turner still very much alive around Virginia when you were growing up?

Styron: Yes.

Conversations: Would people still talk about it as something that happened in their grandparents' time?

Styron: He was certainly, you could say, a minor folk hero. He was so mysterious—no one knew anything about him. You know, the whites regarded him in one way and the blacks in another. The blacks, of course, in those days wouldn't mention it because it was too frightening an apparition for them to bring up. He was certainly not a major historical hero in the sense that Robert E. Lee was, or even, let's say, black figures like Frederick Douglass or Booker T. Washington, who, being an Uncle Tom, was perfectly acceptable. But Nat Turner fascinated me always. From the first time I had ever heard about him I thought: "What an idea for something"—a play or movie or novel or something. And after I finished *Lie Down in Darkness* I remember distinctly thinking that this was the one that I wanted to write next. I remember being in long correspondence with Hiram Haydn at the time; he helped dissuade me and I dissuaded myself. I realized it was a good idea, but I had no comprehension at all of the milieu.

In other words, I was ignorant about what slavery was, and it took quite a few years of random, but careful, reading to install in my mind an apprehension of what the world of slavery was. By this time, in the late fifties and early sixties, there was some very interesting scholarship being created in the field. It had been a dead thing for so many years and misinterpreted. One of our great treasures is our scholarship in slavery. It was beginning then. I felt, though, by the time that I began to write *Nat Turner*, that I had a good handhold on the subject; I knew how to move around in it. I had a good sense of what those times were, and I don't think I ever deviated. I think that, with some possible minor exceptions, I would certainly not touch a line in *Nat Turner* in terms of its historical responsibility.

Conversations: As far as the actual narrative form went, I recall reading somewhere that you'd always felt that this was a problem. You didn't know how to write it until you were reading Camus's The Stranger *one day and hit upon somebody in a jail cell.*

Styron: That was a kind of touchstone. I remember I hadn't read *The Stranger* before, but I was quite impressed by it; it's quite a remarkable short novel. I was very affected by the plight of this man going to his death, being executed. That in itself was an original theme, but it sort of coalesced the thing for me, and I suddenly saw Nat Turner in the jail cell before his execution. It just seemed to be the perfect place to embark on a tale.

Conversations: Another catalyst, I understand, was James Baldwin came to live with you for a while, and you felt that you were able to come closer to a black consciousness as a result.

Styron: Yeah, that was a very important factor in the evolution. I was born, after all, in Virginia during the days of segregation, and it was part of my consciousness. I regret that I was brought up as bigoted as most of my contemporaries. I don't mean to say that I was a red-neck, but I had all the classic Southern hang-ups about black people.

Conversations: It was difficult to conceive of a Negro with, say, a poetic sensibility or high intelligence?

Styron: I was emancipated to the degree that I thought they were human. But I never thought they would have been capable of—

let's call it a higher work, until meeting Jimmy and knowing him, as I did and do, quite well. I suddenly felt this dazzling intellect and this extraordinary prose style. After that, it was a total repudiation of all one's prejudices. And that was a great leap forward for me, just to have that kind of friendship. He lived in that little house over there for about six months. He wrote a lot of *The Fire Next Time* over there and *Another Country*. He stayed up here for a while. He was down-and-out. He had not really made a big success at that time. He was well known in literary circles, but he was just on the verge of becoming the extraordinary prophet that he became. I saw a lot of him, and we got to know each other very well.

Conversations: Well, Nat Turner, I think, was probably the book that first had an impact on the American consciousness about slavery, almost to the same extent that Roots *later came to have. It was an enormous best seller.*

Styron: Yeah.

Conversations: Everybody was discussing it for a long time. What's your own opinion of the impact Roots *has had? It seems to me a far more simpleminded sort of approach than yours— less complex and less rich.*

Styron: I think it's certainly an honest book. I don't think it's a very accurate book. When I say accurate I'm not leaning on the necessity for accuracy in every detail, because I don't think that's an important component of a work of its kind. But I think confusion lies in the question of whether it is a work of fiction or nonfiction. It's sold as a work of nonfiction. This seems to me to require more accuracy than if it were being sold as fiction. I thought the television series was—by and large, and with some exceptions—a kind of disastrous performance. I think it misused the worst elements of the book to create a kind of soap opera cliche. Somebody said, very cruelly, "Mandingo for the bourgeoisie." I think that's a little harsh. I think the guy is terribly well meaning, and I don't mean to be condescending, because he obviously has created something that people respond to. But as a book with—again that word—an overview, I think it doesn't have a substantial philosophical substructure as a work of fiction or nonfiction, whatever it is.

271

William Styron

I don't think it coheres, in other words, as an important statement about slavery. It's episodic. It tells very little that is new. The saddest part about it, it seems to me, is again—I hate to sound like I'm beating my own drum—but I did draw, I think, successfully and as faithfully as I could, on all the rich scholarship that was just coming out about slavery, even in the sixties. I don't think that *Roots* does that. I think it's going over very, very old ground and, therefore, is not a revealing book in the sense that one wants books of that sort to reveal, to tell you something new.

Conversations: Could you imagine the response to your own book being different if Roots *had appeared first? As you know, it did run into a certain amount of cross fire, particularly from some black historians.*

Styron: Oh, yes. *Nat Turner* received a horrendous counter-reception from the blacks, which, oddly enough, did not bother me as much as I thought it might because it came out at a time in which it was imperative in the minds of blacks that they recreate their own experience, their own sense of identity. For a white man to come along and ostensibly do that was more than they could really take. So if the book had come out four years earlier, I would have been considered one of the great white writers by blacks; or if it had come out four years later, certainly the book would have gotten an entirely different reception. I don't know how it would have fared vis-a-vis *Roots*; I can't speculate on that. But I do know that *Nat Turner* came out at a kind of ambiguous time. It was fortuitous in many ways that it came out because certainly the mind of America was on black people at that time. It was the time of the burning of Newark and Detroit.

Conversations: And the campus revolt, and the setting up of black studies.

Styron: Yeah, the whole thing. So on that level there couldn't have been a luckier time for its appearance; but, on the other hand, it did receive this wildly abrasive reaction from blacks.

Conversations: What are you working on now? You've been working steadily away at something now for about what, ten years?

William Styron

Styron: Well, that's not quite true. I'd like to clarify that. For several years after *Nat Turner* came out, I fell into an awful slump and didn't write anything much, except a few articles and essays and so on. I was keeping busy. And I started a book about the Marine Corps, part of which was accepted by *Esquire*. Something about that time— I don't know what it was, the war in Vietnam or something . . . I tired of that. I fell into another slump. I abandoned that book, though I intend fully to go back to it, after having written thirty or forty thousand words. And suddenly I conceived about three and a half years ago the book I am writing now, which, in a word if you can use a word, is about Auschwitz; again, an alien subject for me, but one that I now have written 500 pages about.

This is the book, I think, which, more than any of my work, is trying to pull together a point of view about the twentieth century. It's a very complex book; it's autobiographical in tone, having to do with myself working and publishing in 1947 at McGraw-Hill. The Auschwitz element comes in through the meeting of the narrator with a Polish girl who has been a survivor—a victim and a survivor—of Auschwitz, and the complications surrounding this gradual revelation of her past and so on. That's a very confused way of trying to describe what the book is about, because it's quite complex. Ever since I met this girl, who came into my life and then vanished rather quickly—I was quite young; I was about twenty-two—it has haunted me. Almost in the same way that slavery haunted me, this vision of Auschwitz has haunted me, too.

Conversations: Is it a place that you've visited?

Styron: Yes, I did, a couple of years ago when I went to Poland. I don't know why—I certainly am not the first to feel this, but it seems to me that what happened there, in the sense that it epitomizes what happened in the other places like Buchenwald and so on, is a sort of central issue of the twentieth century. I mean this is what human beings have come to after vaunted progress and enlightenment. It bears all sorts of philosophical considerations, just as slavery did, and has so obsessed people. We learn the wellsprings of human experience, it seems to me, through the attempt at an understanding of what went on there. That's why I am writing about it.

William Styron

Conversations: Is it a question of lost innocence? Do you think there was a time when men were better than they are now . . .

Styron: No, I don't really think so.

Conversations: . . . . A time of standards and honor and decency and uprightness—or when an attempt for such things could be made, at least?

Styron: I think that history fluctuates in that way. I think you can isolate areas of history in which idealism flourishes and men are content, relatively content, that is, and things seem sunny and bright. Most of the nineteenth century was that way. That is the problem: Why is it that men in the nineteenth century had this? It was an extraordinary age of optimism, really, with shocks, terrible shocks going along parallel with it—Darwinism was terrifying everyone. But it was a time of a general lack of anxiety, really.

Conversations: Underlying optimism—and a belief, I suppose, in perfectibility?

Styron: Sure, right. To have that flower into the twentieth century, which also has had its little pockets of beatitude but has really been the most horrifying time in the history of the human race. This is what makes the question, which is a very good one, very difficult to answer: Why is it that human beings are at endless war with themselves when they have such great potential to be all the cliche things—brothers? Why do they enslave each other by constant strife? Why do they develop more and more frightening and murderous barbaric instruments to destroy each other? We've come to that in the twentieth century.

Conversations: Too many of us. Is that it, perhaps?

Styron: That's partly it.

Conversations: That was one of the ostensible reasons for Hitler, after all: Lebensraum and expansion.

Styron: Sure. He used the most virulent form of philosophical racism to justify *Lebensraum*. Certainly the idea of overpopulation is part of it. But if so, it doesn't help our condition at all. It seems to me, however, that Auschwitz transcended that. It became something so profoundly evil that we're still in the throes of shock over it. We're still trying to make sense of it. After all, it wasn't that long ago; it was very, very recent, just yesterday, in fact. And, you know, the horrors which were inflicted there defy reason. That is why, I think, I have been attracted to it.

I also think I have been attracted to it because of my own interest in slavery. I think it's becoming more and more clear that the Germans had parallel goals with the slave owners. One was to exterminate millions of people or to enslave them, at a time when we thought we had long ridded ourselves of slavery as an idea which civilized men could entertain. But Auschwitz was an institution devoted as profoundly to slavery as it was to extermination. And this is another thing that fascinates me.

Conversations: It's also a subject on which a number of Jewish writers have written very eloquently but, by and large, Protestant writers have neglected. We've had, you know, writers like Elie Wiesel and so on.

Styron: I think it's because of a misapprehension of what it was all about. I don't think anyone can deny that the Jews received the brunt of the horror. But I think so completely lost in the shuffle is: first, the fact that hundreds of thousands, if not millions, of non-Jews, mainly Slavs, Russians, and Poles, were killed just as ruthlessly; and then, even more importantly, the *futurity* of Auschwitz. Namely, that once the last Jew had been destroyed, they were going to do the same job on the Poles. We know; we've seen the documents, the plans. Heinrich Himmler could scarcely discriminate between a Pole and a Jew.

This is a very important matter that has to be examined historically, because if we can say that only the Jews were going to get it—and certainly they got it—it's to minimize the evil: It is simply to preconceive a moment in which Hitler, Himmler, and company—had they been more successful—would have, you know, patted their hands and simply said, "Boys, this is the end of the evil." We can't conceive of that; the evil had to go on, and it would have successively involved forty or fifty million Poles, and as many Russians as they could fit into the gas chambers. It's this, as I say, the sense of that futurity, which seems, to me, more demonic in its prefiguration of what might happen to the human race than if only Jews were victims.

Conversations: Yes. That hasn't been dealt with at all.

Styron: Hasn't been dealt with at all. And it's a very central fact that you can't ignore. I am the first to be apprehensive. I'm married to a Jewish girl, and my children are Jewish in the eyes of Israel. So, therefore, I have a private stake in that consideration. But also in a place as heavily Jewish as New York, it's still a matter of astonishment to some people when you bring up the fact that 1,000,000 non-Jews died at Auschwitz—over a third were not Jewish. It's a matter of absolute astonishment; you know, "You don't mean it. Are you sure?" Of course one is sure—the records are there. And it's not in any sense to denigrate the terrible martyrdom of the Jews, because it was central. No one could ever wink at it, but it seems to me that this other dimension is absolutely crucial to the historical understanding of what was going on there.

Conversations: There was no exclusivity in the suffering, in fact, is what it amounts to?

Styron: Right. Also this total misapprehension that somehow.... I'm not defending Christianity, the anti-Semitism embedded in Christianity, which is definitely there and was somehow the cause of the Nazi atrocity. But, in reality, the Nazi offense, the Nazi atrocity, was a *negation* of Christianity as profoundly as it was an anti-Semitic movement in its own right. Otherwise you simply can't justify the horrors visited on Christians. In my work, you have seen I can bear down very heavily on Christians, especially hypocritical clergy and so on. I'm not about to try to defend Christianity. But it's a slander on Christianity to make it the prime mover of the Nazi holocaust and the whole Nazi outrage.

Christians were as deeply victimized as the Jews. This is another thing which is very tough for people to get an understanding of. It's a very important historical fact. My heroine, for instance—Sophie is her name—is not a Jewish girl. She's a Catholic who loses her religion as a result of what happens to her in Auschwitz. In no way am I trying to minimize the massacre of the Jews. That is essential to the book, too. But it has to be occasionally put in a broader panorama.

Conversations: Is this work coming on well? Are you pleased with it?

Styron: It's been the toughest, I guess, of all the books I've ever had to write, but it's coming along beautifully at the moment. I've got, as I say, well over 500 pages with which I am, at least provisionally, quite satisfied. I think it's possibly going to cause another furor because. . . . What you said just now impressed me; I mean your understanding of the fact that Elie Wiesel and people like that have done it. Well, this is quite true; it's been a Jewish province.

Conversations: Exactly, to the extent that people say, "Another book about the Holocaust. Who needs it?"

Styron: And, you know, Andre Schwarz-Bart—and so on. People who are often very, very competent witnesses. But again, one of the challenges here was to say to myself—I don't mean recklessly or capriciously: "Why can't a Virginia-born Protestant deal with this as well as an Austrian-born Jew?" This is what art essentially is about, so long as you have a certain passion of conviction about the historical necessity of writing a thing like this. So that's where I am now.

Conversations: When do you expect to publish?

Styron: Well, I'm not sure. I'm at a very interesting point now where I'm, like, over the brow of the hill.

Conversations: Beginning to coast down?

Styron: Yeah. It's getting a bit easier to write, because I'm seeing where all my options are now. All this is fairly well laid out, so I'm feeling very good about it. I'd love to have the idea that I could finish it this year. That would give me the deepest sense of satisfaction, because novels strangle with murderous hands. Nothing better than getting rid of a novel.

Conversations: Can you see beyond it, or does it fill your whole foreground at the moment?

Styron: Right now, if I can get this done, I will be the happiest man I know. After that, I don't know. I do think that I will get back to this book which I temporarily abandoned.

William Styron

Conversations: The Marine one?

Styron: Yeah. Because again, I think I've gotten new insights into that. I think it was wise of me to leave off with that and get back to it. It's also nice after having finished one book to have a partially completed book. So that makes me very satisfied.

Conversations: When we were setting the date for this talk, you mentioned your peculiar work habits, which involve starting determinedly at around the middle of the afternoon. Tell me a little more about those, if you will.

Styron: Well, I'm kind of a night person. My mechanism really doesn't start up in the morning. I mean, I'm in a terrible fog when I wake up, which is usually a little later than most people. I wake up around ten, because I often go to bed as late as 2:30 or so. It gets earlier as the weather progresses. In the spring I'll get up considerably earlier. I'm not one of these people who can conceivably sit down and write anything if I get up at ten, say, or eleven. I'm too depressed. I could write a suicide note, I guess, at that hour, but nothing much more.

Conversations: Or a note to your publisher?

Styron: A note to my publisher saying I'm quitting. So gradually I find that over the years I've evolved this thing with the late afternoons as one of my better writing times; anytime after four up till eight. Even out here we tend to dine at a late hour. So that's pretty much the schedule. And I have no real reason to regret it. The main thing is to be able to write something each day. That seems to me the most valuable thing.

Conversations: If nothing comes to you on the book you're working on, will you just dash off a bit? Do you keep a journal, for instance?

Styron: I keep notes, yes.

Conversations: A sort of notebook of ideas and observations?

Styron: Yeah, very valuable. Also, to be quite honest, I get some of my best ideas when I'm not writing, which is to say those late hours when I'm up pondering, cogitating, with no intention of writing—maybe with a couple of Scotches under my belt

278

liberating the imagination. I will suddenly get some of my really most valuable notions, which must never be sneezed at. I think writers obviously all have their own techniques about work, and far be it from me to even suggest what other writers should do. But I myself am not one of these people who necessarily is getting his best ideas at the moment that he sits down to work; often they come later. Then, as the clock comes full circle, I apply what I've thought of yesterday to what I am going to do today.

Conversations: You can hang onto it?

Styron: Yeah. I usually make a few notes. And that's very valuable, too. For instance, just last night I found myself in one of these moments of what I consider to be imaginative efflorescence, or something like that. It was astonishing, because I suddenly saw a way to break through a very difficult part of the book. I suddenly saw a way to condense the whole—I won't go into it.

Conversations: But you hadn't been consciously pondering; this just came to you?

Styron: It came to me, yeah. A kind of liberating something that happened in my head at a point where I was rather discontentedly aware that what I was doing was perfectly all right, but it was losing some of its horsepower. I know very little about music, but I do know enough about it to be able to sense what a musician must do at a certain time. He goes into another key or he will change tempo in a composition, and this is what I was doing analogously. The thing was like a long Mahler movement that was getting much too long, slow, leisurely, and boring. In some kind of unconscious need to rectify this, all of a sudden I saw I just had to cut it short, shift into a new key: shift from past to present tense, which is.like shifting a key. And suddenly it was all solved. It may go haywire, but I have such confidence in what I've done so far, in being able to sense when I'm on the right track, that I think it will work.

But this is something I could not have done at my writing desk. It had to be done in some other mood, another context. It bubbles up. The knack is to be able to be receptive to an idea, to find out when it's coming and to want to find it. I know enough from my past experience to know that a lot of my best work has come that way: not in this methodical sitting down and doing those daily lines, but in waiting for these moments.

Conversations: You're a compulsive polisher, I believe. You work very hard at getting every line right before you move on, rather than sort of rattling it all out and going back to do new drafts.

Styron: Yeah. That's one small consolation, because once I have a stack of manuscript, it very, very rarely ever happens that I'll rewrite. I'll change a few words. Of course, with this book, because there are a whole lot of contemporary historical references, also a lot of linguistic stuff in various languages, it will require a lot of polishing and honing. But that's just spadework; it's not imaginative. I'll have to go through the manuscript carefully after it's all done, but the major part of the work is done; the day I put it together, the very last day, it's all done. That is a consolation—no rewrites.

Conversations: How much of your contemporaries do you read? Do you try not to read too much while you are actually working on something?

Styron: I read most of my contemporaries. I shy away from a great deal of reading of fiction while I'm working. But, for instance, I'm right in the middle of Cheever's book, *Falconer,* which I like very much and admire very much. Often, though, I'm constantly reimmersing myself in work on contemporary history, as I was when I was writing *Nat Turner.* I never stopped reading about slavery. I don't mean I read methodically, but rather haphazardly. The same applies here. I'm constantly trying to reinforce, in the best sense of the word, my insights into the Nazi story. Therefore, that's the kind of reading I find myself gravitating toward. I read most of this new book on Hitler, *Hitler's War.*

Conversations: That presents the rather odd notion that Hitler didn't really know what was going on about the Jews.

Styron: I don't think he proves his thesis. I have often thought, as he seems to support, that probably the evilest man who ever lived was Heinrich Himmler, and that Himmler certainly was basically responsible for a lot of the technological death that happened. But I also think that Hitler was very, very much aware of what was happening. The point is academic: if Hitler made one speech such as he did about the Jews—and he made fifty or 100 of them—he's as responsible as Himmler is. But the book has a lot of interesting stuff in it, and that's the kind of thing I do read. I've been reading some Polish documentation on camps and so on; raw material from those I've got pretty much in my head. I've read people like Trevor-Roper a lot, because I think he really and truly caught, even almost comically in a way, the sense of the madness of Hitler's Germany. So I don't consciously shun fiction, but it's not the kind of reading I move toward while I'm writing. It's too hard to keep the other stuff going.

Conversations: Are you doing any reviewing at all these days?

Styron: I told Bob Silvers at *The New York Review* that I would do a review of this book called *A Rumor of War*. It's about the Vietnam War. I haven't finished it yet, but I probably will review it. I don't find it terribly profitable—I don't mean in a financial sense—to do much reviewing. I think it takes away valuable time. But occasionally I'll do it when a book like that strikes my fancy. What struck me about that book is that line-for-line I could have written the first paragraph twenty years before. Where he says he came out of college with Shakespeare as his intellectual baggage and learned to be a Marine in Quantico, Virginia—well, that's just what I did. So the comparison of his experience and mine I found interesting.

Also the chilling apprehension of this war seems to be one of the standard features of the century. Here I am, not yet an aged fellow—not yet, heading toward it, but still feeling fairly chipper—and I find that in my lifetime there have been three wars. And I fought in two of them. It's chilling because it seems far more probable, since that's the track record of the last thirty-some years, that we're more likely to have one again than not.

What gives us this incredible optimism to think we're shut of these wars? I felt that we were shut of these wars in 1945, when the atomic bomb was out. And then to find myself in the Korean War was a horrible shock to my system. And then within twelve or fifteen years to have another war cranked up, which I was not

William Styron

in—the war of Vietnam. It seems to be a cyclical thing. It seems far more likely that we will have a war than not.

Eudora Welty was born in Jackson, Mississippi, an area from which she draws much of her material, and where she lives today. Her reputation as a novelist and short story writer is based on a body of very highly regarded works including A Curtain of Green *(1941),* The Robber Bridegroom *(1942),* The Wide Net and Other Stories *(1943),* Delta Wedding *(1944),* The Golden Apples *(1949),* The Ponder Heart *(1954),* Losing Battles *(1970),* The Optimist's Daughter *(1972). Miss Welty has won many literary awards, among them the William Dean Howells Medal (1955), the Gold Medal for Fiction (1972), and the Pulitzer Prize for Fiction (1973).*

Eudora Welty

Eudora Welty was interviewed by Jean Todd Freeman on the morning of 29 July 1977 at the Welty family home, which parallels the Belhaven College campus in Jackson, Mississippi. Miss Welty had just returned home from several hectic months of traveling and said she was "burning" to get back to work on a piece of fiction. She sat on a small, pale yellow sofa next to a table on which several books rested, including the latest publications of Reynolds Price and Katherine Anne Porter.

Conversations: I read your collection of stories, **A Curtain of Green,** *shortly after it came out; then I read* **The Wide Net;** *and, unfortunately, I missed* **The Robber Bridegroom** *somewhere along in there—*

Welty: Everybody did; I swear everybody did.

Conversations: Although your latest two books have been novels rather than short story collections, I think of you primarily as a short story writer.

Welty: Thank you, so do I. I certainly do. My novels have happened by accident. Every single one.

Conversations: Katherine Anne Porter in her introduction to A Curtain of Green *has suggested that you might get pressure from publishers to write novels.*

Welty: Oh no, there never was that. That's because, I think, Diarmuid Russell stood between them and me.

Conversations: Diarmuid Russell was a wonderful agent, wasn't he?

Welty: He was wonderful and, of course, if it hadn't been for him, I wouldn't have ever been published anywhere. That's true.

Eudora Welty

Conversations: How did that come about?

Welty: Well, I was his first client, I think. I believe I was. He wrote me when he first opened the agency, just as he wrote to lots of young writers whose works he'd read that he liked and whom he thought might not have an agent. And I had had some stories in the little magazines and the quarterlies. He wrote and asked if I would like him to be my agent. I'd never heard of a literary agent, but I liked his letter so much that I wrote back by return mail and said, "Yes! be my agent." Well, his first letter showed me what he was like. And also his second because when I wrote and said, "Yes, be my agent," he wrote back and said, "Now don't be too quick. You don't know anything about me; I may be a crook for all you know." He spent about a full year or maybe two full years trying to get my stories in national circulation magazines and finally made it with the *Atlantic.*

Conversations: The Atlantic, *then, was the first major magazine that published your stories?*

Welty: Yes, through his work.

Conversations: Which story was that?

Welty: That was—they published two: One was "Why I live at the P.O."; and one was "A Worn Path." As soon as that happened why then the way was clear for other magazines to be interested. And that made the first book possible, which would otherwise never have happened, you know, never.

Conversations: You had been published before in literary magazines?

Welty: Yes, I'd been sending these stories around about six years. I'd had good luck being published in the *Southern Review* and little magazines—*Accent, Prairie Schooner.*

Conversations: I think your first story was published in a magazine called Manuscript.

Welty: Right. The man who did it, John Rood, has been dead for quite awhile now, and he left publishing anyway and became a sculptor. I owe *Manuscript* a great deal.

Conversations: I'd like to go back a little bit and talk about your childhood. This is a beautiful house we are sitting in. Is this the house you grew up in?

Welty: It's the second house my family built, but I was in school by then. This was sort of in the country when we built it in 1925, I guess. Before that I lived in the house in Jackson where I was born.

Conversations: You had two brothers, is that right?

Welty: Yes. They were younger.

Conversations: Do you consider that you had a normal kind of a childhood?

Welty: I had a happy childhood and I was very fortunate in my family. It was always a congenial house with plenty going on. But, also, we always had all the books we wanted. We always had books and my earliest presents were books, which I loved. And I remember we had an encyclopedia always, and it used to be in the dining room: if someone asked a question at the table, you could jump up and prove right away that you were right or find you were wrong. It's always been a family full of curiosity and interest in the world.

Conversations: Did your brothers read, too?

Welty: They didn't read as much as I did; they were more athletic. They liked reading, but one of my brothers became an architect and he was musical; they were other things.

Conversations: Was your mother interested in artistic pursuits?

Welty: She was a teacher when she was young but she was also a great reader all her life, and, even after her eyesight failed, loved books. And so did my father. So, what hopeful writer could be more lucky? From the first I was able to read.

Conversations: Who were your favorite authors back then?

Welty: Of course, I read lots of fairy tales and all the childhood books. And I also liked Mark Twain. We had a set of his work; it's still over there in the bookshelves. I read practically everything, the way I do now. You know, a ferocious, voracious reader.

Eudora Welty

Conversations: I notice there's a new book by Reynolds Price right here on this table. He's another Southern writer.

Welty: Absolutely, and a good friend.

Conversations: Did you have a large peripheral family of cousins and aunts and uncles or was it rather small?

Welty: No, not in Jackson because both of my parents came from away. My mother came from West Virginia—

Conversations: That's pretty obvious in The Optimist's Daughter.

Welty: Yes. That was literal memory, up on the mountain and the sounds and sights up there.

Conversations: I've always been curious as to how West Virginia got in that novel so strongly.

Welty: Well, we spent every summer visiting the families. My father was from Ohio and we went to his father's farm down in southern Ohio, and to the house on the mountaintop in West Virginia. That's where all of our kinfolks were, not here. Not any here, except the immediate family.

Conversations: So you never had the experience that many Southern children have of being "trapped" in a room where all the relatives are talking and telling family stories.

Welty: I've experienced that but only as a treat, you know, in the summer. I had to make all that up for *Delta Wedding*.

Conversations: How did you manage to cope with such a large cast of characters in Delta Wedding? *Have you ever counted them?*

Welty: I wonder, myself. I had to make family trees and chronologies, to be sure I had everything right. But you touched on a tender subject when you asked had I ever counted, because when Edward Weeks serialized *Delta Wedding* in the *Atlantic*, he found out, as my editor, that I had miscounted the children, and set me right. It was a stern lesson to me; I made my mind up never to let that happen again. I said, "Here I've had nine children" or whatever it was, and it was really ten. Of course I knew them all, but I hadn't really said one, two, three, four, five, six. . . .

Conversations: When did you actually start writing?

Welty: You know how we all write when we are little. I think always I loved writing because I loved reading. I don't mean I get my stories out of books—I don't. They spring from living. And not that I literally take things from real life, but it's living that makes me want to write, not reading—although it's reading that makes me love writing.

Conversations: You have never consciously emulated another writer?

Welty: No. It is a way to do, but I have never . . . I don't think consciously that I've ever used that method.

Conversations: Can you remember the first piece of writing—a story or something—that you did as a very young child?

Welty: You know how you made up little booklets to give your mother for a present. Mine were surely sappy. It seems to me I can remember my illustrations more than what I made up. I seem to remember an Easter rabbit on the telephone, that kind of thing.

Conversations: You were interested in both painting and drawing, weren't you?

Welty: I have a visual mind but I had no gift for painting.

Conversations: This may be why the imagery in your writing is so vivid.

Welty: It may be. I am interested in the visual world.

Conversations: Have you always been interested in people, in what makes them tick, and in what brings them together or drives them apart?

Welty: I think so. I was probably a troublesome child with my curiosity, because I asked a lot of questions and I loved to just sit in a room with grown people talking, anyone talking. My mother has told me how I would sit between two people, setting off for a ride in the car, as we used to do on Sunday, and say, "Now start talking!" My ears would just open like morning glories.

Conversations: You have an awfully good ear, too, for dialogue; you're universally praised—

Welty: I do work hard at that. Of course, a lot of conversation in the South, as you know, is of a narrative and dramatic structure and so when you listen to it, you're following a story. You're listening for how something is going to come out and that, also, I think, has something to do with the desire to write later. We would listen to talk forever. When you go up North, they don't **want to hear it, you know. They don't want to hear in the** starting-at-the-beginning-going-all-the-way-through style. They just want to hear the results.

Conversations: You went to public schools in Jackson and then to Mississippi State College for Women.

Welty: For two years, then I went to the University of Wisconsin.

Conversations: What steps took you there?

Welty: That was my father's preference. He was from the Middle West, and he had the idea that the big Middle Western universities were the most progressive. I think at that time he was probably right. I was considered too young to start off there. You know, in those days we went to college at sixteen, which I was, and I would have been too much of an infant to go to the University of Wisconsin. Well, I think I was too much of an infant to go to college.

Conversations: Did you like MSCW?

Welty: I liked it; I had a good time.

Conversations: After you went to the University of Wisconsin, you then went to Columbia and studied advertising?

Welty: That's right. Well, by that time, I knew I wanted to be a writer. Again, my father who always was pretty wise said, "You'll never make a living as a story writer"—prophetic words. "You'll need to be able to support yourself." I said, "I'm not going to be a teacher." So he said, "Well, then, it should be business." I had longed to go to New York for a year, so that was the answer: I went to Columbia School of Business and had a year in New York.

Conversations: Where did you live in New York?

Welty: I lived in Johnson Hall. All female graduate students under twenty-one had to live there.

Conversations: You didn't do the Greenwich Village scene?

Welty: We didn't live down there, but we went out nightly, you know, to something: the theatre, to dance up in Harlem, down to Greenwich Village. Well, it was the heyday—1931.

Conversations: Did you meet some of the literary people there at that time?

Welty: No, no. I didn't mean we knew anybody. We would just go down there, wandering around in Minetta Lane, to Romany Marie's, and places like that. In that year the theatres couldn't have been more wonderful.

Conversations: Is this when your interest in the theatre started?

Welty: I'd always been interested. On trips with my family, we'd go to the theatre wherever we were. And plays used to come here, you know. In the days of train travel and road companies, Jackson was the stopover between Memphis and New Orleans, so we got a lot of shows here, the so-called Broadway shows. Our parents always took the children; that was another good thing.

Conversations: There was really quite a lot of cultural life in Jackson, then?

Welty: Well, we thought there was. And I think that we really did have people come through here that were first-rate.

Conversations: After you left Columbia you came back to Jackson?

Welty: Yes, because the Depression happened. There was no more advertising being done; there were no jobs.

Conversations: Is this when you started working for the government with the W.P.A.?

Eudora Welty

Welty: Pretty soon. That was also the year my father died—he was fifty-two. My mother was left with two sons in high school and college, so I came home and worked in Jackson at whatever I could do. You know, it was poor pickings in those days. But I, again, was lucky. I worked for the radio station here and did, oh, various meager work on newspapers—whatever I could get. Then when the W.P.A. came along, I was offered a job as a publicity agent.

Conversations: What exactly did you do? I know that you took pictures.

Welty: I did reporting, interviewing. It took me all over Mississippi, which is the most important thing to me, because I'd never seen it—except Jackson and Columbus—never. And the coast, I guess, once or twice.

Conversations: Did the people that you met become "characters" in some of your early stories?

Welty: Not as themselves, and not directly. But some of the places are real—and the landscapes. And you're certainly right in that that experience, I think, was the real germ of my wanting to become a real writer, a true writer. It caused me to seriously attempt it. It made me see, for the first time, what life was really like in this state. It was a revelation.

Conversations: Did you really get to know people like the characters in your stories, like "Keela the Outcast Indian Maiden" and "The Petrified Man"?

Welty: Not the particular people, but I got an insight into human beings that I'd never had. I realized later what a protected life I'd led. You know, I thought I had been so sophisticated in New York, and I didn't know a thing. I didn't know what people were really like until then.
   "Keela," which you mentioned, came about in a special way. In my job I would go to different county fairs and put up booths for the W.P.A. Once some of the people on the midway—I used to go out and drink coffee with them and so on—they were talking about the sideshow act of something *like* Keela, the outcast Indian maiden. I don't remember now, but it

292

involved a little black person that had been carried off. Well, of course, my story is not about that; it's about the moral response to it made by three different people. It troubled me so and I tried to write my story in response to that situation. In a way that's a very simple example of the way I always begin in making a story.

Conversations: You don't try, then, to take a person you have met and put that person, exactly as he is, on the printed page?

Welty: It would be impossible. You never know enough for that, to begin with. But also, you have to invent the character to suit the purpose of the story that you are trying to tell. That is his circumference and his point and his reason for being. I mean the character of a short story, not a novel.

Conversations: In your introduction to One Time, One Place *you say: "I learned quickly enough when to click the shutter, but what I was becoming aware of more slowly was a story-writer's truth: the thing to wait on, to reach there in time for, is the moment in which people reveal themselves." Would these people that you met open up to you and talk?*

Welty: Maybe I considered that they had, because I began to understand a little. I hadn't thought of this until you asked me, but maybe I was speaking too subjectively in that remark. Of course, some people did open up; you got an idea of their lives anyway, by one way or the other, by something they'd said, something you saw, something that made you feel where your sympathies were going.

Conversations: I know you dislike the tag of "regional writer."

Welty: Oh, I don't mind.

Conversations: Most of your fiction is set in the South and your writing conveys a strong sense of place. Do you consider this an important element of your work?

Welty: It seems very important to me. I think Southerners have such an intimate sense of place. We grew up in the fact that we live here with people about whom we know almost everything that can be known as a citizen of the same neighborhood or town. We learn significant things that way: we know what the place has made of these people; what they've made of the place through generations. We have a sense of continuity and that, I think, comes from place. It helps to give the meaning—another meaning to a human life that such life has been there all the time and will go on. Now that people are on the move a lot more, some of that sense of continuity is gone, but I feel . . . I believe it will always be in our roots, as Southerners, don't you? A sense of the place. Even if you move around, you know where you have your base. And I just think it's terribly important.

Conversations: On the inside of Delta Wedding *there's a map—*

Welty: Well, that was just done as a decoration by Doubleday. But maps—they're of the essence. I drew my own map for *Losing Battles*. I had to; I used it when I was working. I had to be sure just for one thing that I had people turning left or right correctly, when they charged up and down. To be sure I got all those routes right. Oh, it was just a delight. I loved being able to do my map.

Conversations: Was Delta Wedding, *your second novel, fairly easy to write, after having written mainly short stories?*

Welty: Yes, well, again, that's something I owe to Diarmuid. I sent what I thought was a story in to Diarmuid called "The Delta Cousins," and he wrote back and said, "Eudora, this is chapter two of a novel. Go on with it." He recognized that it had a possible scope to it or something. It hadn't occurred to me; it might never have occurred to me. And it never occurred to me that I could write a novel, but he spotted it. His judgment was so acute and I trusted everything that he said, absolutely. You know, I would have given it a try after he'd said that, no matter what had happened. So I just went on from there, and "The Delta Cousins" became *Delta Wedding*.

Conversations: Many of your books center around an incident and involve a great many people, all commenting on that central incident almost like a Greek chorus.

Welty: I know. I seem to have these unconscious patterns. Does everyone? I didn't realize that myself for quite awhile. I suppose it's more or less an obvious kind of way to bring people together and have things emerge.

Conversations: It's like writing a play, especially in Losing Battles *where you use so much dialogue and your point of view is objective.*

Welty: I really do work at it, do a good deal of rewriting. I didn't do so much in *The Optimist's Daughter*, but it's never as hard for me to write something that's an interior story. Although it was a more complicated and deeper story, *The Optimist's Daughter*, and it meant more to me personally, it was easier to write. But I had set myself to do *Losing Battles* to see if I could, to try to see if I could do everything objectively. I wrote, oh, so many scenes over and over again to condense them, shape them to sharpen up what I was trying to do.

Conversations: Didn't it take you about fifteen years?

Welty: Well, I wrote it over a period of ten years, but then, of course, I was working on other things too. I couldn't work on it consecutively because of affairs here at home. I worked on short things and I was giving lectures. I also wrote *The Optimist's Daughter* before I finished *Losing Battles*. I really loved writing *Losing Battles* because of the problem it set: trying to do something strictly through dialogue and action. And another problem was to keep the spark, you know, that was what scared me when it took so long. I thought: the spark may have died; it may not still be alive, and there was no way to know until someone had read it.

Conversations: I felt that there was a shift in style in Losing Battles. *The first part seems to be very poetic; and then it seems that your book becomes less poetic, less concentrated. The narrative moves faster forward. Were you aware of this? Was this something you had in mind?*

Welty: I must—no, I think that's astute on your part. I can think of two reasons why that would be true. First, I thought it was going to be a short story—I do every time. I wrote the first part thinking that was to be the story: the family gathered and telling the story about Jack, what he had done; and then I was going to end it with Jack coming home and asking them what in the world is the matter with *them*. It ended with his appearance, that is. Well, goodness, by that time—

Eudora Welty

Conversations: You were hooked on him.

Welty: I was hooked. Also, I went back at the very end and rewrote that very beginning many, many times. It was the hardest thing in the world for me to lead into what had come out of it, and it may be too rewritten, you know. In the opening part that you're talking about, with all the similes and so on, I was trying to see if I could condense all that was ahead into just such terms, in a very concentrated way to give a picture. I could have overwritten it and overdone it; some people didn't like that beginning. Whether people liked it or not was not the thing I was worrying about; that never enters your mind.

Conversations: Have you ever written any poetry?

Welty: No, I can't write poetry at all.

Conversations: In reviewing Delta Wedding, Time *took you to task for writing about an aristocratic Southern family without criticizing the aristocratic Southern way of life. The reviewer closed with something like, "Such writing is to be expected from one who is the daughter of an insurance company executive and a member of the Junior League." Does this sort of comment make you angry?*

Welty: Sure. Sure it made me mad. I used to get mad at *Time* for everything they said about the South in those days; it was a good deal of a pattern. I never write stories or novels with the object of criticizing the people. I want the reader to understand the people, and people as individuals. I'm not condemning people at all and *never* have. I think it's the business of a fiction writer to reveal life as he sees it by letting the characters reveal themselves and letting the reader draw his own conclusions. It doesn't matter whether I live and write in the South or East India or the North Pole, I would still feel that way.

Conversations: Yet in your earliest collection, A Curtain of Green, *there are stories which show people being exploited, people suffering; these were hardly "Junior League" stories.*

Welty: Yes. And when I was one of the writers who was receiving middle-of-the-night, dead-of-night telephone calls about the troubles in the sixties, when I was harangued by strangers saying,

"Why are you sitting down there writing your stories instead of out condemning your society," I felt like saying I didn't need their pointers to know that there was injustice among human beings or that there was trouble. I had been writing about that steadily right along by letting my characters show this. I don't believe in pointing my finger and shaking a stick at people and saying, "Look here—" As a fiction writer I never would do that.

Conversations: Didn't you write an article defending this position?

Welty: In 1965 I wrote a piece for the *Atlantic Monthly* called "Should the Novelist Crusade," in which I tried to express this. Not only on my behalf, but on the behalf of all writers at all times. Some writers may see that as their business, which is their privilege, but I see as my privilege writing about human beings as human beings with all the things that make them up, including bigotry, misunderstanding, injustice, and also love and affection, and whatever else. Whatever makes them up interests me. I try to write as I see real life, which doesn't allow stock characters who get up and illustrate something in the abstract—that was going on a lot at that time.

Well, one thing that I did do which pertains to this, I guess, was in result of the one really bad thing—one of two really bad things—that happened in Jackson during the 1960s as far as race incidents went. It was the murder of Medgar Evers. I did write a story the night it happened. I was so upset about this and I thought: I live down here where this happened and I believe that I must know what a person like that felt like—this murderer. There had been so many stories about such a character in the stock manner, written by people who didn't know the South, so I wrote about the murderer intimately—in the first person, which was a very daring thing for me to do.

At that time, of course, he hadn't been caught; I mean, no one had been arrested, much less tried. In between my writing that story and its publication, which was done very quickly in *The New Yorker*—they set it up and printed it almost right away, just two pages long—there had been an arrest. William Maxwell, my editor, called me up and we made the changes over the telephone. The story had to be gone over with a fine-toothed comb by the magazine's lawyers in case I had inadvertently jeopardized somebody. And it was odd how many things I had guessed right, though I was wrong in the social level of the man accused—that's interesting, isn't it?—but, I think I still knew what the man thought. I had lived with that kind of thing.

Conversations: First person was a very daring approach.

Welty: Well, I felt that desperate about it.

Conversations: That story should have silenced some of your "social" critics!

Welty: Well, but that was using my skill as a writer and not lecturing. I was trying to let the story itself speak for its point, you know.

Conversations: I noticed that your number is no longer in the phone book, whereas it was for a long time.

Welty: Well, that was sort of as a result of those midnight calls. I'm sorry not to have it in there although it helps me in a way, because I work at home and I like to work pretty concentratedly through the day. I try to give my number to everyone who could possibly want it, but sometimes I miss out on the visit of a friend who is unexpectedly passing through and I'm sorry.

Conversations: Various people have commented on how accessible you are as a writer—

Welty: Real accessible.

Conversations: You give interviews—maybe you don't like to, but you do; you give lectures—you have just come back from a lecture tour.

Welty: Well, it really wasn't a lecture tour. That is, I came back to home base in between everything. There was a time when I did a lot of this, and it pleased me to get invitations from some of the same places where I went before. It's mostly readings from my work and answers-to-questions periods. I like best the give-and-take with the students. I enjoy it but I don't try anymore to write and do that at the same time.

Conversations: You appear on educational TV; you appeared with Jim Hartz when NBC's Today *show came down here to Mississippi—*

Welty: I know, but I was so disappointed in their idea of coverage. It was just that they had such a chance to find out things for the rest of the country about Mississippi. I told Mr. Hartz and some of the others that in one or two sentences I, for instance, could give them a picture of the great amount of work in the arts that's going on here—writing—painting—music—and they said, "Well, we don't have time to go into anything. We've got to get to Arkansas." I really was so cross, because everybody here was trying and ready to help them with things: show them the backgrounds and give information.

Conversations: How do you manage to keep out all the people who make you mad, or do you?

Welty: Oh, I really do what I like to do. For instance, I wanted to see you, but I don't have time or energy to give many interviews. And when I work, I do nothing else. For instance, after we finish our interview I'm going to dive right in. I've not been able to wait to get home from these lectures and so on, and get into some work which I interrupted to go off—some writing.

Conversations: Well, when you don't want to see people, what do you do? Do you take the phone off the hook?

Welty: Oh, no, I answer the telephone. I can't not do it. And, of course, I want to see people and my friends; I can do that in the evening. My friends are understanding: if they know I'm working on something, they usually don't call me in the morning—that's when I like to work. People have always been understanding of me here in Jackson. But it is necessary, as you know, to have consecutive time ahead. You can't take an hour this morning, an hour this afternoon, thirty minutes after supper.

Conversations: How do you work? Do you have any peculiarities?

Welty: Oh, no, I don't think so.

Conversations: You do work on the typewriter?

Welty: I work either way, but I have to type it early in the process. I guess my journalistic training taught me to want to see something on the page, objective, in type.

Conversations: Do you do any revision as you're working or do you tend to go clear through a long chunk of writing, and then go back and rewrite?

Welty: I guess a combination of both. Or either, depending on how I worked at it. I revise a lot, at one time or another.

Conversations: Did Diarmuid Russell ever, ever, ever send you anything back and say, "Brood over this for a while"?

Welty: That's his favorite word, isn't it? I don't believe he ever sent a story back; I don't believe he ever did. But, you know, his terms were not uncertain; you knew how well he liked something or how well he didn't. I just can't tell you what it meant to me to have him there. His integrity, his understanding, his instincts—everything was something I trusted.

Conversations: You never had the feeling that he would sell a shoddy piece of work just to make money.

Welty: No, nobody's. And neither would he send a publisher a shoddy piece of work. They knew he was going to send good things; the writers knew he would send it to the right place. Editors and publishers have remarked to me that they opened his things first. It's so nice to know that two people who started off with those wonderful ideas succeeded. You know, Diarmuid and Henry Volkening started off on a shoestring and just the two of them—they always wanted to keep their own clients; they kept the firm small; the client list small; so they could always handle it personally. And can you imagine anything more lucky than just walking into their agency?

Conversations: Was there anyone else—what about publishers— who helped you?

Welty: Are you old enough to have known John Woodburn? Well, he was marvelous. He was with Doubleday to begin with. He gave my name to Diarmuid Russell when he was starting an agency. Diarmuid finally sold my first book of stories to John

Woodburn. And, you know, for Doubleday to publish a book of short stories by an unknown writer was really extraordinary in those days. Or, maybe, at anytime for anyone to. So when John moved to Harcourt, Brace I moved with him, because it was to him that I had the allegiance.

Conversations: And you stayed with Harcourt, Brace until—

Welty: Until *Losing Battles*. That came after such a long interval and everyone I knew at Harcourt had left. And I didn't feel close to them anymore, whereas at Random House there's Albert Erskine, who was on the *Southern Review* when they published my beginning stories. So when I came to Random it was another full circle. I really have been a lucky writer as far as my professional associates have been concerned, all the way through.

Conversations: You never have had any bad experiences with publishers and certainly not with Diarmuid Russell.

Welty: No. And then, Mary Louise Aswell, who was on *Harper's Bazaar* and still a close friend of mine, published some of the early stories. She was so good; she would keep the powers from cutting her fiction to make room for an ad, you know, that kind of thing. She fought for her writers. William Maxwell is close to me as my editor and my friend of many years.

Conversations: Well, you've had a lot of friends but I don't know that you really needed much help—

Welty: Oh, boy, who doesn't! Who doesn't.

Conversations: The Ponder Heart was produced in 1956, wasn't it?

Welty: I believe it was. I didn't write the play, as you know.

Conversations: Have you ever written a play or tried to write a play?

Welty: Not to show other eyes. I've worked on it, but torn up everything. I discovered exactly what my trouble is: the difference between dramatic dialogue and dialogue on the page. You know, it's completely different in function and everything else.

Conversations: And yet, I would think that anything from Losing Battles *could be read straight out and would sound like stage dialogue.*

Welty: I don't know—but think how short a play is and how every single line of dialogue has to advance the plot. You can't have any digressions and—

Conversations: You're very good at digressions!

Welty: Well, my great weakness! And also, it was a liberty I could take in *Losing Battles*; in a play you could take no liberties. I would love the discipline of writing a play; I still would like to do it.

Conversations: There were two versions of The Ponder Heart *produced, were there not? Wasn't one done by Frank Hains here in Jackson?*

Welty: Oh, yes, absolutely. At New Stage.

Conversations: Which one of the versions did you think was truer to your novel?

Welty: Oh, Frank's. Of course, we gave it paying our royalties to Chodorov and Fields and so on, because it wouldn't be allowable to write or publish another version. I loved the one they did here; I wish you could have seen it. They've done it about three different times. Frank wrote it; directed it; made the sets; wrote the music for it—did everything. He said he knew that he broke every rule of dramatic construction, but it seemed to work.

Edna Earle, who is the chief character in my story, was still the chief character and what happened was all presented from her point of view. The Broadway play made Uncle Daniel the main character and Edna Earle receded to the background. It was perfectly legitimate for the play to do that, but it was not my story.

Conversations: No, well, the whole strength of The Ponder Heart *is the central intelligence which is Edna Earle telling the story—*

Welty: The way she saw it. It was done as really a labor of love by New Stage here; Frank and the whole crew, and the beautiful performances—especially by Jane Petty and Tom Spengler who acted the leads. That story was very blessed.

Conversations: Have you had any other theatrical productions?

Welty: Well, *The Robber Bridegroom.* I, of course, didn't write that either. That was this past fall; I gather it's about to go on tour.

Conversations: Wasn't there a ballet based on your juvenile book, The Shoe Bird?

Welty: Oh, yes, there was, by the Jackson Ballet Guild.

Conversations: I think that was charming, too.

Welty: It really was. Rex Cooper and Albia Kavan did the choreography, and Lehman Engel wrote the music for it. The costumes were charming. I was very proud that they did it—and pleased.

Conversations: In earlier interviews you have warned readers about the dangers of overanalyzing stories. Yet a lot of critics have talked about the mythological content in your stories, such as the name "Phoenix" in "A Worn Path," and in "Death of a Traveling Salesman" the idea of Sonny as Prometheus, the bearer of light, and his wife as the great Earth Mother. Are you consciously using this material symbolically?

Welty: Yes, I know. I think that sounds like a literal way to take it. In the case of "Death of a Traveling Salesman," I had no idea of any of that which you were just saying.

Conversations: When the mule's face looks in the window there's been. . . . Somebody wrote a scholarly article about just what this mule's face meant.

Welty: It meant a mule was looking in the window. Well, the thing I feel about all symbolism, in general, I can easily say very simply and that is: if a symbol occurs to you organically in writing the story, you can use it. For instance, I wouldn't have used the word "phoenix" in "A Worn Path" if it hadn't first come to me as an appropriate Mississippi name. I'd heard of old people named Phoenix; there's a Phoenix town. I thought it was legitimate as a symbol, because it is also true. I couldn't have called her "Andromeda" or something like that, you know, in order to make her a symbol. It would take away her life. If it comes in naturally, then it can call up some overtones and I don't mean to do any more than that.

Conversations: Would that also apply to "Beulah" as the name of the town that Bowman is heading for in "Death of a Traveling Salesman"? "Beulah Land" has a biblical connotation, but there is a Beulah, Mississippi, isn't there?

Welty: Mississippi is full of Beulahs. I used it again in *The Ponder Heart* without remembering that I'd used it before—it doesn't matter. The Beulah Hotel—and someone wrote in to ask me if the whole thing was a Christian allegory. That kind of thing makes me uncomfortable. You try to suggest, to arouse people's imagination. But then, I don't like to be held responsible for making their ideas neatly work out. Some are far-flung! There's the sense of proportion to go by, too, in letting in symbols.

Conversations: I was going to ask if you had read a lot of mythology.

Welty: I certainly am interested in myths and I've always used them; I read and loved them as a child. In *The Golden Apples* I used mythology, but the stories weren't meant to illustrate a myth. I just used mythology, just as I used Mississippi locations and names. In *The Robber Bridegroom* I used fairy tales and real folklore and historical people and everything alike and simultaneously. I think it's there; I think it's right there—so why shouldn't I avail myself? But it is kind of frightening to think that people see ponderous allegorical meanings—

Conversations: And even would take to worrying about that old mule looking in the window.

Welty: I know; I don't think that's fair; I really don't. Not fair to that mule. This isn't to say I don't appreciate genuine criticism—

Conversations: You have been praised for your ability to reconcile the tragic and the comic and to balance them simultaneously. Do you see life basically as a comedy or a tragedy or, perhaps, as a tragicomedy?

Welty: Well, I guess it's like what I just said about the myths and the folklore and everything: it's there. It's in the fabric of life— and I try to show what I see or find there, sometimes comedy, sometimes tragedy, and sometimes both. I don't see what else you can do, except try to show in the most honest way you can what you see.

Conversations: You have also been accused of being obscure. Would you agree with this criticism?

Welty: Well, I think it would be the worst sin I could commit, if I were. I certainly don't do such a thing on purpose. If I'm obscure, it's where I've made a mistake somewhere in trying to be clear, because I abominate deliberate obscurity.

Conversations: When you're dealing with what Robert Penn Warren has called "love and separateness," you can't help being a little bit mysterious—

Welty: Well, mysterious is something else; I don't mind being mysterious. I think life is mysterious. But to be obscure would be a fault in the teller of the story; and that is something I would have avoided, or overcome, as far as I'm able.

Conversations: Would you agree with Robert Penn Warren's statement that your writing is often about love and separateness?

Welty: I guess it is. He's a most marvelous critic. I haven't read that piece in a long time because he wrote it a long time ago, but I'm grateful to him for whatever he would say. I would trust him to be right.

Conversations: It seems to me that your story, "The Landing"—

Welty: *That* has lots of faults to it; *that's* obscure. I was really trying to express something that I felt in that *place*. It used to be really lost down there. A ghost river-town. It was magical to me and I was trying to express some of that lostness and the feeling of enchantment. Maybe I got too carried away by my own words.

Eudora Welty

Conversations: Another thing that you seem to come back to besides love—the expression of or the failure to express—is family loyalty and unity. Would you say that this is one of your recurring themes?

Welty: Well, I think it goes with your sense of family, however that loyalty or unity works out. In *The Optimist's Daughter* there is Laurel's loyalty to her father and her mother, and Fay's family swarming in is another aspect of the same thing. They are together, for heaven's sake—a knot. Just as sure as Laurel's family is a knot. I do think the family unit can hold just about all the stories of man, don't you? It can embrace them.

Conversations: You've won a staggering number of awards and prizes, including the Pulitzer Prize in 1973. Would you go out on a limb and say which of these awards meant the most to you, personally?

Welty: I don't know; I don't know. Of course, I was so *astonished* at the Pulitzer. I had no—

Conversations: How did you find out about it?

Welty: Frank Hains down at *The Daily News* called up and said, "Well, how does it feel—" or something. I thought he was talking about something else and while I was talking to him I saw these two strangers with a camera coming up my walk. I said, "Frank, what's happened?" He told me it came over the AP wire. About two or three days afterwards, I think, I got a telegram. So that was my biggest shock, the Pulitzer Prize.

I was very proud of the Gold Medal for Fiction from the National Institute of Arts and Letters, because this is a body made up of artists who are my own contemporaries—people doing what I'm doing. And also because it was for a body of work instead of for something that—some one effort. It meant a great deal to me for those two personal reasons.

Conversations: When was this?

Welty: I think it was in 1972. I've had great descents of good fortune.

Conversations: Well, but you do work at it!

Welty: I do work hard; I do work hard, but it doesn't always follow, you know, that people even read your work, much less like it. The whole world could have been like *Time* magazine in 1943.

Conversations: Have you served on any boards that grant awards?

Welty: Well, I am a member of the Institute and the Academy and we all do a shift at some committee like that, and I have been a judge on their awards, and a number of others.

Conversations: Does this mean you're reading a great number of books?

Welty: Yes, constantly, constantly reading.

Conversations: Could you give a rough estimate of how much?

Welty: I don't know. If I'm serving as a reader for such a thing, it seems to me that wherever I go, like to get my hair done, wait in the dentist's office or anywhere, I try to get a part of a novel read. I don't know how people who review regularly in a weekly do it. It's different from constantly reading on your own.

Conversations: You do a lot of reviewing, too. Do you work exclusively for The New York Times?

Welty: I do do a good bit of reviewing. No, they're the ones that seem to ask me the most. I've just finished reviewing Katherine Anne Porter's book which she wrote on Sacco and Vanzetti. Did you see—it came out in the *Atlantic*. I didn't know that she was one of those writers who went up to Boston and demonstrated with Edna St. Vincent Millay and John Dos Passos and all of them. She took notes at the time, but had not found herself able to really make a book, a complete thing of it until now, this last year.

She's eighty-seven years old and this is an extraordinary book: it's sixty-three pages long—utterly concentrated and pure and honest and straightforward reporting, in the light of her subjective feelings which she has tried to clarify through the years. It was a privilege to review it. I just mailed it yesterday.

Eudora Welty

Conversations: Have you and Katherine Anne Porter been friends? I know that there's a disparity in your ages, but I also know she was one of the earlier writers to recognize your talent.

Welty: She was one of the first people. She was living in Baton Rouge at the time that I was sending my first stories in to *Southern Review.* She wrote me a letter out of the clear blue sky and said that she liked my work, and invited me to come down to see her, and offered anything she could do. Isn't that amazing? It was just wonderful. It was also her way. So, of course, we've been friends ever since. I owe her a great deal and admire her whole life's work a great deal and, of course, love her.

Conversations: Which of your stories is your own personal favorite and which of your novels?

Welty: Whatever I'm working on at the time seems to matter the most with me, and all the others are forgotten. But I think really that book of stories called *The Golden Apples* is, on the whole, my favorite. Somehow that's very close to my heart. It has some of the stories I most of all loved writing. And then it excited me, because I discovered only part way through that the stories were connected. All this time in the back of my head these connections had worked themselves out. I had just to get the clue like a belated detective: this story's people were that story's people at a different period in their lives.

Conversations: That's fascinating.

Welty: It was to me. And also, Diarmuid liked that; he even telephoned me, which is very unusual for him, you know. After he finished reading it he said, "I think this is a very, very good book." That meant a lot to me—the reader, you know, speaking from the other end. It stayed with me as something that really made me happy.

Conversations: So things do happen in your writing that you are not expecting to happen, such as these connections.

Welty: Yes and I trust them.

Conversations: So you don't go through and plan, plot out everything exactly as you expect it to go. Then how do you know if a story is going well?

Welty: You do get a story to a point where it, on its own momentum, can sort of work for you. That's a mark that you are doing it right. I do think that if the story is any good, it has a life of its own, don't you? And a momentum. And it helps you and you help it sort of at the same time. I find in every story that I write it's teaching me how to work it out as I go, which is why I love to write. I really love the work involved and what happens.

Conversations: A lot of writers claim to write with pain and agony—

Welty: It's hard, but I like it to be hard. In fact, that's another mark that it's any good, but I love it. Really, it just delights me to write. Sometimes I think about P. G. Wodehouse, who was said to laugh as he wrote. Well, sometimes I do too.

Conversations: What do you think about the current literary scene? Are there any writers whom you are particularly interested in right now?

Welty: That's a hard thing to answer off the top of your head. I think it's very important to us what is going on today, and I am interested in finding out about young writers coming along. As well as the new work of us older ones.

Conversations: What do you think about Walker Percy?

Welty: He's very interesting to me. I don't always understand his work right off and have to go back and read again. Or that's the way I read Lancelot. I still prefer The Moviegoer to all of them. When I was reading Lancelot it interested me and compelled my admiration, and still I kept thinking, "But I like The Moviegoer."

Conversations: I think Walker Percy has a philosophical idea that he's trying to express through fiction. Do you have that feeling?

Welty: I do too, and I'm sure that whatever it is it's full of interest and complications. I'm just not certain I can follow. I thought he did something of the same thing, but more by suggestion, in The Moviegoer. In Lancelot it's sort of wide open: actual symbolic playing with things, and the movie mechanism of pictures within pictures within pictures, and media being the meaning and so on. I admired how he was able to do this. I'll be interested to see what he will do next.

Eudora Welty

Conversations: And Reynolds Price?

Welty: I am deeply interested in him. He's just rewritten or reconceived his first book as a play. I read an earlier version of it, but not this finished one that just came out, *Early Dark*. Yes, I think he's full of books to come. With all his fine accomplishments, his absolutely first-rate work so far, you feel there is so much more there. He teaches at Duke University and he's a person of great vitality and independence of mind, who knows exactly what he wants to do. I feel the same way about Elizabeth Spencer, you know: she's just a born writer with all sorts of resources already shown and to come. Abundance!

Conversations: What about Ellen Douglas, who you think is a fine writer.

Welty: Yes, I've read all of her work. She has so much power, hasn't she? Tremendous strength. She writes with a lot of passion, too, which is the essence. A passion of knowing and understanding, able to give a true reflection of life in a particular part of the world. Peter Taylor has it too, another writer I like enormously—he finds his essence in the life he knew in Tennessee.

Conversations: I kept trying to make Peter Taylor a Mississippi writer, but he's over the border.

Welty: Oh, he's over the border, very *much* so. If you'd say Mississippi to him, he would say, "Are you crazy? It's Tennessee!"

Conversations: Of course, there are other writers besides Southern writers—

Welty: There are indeed.

Conversations: I was thinking of Saul Bellow, for instance, who is another Russell and Volkening client, is he not?

Welty: Yes, he is. I think he was Henry's. And, of course, he is a very knowledgeable and skillful writer. He has won all the honors in the world.

Conversations: What do you read for pleasure?

Welty: I've just finished reading a whole year of Chekhov which was pure bliss. The one lecture I gave this year was on Chekhov, so that gave me a wonderful reason to—as if you needed one—to reread everything and track down everything that I had not read. Reading Chekhov was just like the angels singing to me. Often, if you're asked to do a piece on somebody, I think the reason you accept is that you know it's your chance at something that you've always wanted to do: that is, read one person through and no one else and everything they've written. I did the same thing with Willa Cather, to my great delight.

Conversations: I have never done that with Cather.

Welty: Neither had I before. You know, I hadn't even read all of her books. I thought I had, but had not. So that was a wonderful new experience.

Conversations: I did that with Jane Austen once. I understand that she is one of your favorite authors.

Welty: She is. And I did the same thing. More than once, because she only has a short row of books and you can't stop when you start her anywhere. If you ever start her, you read them all.

Conversations: It is astonishing to me in this day and age of explicit sex, violence, and so forth, how Austen can keep you hanging, waiting for the hero to call the heroine by her first name.

Welty: Absolutely. Exactly. Well, it's symbols either way—the whole thing means coming intimacy or intimacy arrived. Today's explicit sex and Jane Austen's calling by the first name speak of human beings reaching the same thing, within the dramatic possibilities of the day. So there you are.

Conversations: Who are some of your other favorite writers—not necessarily contemporary?

Welty: Henry Green! I'm crazy about him. I just got hold of his first novel—the one he wrote while he was still at Eton—called *Blindness*. I knew he had written it, but, to me, it was a mythological book that had never reached this country. I knew it had been out of print in England for ages. While I was in Santa

311

Eudora Welty

Barbara a friend who has a bookstore told me that he had come by this book, and so I bought it from him. I don't usually buy rare books, per se, but I just had to have this, and now I've read it.

It really is extraordinary. Only a seventeen-year-old boy would have the daring to start off like that: his hero, a young boy, is blinded when struck by a child throwing a stone through the glass of a moving train. And the boy's ordeal . . . his going on home and trying to adjust to his life. This is the novel. Isn't that amazing? I've heard it said that afterwards Henry Green disowned it; I don't know on what basis. Anyway, I've now read everything that he's ever written, closely and with love.

I love E. M. Forster and Elizabeth Bowen very much. I revere Virginia Woolf but I don't want her preeminence now—everyone reading her and writing about her—accidentally to put Elizabeth Bowen in any kind of shadow because I think she was fully as good. And, in a rewarding way, more robust, human, and rounded. I'm not dreaming of trying to see them as competitors, which they *never* were. You can't look at writing like that. But Elizabeth died recently, and I don't want her books suddenly for that reason to drop behind, even briefly.

Conversations: Well, it's a little unfortunate that we get these cult figures—

Welty: It's not fair to either one.

Conversations: No, not fair to the person who inspires the cult, either. I am thinking of Sylvia Plath and, of course, Truman Capote for a long time. And I've wondered if Harper Lee was stopped from writing more by having so much attention, so early on with To Kill a Mockingbird.

Welty: I know nothing at all about her case, but I do know that this happens because I've seen it. It could be the most unfortunate thing in the world, I guess, to have something happen to you too soon. It's a matter of timing in your life. It's really not fair, either, that somebody's first book, written at a very tender age, gets the acclaim it deserves but yet at the wrong time for that person; so that whatever happens after that, people will always say, "Yes, but it's not what we expected when we read so-and-so." Why should it be?

Conversations: I suppose nothing could be more maddening for a writer than to have his or her very first work praised over anything he writes during the next fifty years.

Welty: It's happened to us all, including me. Somebody told me—Reynolds Price told me this past spring that he thought "Death of a Traveling Salesman" was the best story that I had ever written, the first one that I ever wrote. Anyway, it's nice to know that people still like your old work. I guess you don't think of it in chronological terms much. That is, I don't consider that I am progressing or regressing from story to story; I've just reached something different.

Conversations: You've done a great deal of experimenting with point of view.

Welty: Well, I feel that each story has its own demands and that's why I say: it may not be better or may not be worse; it's just something new. I mean new to the writer, not necessarily to the reader. That's the fascination of working with the short story.

Conversations: You did recently write an essay for a book about short story theory edited by Charles LeMay. In it you said that the short story was vital and was going to last partly because of the short story's infinite variety which offers so much scope for experimentation.

Welty: I do feel that very strongly.

Conversations: Well, there are a considerable number of people who feel that a short story is somehow inferior to a novel, simply because it's shorter.

Welty: Isn't that a bore? "Well, I couldn't find *anything* at the library; I just had to bring home some short stories." I love the short story!

Conversations: Then you plan to continue to write short stories?

Welty: Yes! As I told you, I've never started a novel knowingly. What I thought *Losing Battles* and *The Optimist's Daughter* both were going to be is really my favorite form which you can call the "long short story." I guess *The Ponder Heart* is really that and *The Robber Bridegroom* as well—they aren't novels. Ninety pages or

100 pages, that is my favorite length. But I write them as I do a short story, in a sustained, one-piece manner.

Conversations: Whereas with something like Losing Battles, *obviously, you could not do that way.* The Optimist's Daughter *is a very, very strong novel.*

Welty: Thank you. It came to be a kind of essence of what I've been trying. . . . I was glad that I wrote it. Oh, you know, I can see things that I wish I had been able to do better in it. But I felt that I. . . . I guess through discipline or experience or something, I had learned a little bit about how to give the story the shape I wanted. I felt that it was cohesive.

Conversations: I assume that you will go back to working on a short story, and not a novel.

Welty: I hope so. It's begun and it's in lots of pages and notes. What I want to do with it is to look at it fresh and to start from the beginning, and get it all in one. I have just finished making a collection of my nonfiction, which I had to get off first. Pieces that I wrote all through the years starting back in 1944, reviews and lectures and what they call "occasional pieces."

Conversations: That's quite a job to get all of the material together, isn't it?

Welty: I had to hunt everything up and make Xeroxes.

Conversations: Will this be a Random House book?

Welty: Yes. They've got it up there now. I have a couple of stories that are still uncollected that have been in *The New Yorker*, but never have been in a book; so I have a start on a book of stories. Now to write my new story.

Conversations: You have taught writing classes; you've been the writer-in-residence—

Welty: Something like that.

Conversations: Do you really think that writing can be taught?

Welty: No, I don't and I always say that at the beginning. I don't think you can tell anyone how to do it, but I do think that with specific works it may do something for a writer to have his work put out on the table, out before him in the open. Once he's finished it. I think that the writer helps himself; I've seen this work and I'm sure you have too.

I had a little class like that at Millsaps for a year and a half. A nice group of about sixteen people, talented, bright. They would bring their stories in, and I was trying to learn as well as they were how to proceed in class. They would read them out loud and the rest would respond. That was it. As the writer reads his own work out loud, he hears it objectively for the first time. And you begin that way to teach yourself. I found that out, too, when I began reading my stories out loud, on my college visits. I could see all these weaknesses that had been in there all these years and I didn't know it. You know, sentences that should have been cut; paragraphs, bits of narrative that should have been transposed— mistakes that were just as clear as day. Finally!

Conversations: You feel that not only poetry, but short stories, too, should be read aloud?

Welty: Well, I find that for me that's a way to learn. No, I think their place is really on the page. That's their destination. But before that's reached, learning by reading aloud seemed to work all right in our class. Since the class was an excellent one, there was a good playback, you know, a good sounding board.

Conversations: Then you do feel that a writing class has its value, has its place?

Welty: Well, they seemed to think that it went off all right.

Conversations: Did you ever take a course in writing?

Welty: No. I didn't write any stories while I was in college—well, I don't think so.

Conversations: You were preparing to be a businesswoman.

Welty: No, I mean, I was thinking about my major. I was majoring in English literature, and I'm terribly glad I had the sense to.

Conversations: But there was no class in "creative writing"?

Eudora Welty

Welty: No. I was from the start on my own. And that's the way it needs to be. I think it's so much a personal matter. As you know, writing's an interior business, and you have to tell yourself, in the long run, only you can help.

CONVERSATIONS WITH
 WRITERS II.

DATE DUE
